Avoiding and Enforcing
Repetitive Structures in Words

Dipl.-Inf. Mike Müller

Dissertation
zur Erlangung des akademischen Grades
Doktor der Naturwissenschaften
(Dr. rer. nat.)
der Technischen Fakultät
der Christian-Albrechts-Universität zu Kiel
eingereicht im Jahr 2014

Kiel Computer Science Series (KCSS) 2014/8 v1.0 dated 2014-11-26

ISSN 2193-6781 (print version)
ISSN 2194-6639 (electronic version)

Electronic version, updates, errata available via https://www.informatik.uni-kiel.de/kcss

The author can be contacted via mail@mikemueller.name

Published by the Department of Computer Science, Kiel University

Dependable Systems Group

Please cite as:

▷ Mike Müller. *Avoiding and Enforcing Repetitive Structures in Words*. Number 2014/8 in Kiel
   Computer Science Series. Department of Computer Science, 2014. Dissertation, Faculty of
   Engineering, Kiel University.

```
@book{MMueller14,
  author    = {Mike M\"uller},
  title     = {Avoiding and Enforcing Repetitive Structures in Words},
  publisher = {Department of Computer Science, CAU Kiel},
  year      = {2014},
  number    = {2014/8},
  isbn      = {978-3-73474-197-5},
  series    = {Kiel Computer Science Series},
  note      = {Dissertation, Faculty of Engineering, Kiel University}
}
```

Herstellung und Verlag: BoD — Books on Demand, Norderstedt

About this Series

The Kiel Computer Science Series (KCSS) covers dissertations, habilitation theses, lecture notes, textbooks, surveys, collections, handbooks, etc. written at the Department of Computer Science at Kiel University. It was initiated in 2011 to support authors in the dissemination of their work in electronic and printed form, without restricting their rights to their work. The series provides a unified appearance and aims at high-quality typography. The KCSS is an open access series; all series titles are electronically available free of charge at the department's website. In addition, authors are encouraged to make printed copies available at a reasonable price, typically with a print-on-demand service.

Please visit http://www.informatik.uni-kiel.de/kcss for more information, for instructions how to publish in the KCSS, and for access to all existing publications.

1. Gutachter: Prof. Dr. Dirk Nowotka
                     Christian-Albrechts-Universität zu Kiel

2. Gutachter: Prof. Dr. Narad Rampersad
                     University of Winnipeg

Datum der mündlichen Prüfung: 17. November 2014

Zusammenfassung

Der Fokus dieser Arbeit liegt auf der Untersuchung sich wiederholender Strukturen in Wörtern, einem zentralen Thema auf dem Gebiet der Wortkombinatorik. Die in der vorliegenden Arbeit präsentierten Ergebnisse zielen darauf ab, die bestehende Theorie bezüglich des Vorkommens beziehungsweise Fehlens solcher Strukturen zu erweitern.

Im ersten Teil untersuchen wir, ob derartige Strukturen zwangsweise in unendlichen Wörtern über endlichen Alphabeten auftauchen. Die Form von sich wiederholenden Strukturen, die wir untersuchen, beinhaltet funktionale Abhängigkeiten zwischen den wiederholten Teilen. Insbesondere gehen wir dabei Vermeidbarkeitsfragestellungen von Mustern nach, deren sich wiederholende Struktur durch die Anwendung einer Permutation verschleiert wurde. In diesem neuartigen Szenario tritt der überraschende Effekt auf, dass bestimmte vermeidbare Muster in einem größeren Alphabet nicht mehr vermieden werden können. Der zweite und umfangreichste Teil dieser Arbeit befasst sich mit Wortgleichungen, die eine bestimmte, auf Involutionen basierende, sich wiederholende Struktur in ihren Lösungsmengen erzwingen. Czeizler et al. (2009) führten eine verallgemeinerte Version der von Lyndon und Schützenberger untersuchten klassischen Wortgleichungen $u^\ell = v^m w^n$ ein. Wir lösen die beiden letzten und anspruchsvollsten Fälle und vervollständigen damit die Klassifikation dieser Gleichungen bezüglich der sich wiederholenden Strukturen, die in den Lösungen auftreten.

Im letzten Teil untersuchen wir die Auswirkungen des Mischens auf wiederholungsfreie Wörter. Wir konstruieren sowohl endliche als auch unendliche quadratfreie Wörter, die mit sich selbst so gemischt werden können, dass ein quadratfreies Wort entsteht. Zusätzlich zeigen wir, dass die sich wiederholende Struktur, die beim Mischen eines Wortes mit sich selbst entsteht, in unendlichen Wörtern vermieden werden kann.

Abstract

The focus of this thesis is on the study of repetitive structures in words, a central topic in the area of combinatorics on words. The results presented in the thesis at hand are meant to extend and enrich the existing theory concerning the appearance and absence of such structures.

In the first part we examine whether these structures necessarily appear in infinite words over a finite alphabet. The repetitive structures we are concerned with involve functional dependencies between the parts that are repeated. In particular, we study avoidability questions of patterns whose repetitive structure is disguised by the application of a permutation. This novel setting exhibits the surprising behaviour that avoidable patterns may become unavoidable in larger alphabets.

The second and major part of this thesis deals with equations on words that enforce a certain repetitive structure involving involutions in their solution set. Czeizler et al. (2009) introduced a generalised version of the classical equations $u^\ell = v^m w^n$ that were studied by Lyndon and Schützenberger. We solve the last two remaining and most challenging cases and thereby complete the classification of these equations in terms of the repetitive structures appearing in the admitted solutions.

In the final part we investigate the influence of the shuffle operation on words avoiding ordinary repetitions. We construct finite and infinite square-free words that can be shuffled with themselves in a way that preserves square-freeness. We also show that the repetitive structure obtained by shuffling a word with itself is avoidable in infinite words.

Acknowledgements

"Knowledge is in the end based on acknowledgement."

LUDWIG WITTGENSTEIN

First and foremost I want to thank my supervisor Dirk Nowotka for introducing me to this interesting field called "combinatorics on words", that I had never heard of before, and for providing me with both the freedom and the necessary funding to spend three and a half years pursuing my research interests in this area.

I would also like to thank Narad Rampersad for honouring me with his service as external reviewer of my thesis. Furthermore, I wish to express my gratitude towards him for being part of my examining committee, together with Steffen Börm, Otmar Spinas, and Thomas Wilke, whom I sincerely wish to thank as well.

I am delighted to thank all people that were and are still engaged in the Dependable Systems group at the Kiel University, that is Florin Manea, Robert Mercaş, Tim Grebien, Philipp Sieweck, Thorsten Ehlers and Gesa Walsdorf, for being wonderful colleagues, providing a great environment to work in, and also sharing plenty of after-work hours with me.

Thanks are also due to the staff of the Department of Mathematics and Statistics at the University of Turku, where I had the pleasure to work one autumn and winter long. The people there made this Finnish winter so much nicer than it may sound. In particular, I would like to thank Juhani Karhumäki, Luca Zamboni, Svetlana Puzynina, and Yury Nikulin for hosting me, all the fruitful discussions we had, walls that we climbed, and in general the time that we shared. My deepest gratitude goes to Tero Harju with whom I had the unique pleasure of staring at a blackboard for countless hours, during which I learnt priceless lessons from him, not only about research, but life in general. It is certainly not exaggerated to say that this thesis owes its existence in large part also to his guidance and encouragement. I would like to deeply thank Dirk Nowotka again for making this collaboration possible.

Thanks also go to all my former colleagues at the University of Stuttgart, namely Volker Diekert, Ulrich Hertrampf, Manfred Kufleitner, Jürn Laun, Steffen Kopecki, Alexander Lauser, Heike Photien, and Horst Prote.

I would like to thank all coauthors that worked with me on the topics presented in this thesis; apart from those already mentioned these are Michaël Rao and Shinnosuke Seki. The latter also voluntarily proofread parts of this thesis, for which special thanks are in order. Any errors that might have remained are of course my sole responsibility.

Besides all the people that directly influenced my work, I would also like to thank everyone that made my private life enjoyable while working on this thesis. Therefore thanks to all friends and family members, flatmates and companions in Kiel, Stuttgart, Plüderhausen and surroundings for reminding me that there is more to life than work. Thank you, Tom and Joanna, Peter and Svenja, Tobi and Anne, Hanno, Malte, Max, Sven and Birte, Neel, Maika, Sonja, Axel and Monika, Jürgen and Anja, Leander and Alissa, Christoph, Marcel, Marco, Henning, Günther, and Thorben.

I owe special thanks to my parents, Roland and Elfriede, who were always there for me and always supported the choices I made, despite the fact that they couldn't explain to others what exactly their son is working on.

Last but not least, I want to thank Izabela for her endless support, for believing in me even when I didn't, and for patiently listening to all the problems I have been working on and my ideas how to solve them - both the good ones and the bad ones.

Contents

1 Introduction   **1**

2 Preliminaries   **5**
   2.1 Words 5
   2.2 Periods, repetitions & basic equations on words 6
   2.3 Morphisms and antimorphisms 8
     2.3.1 Morphisms 8
     2.3.2 Power-free morphisms 10
     2.3.3 Antimorphisms and involutions 11
   2.4 Patterns and avoidability 13

3 Cubic patterns with permutations   **15**
   3.1 Introduction 15
   3.2 Preliminaries 17
     3.2.1 Definitions 17
     3.2.2 Avoidability of patterns under permutations 18
   3.3 Cubes with morphic permutations 18
   3.4 Cubes with antimorphic permutations 27
   3.5 Conclusions and open questions 37

4 Extended Lyndon-Schützenberger equations   **39**
   4.1 Introduction 39
   4.2 Preliminaries 41
   4.3 Overview and general assumptions 42
   4.4 The first open case: $\ell = 3$ and $m, n \geqslant 5$ 42
     4.4.1 The case $u_1 u_2 u_3 = uuu$ 43
     4.4.2 The case $u_1 u_2 u_3 = uu\theta(u)$ 81
     4.4.3 The case $u_1 u_2 u_3 = u\theta(u)u$ 82
     4.4.4 The case $u_1 u_2 u_3 = u\theta(u)\theta(u)$ 82
   4.5 The case $\ell = 3, m = 4$, and $n \geqslant 3$ odd 89

Contents

    4.5.1   The case $u_1 u_2 u_3 = uuu$ 89

    4.5.2   The case $u_1 u_2 u_3 = uu\theta(u)$ 93

    4.5.3   The case $u_1 u_2 u_3 = u\theta(u)\theta(u)$ 98

  4.6 Conclusions and open questions 103

5 Shuffling square-free words   **105**

  5.1 Introduction 105

  5.2 Preliminaries 106

  5.3 Square-free shuffles of finite words 107

  5.4 Short palindromes in square-free words 110

  5.5 Infinite square-free self-shuffling words 112

  5.6 Avoiding shuffle-squares and shuffle-cubes 115

  5.7 Conclusions and open questions 120

A Square-free shuffles of finite square-free words   **123**

B Code listings   **129**

  B.1 Code for Chapter 3 129

  B.2 Code for Chapter 5 142

Bibliography   **145**

List of Figures

1.1 Bonding of Watson-Crick complementary DNA-strands. 3

2.1 Impossible situation for a primitive word. 7
2.2 Impossible situation for a θ-primitive word. 12

3.1 Avoidability of $x\pi^i(x)\pi^j(x)$ in Σ_2 and Σ_3 for morphic π 25

4.1 Equation (4.2) with $|u| < m|v| < 2|u|$. 49
4.2 A more detailed depiction of (4.2) with $|u| < m|v| < 2|u|$. 51
4.3 Equation (4.2) with $|u| < m|v| < 2|u|$ with m or n odd. 52
4.4 The situation in the case $|u| \equiv d \pmod{|w|}$. 54
4.5 The border between v_j and v_{j-1}. 55
4.6 Equation (4.2) with $m = n = 10$. 58
4.7 Equation (4.2) with $m = 12$ and $n = 10$. 61
4.8 Equation (4.2) with $m = n = 6$. 62
4.9 Equation (4.2) with $m = 6$ and $n \geqslant 8$. 65
4.10 Equation (4.2) with $m = 8, n \geqslant 8$ and $i = 4$. 66
4.11 Equation (4.2) with $m = 8, n = 8$, $i = 4$ and $p - k = 3$. 67
4.12 Equation (4.2) with $m = 8, n = 10$, $i = 3$ and $p - k = 3$. 68
4.13 Equation (4.2) with $m = 8, n = 8$, $i = 3$ and $p - k = 3$. 69
4.14 The two occurrences of w inside $w_6 w_7$ if $w_6 = \theta(w)$. 71
4.15 Equation (4.2) with $m \geqslant 8, n = 6$, and $k = 2$. 73
4.16 Equation (4.2) with $m = 10, n = 6$, and $k = 2$. 74
4.17 Equation (4.2) with $m = 8, n = 6$, and $k = 2$. 76
4.18 Equation (4.2) with $m = 8, n = 6$, $k = 2$ and $w_4 w_5 w_6 = w\theta(w)^2$. . . . 78
4.19 Equation (4.2) with $m = 10, n = 8$. 79
4.20 The situation at the two borders $u_1 u_2$ and $u_2 u_3$. 83
4.21 The two possible cases for (4.7) if $|u| < 4|v| < 2|u|$. 92
4.22 The situation inside u_1. 94

List of Figures

4.23 The situation inside u_1 when $2|v| < |w| < 3|v|$. 95
4.24 Factorisation of $\theta(u)$. 102

5.1 A Young tableau of shape $(5,3,2)$. 118
5.2 Young tableau corresponding to the word 00100110100111. 118

List of Tables

4.1 Known results about the equations $u_1 \cdots u_\ell = v_1 \cdots v_m w_1 \cdots w_n$. . . 41

4.2 Full characterisation of solutions in terms of θ-periodicity. 103

## CHAPTER 1

Introduction

> *"Words are, of course, the most pow-erful drug used by mankind."*
>
> RUDYARD KIPLING

The history of studying repetitive structures in sequences of symbols, called words here, can be traced back to the beginning of the last century, when the Norwegian mathematician Thue published two seminal papers [86, 87] concerning words that do not exhibit some particular repetitive structures.

More precisely, he showed how to construct an infinite sequence using two different symbols that does not contain three consecutive identical blocks, and how to derive a sequence on three symbols from it where every two consecutive blocks of the same length are different. Unfortunately, the venues he chose to publish his groundbreaking work (written in German) were largely unknown to the researchers interested in similar questions, and many of his results were independently rediscovered afterwards.

Various other aspects of words have been studied before, and the list of authors includes such illustrious names as Bernoulli [5] and Gauß [38]. The excellent survey by Berstel and Perrin [9] provides a comprehensive account of the history of word-related research. Nowadays however, Thue's work is unanimously regarded as the first systematic investigation of combinatorial properties of words and, in particular, the first work in general on repetitive structures therein. His results are well-known and a summary as well as an annotated full translation of his papers were written by Berstel [6, 7].

Half a century after Thue's initial work, the study of repetitions and other properties of words emerged into a research area of its own, which is nowadays known as *combinatorics on words*. Three monographs of Lothaire [63–65]

1

1. Introduction

have been exclusively devoted to topics this area is concerned with, and the connections to other fields of mathematics and computer science such as number theory or pattern matching algorithms are highlighted, for instance, in the textbooks of Allouche and Shallit [1] or Crochemore, Hancart, and Lecroq [23].

One topic of interest concerns relations between different words, commonly expressed as *word equations*. Makanin [67] showed that it is algorithmically decidable whether a given word equation is satisfiable, while other research focused on the form of solutions of some specific classes of equations. Lyndon and Schützenberger [66] and Lentin [61] for instance studied equations, whose only solutions consist of words featuring the kind of repetitive structure that Thue tried to avoid.

In some sense, Thue's goal was to avoid repetitions, whereas Lyndon and Schützenberger as well as Lentin tried to enforce them. Both these approaches will be undertaken in this thesis, albeit using a different notion of repetitiveness.

The first kind of alternative repetitive structure, that is not so blatant and hence can be deemed as some sort of hidden repetition, was introduced by Erdős [34], who asked whether there is an infinite word with the property that no block is a rearrangement of the symbols of the following block of the same length. This kind of repetitive structure is nowadays known as an *abelian repetition*, and Erdős' question has been positively answered by Evdokimov [35], who showed that such a word using 25 symbols exists. Evdokimov's result was later improved on by Pleasants [74] and Keränen [58], who lowered the required number of different symbols to five and four, respectively.

In the last couple of years, various other notions of repetitiveness were introduced and studied from a combinatorial point of view. Most of these are based on an equivalence relation on words and consecutive blocks that are equivalent with respect to this equivalence relation are considered repetitive. The k-*abelian* [52], k-*binomial* [83] or the sum-of-digits equivalence [17] serve as examples of relations that were used to define generalised repetitions.

The notion we shall be concerned with in this thesis is inspired by a phenomenon arising in DNA-strands: such a strand, composed of the bases Adenine (A), Cytosine (C), Guanine (G), and Thymine (T) bonds with its *Watson-Crick complement* to form a double stranded DNA helix. Here A is complementary to T and C is the complement of G. Furthermore, the two joint strands are oriented in the opposite way after the bonding, where the orientation is determined using the so-called *3'*- and *5'*-end, see Figure 1.1 for a graphical representation.

Figure 1.1. The bonding of two *Watson-Crick* complementary DNA-strands.

A suitable abstraction of this natural principle is obtained by modelling the DNA-strand as a word over a finite alphabet (for instance $\{A, C, G, T\}$) and the Watson-Crick complement as a function θ on these words. In order to reflect the main properties of the Watson-Crick complement, the function θ is chosen to be an involution, meaning that $\theta(\theta(w)) = w$ for all words w, that also acts as an antimorphism, which means that $\theta(uv) = \theta(v)\theta(u)$ for all words u and v. In this setting, two words are considered to be equivalent, if one is the image of the other under such a function θ, and a repetitive structure in a word is a concatenation of equivalent blocks. This notion of equivalence has been introduced recently and a series of papers has already been devoted to the study of its properties [19, 30, 32, 54–56, 89].

Outline

This thesis contributes to the theory of repetitive structures in words and provides solutions to some problems that were left open in the existing literature.

In Chapter 2 we introduce the terminology and notation from combinatorics on words that is relevant to this thesis, and recall some of the most fundamental theorems on repetitive structures on words, such as Thue's and Lyndon and Schützenberger's, as well as some recent results that will be used in the following chapters.

In Chapter 3 we will follow Thue's approach and study avoidability questions involving functional dependencies between the blocks. We generalise the approach previously taken by Bischoff, Currie, and Nowotka [10], who allowed involutions to be applied to the blocks, by allowing permutations of higher order as well. This enables us to define patterns that are avoidable when using some finite set of symbols but can not be avoided in words using a larger set of symbols. Such behaviour with respect to avoidability is not known to exist using other notions of repetitivity. We provide a full classification of all such repetitive structures involving three blocks and one permutation in terms of symbol sets admitting infinite words avoiding such structures. The results of this chapter are based on joint work with Florin Manea and Dirk Nowotka and have been presented at the 16th International Conference on Developments in Language Theory 2012 [70].

In Chapter 4 we focus on equations enforcing repetitive structure, pursuing Lyndon and Schützenberger's avenue. We close an open problem by Czeizler et al. [30] regarding the generalised repetitivity of solutions of equations of the form $u_1 u_2 \cdots u_\ell = v_1 v_2 \cdots v_m w_1 w_2 \cdots w_n$, where $u_i \in \{u, \theta(u)\}$ for all $1 \leqslant i \leqslant \ell$, $v_j \in \{v, \theta(v)\}$ for all $1 \leqslant j \leqslant m$, $w_k \in \{w, \theta(w)\}$ for all $1 \leqslant k \leqslant n$, and θ is an antimorphic involution. The results of this chapter comprise the main part of this thesis and are based on two joint papers, the first of which was written together with Florin Manea and Dirk Nowotka and presented at the IARCS Annual Conference on Foundations of Software Technology and Theoretical Computer Science 2013 [69], and the second one was the result of a joint effort with Florin Manea, Dirk Nowotka and Shinnosuke Seki and was presented at the 39th International Symposium on Mathematical Foundations of Computer Science 2014 [71].

In Chapter 5 we study how words without repetitive structure behave when they are shuffled. We show how to construct square-free words that can be shuffled with themselves in a square-freeness preserving manner, and prove the existence of an infinite square-free word that can be shuffled with itself to reproduce itself, answering two open questions of Harju [45]. Furthermore, we improve upon a result by Currie [26] regarding positions of palindromes in square-free words. Finally, we give a simple proof showing that a certain repetitive structure called a *shuffle-square* is avoidable. The results contained in this chapter are based on common work with Tero Harju [47, 48], Michaël Rao and Svetlana Puzynina [73], and the theorem concerning shuffle-square avoidability was announced in [22].

## CHAPTER 2

Preliminaries

> *"The secret to getting ahead is getting started."*

MARK TWAIN

2.1 Words

Let Σ be a non-empty, finite set, called *alphabet*. We call the elements of Σ *letters*. A *word* over Σ is a (finite or infinite) sequence of letters from Σ. The set of non-empty finite words over Σ, also known as the *free semigroup* generated by Σ, is denoted as Σ^+. Endowing Σ^+ with a unique neutral element, which is called *empty word* and denoted as ε, we obtain the *free monoid* generated by Σ, which is denoted as Σ^* (hence, $\Sigma^* = \Sigma^+ \cup \{\varepsilon\}$). The set of infinite words over Σ will be denoted as Σ^ω. If $S \subseteq \Sigma^*$ is a set of words, then S^+ and S^* denote the free semigroup and free monoid generated by the words in S.

We make use of the notation Σ_m to describe an alphabet of m letters, which consists of the digits from 0 to $m-1$, so $\Sigma_m = \{0, 1, \ldots, m-1\}$. Words over Σ_2 are called *binary* words, and words over Σ_3 will be referred to as *ternary* words.

For a finite word w, we denote its *length*, that is the number of letters it consists of, by $|w|$. So, if $w = w_1 w_2 \cdots w_n$, where $w_i \in \Sigma$ for all $1 \leqslant i \leqslant n$, then $|w| = n$. The empty word ε is the unique word of length 0.

If $w = uvz$ for some words u, v and z, then we call u a *prefix*, v a *factor*, and z a *suffix* of w. We denote these relations as follows: $u \leqslant_p w$, $v \leqslant_f w$ and $z \leqslant_s w$. If $u \neq w$ and $u \neq \varepsilon$, then u is called a *proper prefix* of w, and similarly z is a *proper suffix* of w, if $z \neq w$ and $z \neq \varepsilon$. We use the notations $u <_p w$ and

$z <_s w$ in this case. A factor that is neither prefix nor suffix of w is called a *proper factor*.

For a word w of length n, we denote by $w[i]$, $1 \leqslant i \leqslant n$ its i-th letter. Furthermore, we denote by w^R the *reversal* or *mirror image* of w, which is defined as $w^R = w[n]w[n-1]\cdots w[1]$ if w is of length n. A word w is a *palindrome* if $w = w^R$.

2.2 Periods, repetitions & basic equations on words

One of the most basic properties of a word is expressed by the notion of periodicity. A *period* of a word w with $|w| = n$ is a positive integer p, such that $w[i] = w[i+p]$ for all $1 \leqslant i \leqslant n-p$. The set of all periods of a word w is denoted by $P(w)$. The smallest period of a word w is also referred to as *the period* of w, and it is denoted as $\pi(w)$.

One of the most well-known, and probably also most frequently used results concerning periods in words, is the Theorem of Fine and Wilf [36]. The theorem reads as follows, where gcd denotes the *greatest common divisor* of its arguments:

Theorem 2.1 (Fine & Wilf, 1965). *Let $u, v \in \Sigma^*$ be words. If $\alpha \in u\{u,v\}^*$ and $\beta \in v\{u,v\}^*$ have a common prefix of length at least $|u| + |v| - \gcd(|u|,|v|)$, then $u, v \in \{t\}^+$ for some word t.*

This theorem can be also rephrased using suffixes instead of prefixes, and sometimes we will apply it to suffixes in this manner. It should be clear from the context which variant is used.

A word w is called a *repetition* (or also *power*), if $w = u^k$ for some word u and integer exponent $k \geqslant 2$. Here u^k denotes the k-fold concatenation of u with itself. If w is not a repetition, then w is called *primitive*.

Example 2.2. The German verb

$$\text{nennen} = (\text{nen})^2$$

is a repetition, but its English translation

$$\text{(to) mention}$$

is primitive.

Repetitions of exponent two are commonly known as *squares*, while repetitions of exponent three are called *cubes*.

Primitive words are characterised by the following well-known property (for a proof see, e.g., Section 1.2 in [23]), usually referred to as the *synchronisation property*:

Proposition 2.3. *If w is primitive and $ww = xwy$, then either $x = \varepsilon$ or $y = \varepsilon$.*

The synchronisation property states that a situation as the one illustrated in Figure 2.1 cannot happen, if w is primitive, or in other words, if this situation appears, then w is not primitive.

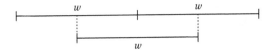

Figure 2.1. Visualisation of the impossible situation for a primitive word w.

Words having no factor of the form u^k for any word u are called *k-power-free*, and in particular *square-free* and *cube-free*, if $k = 2$ and $k = 3$, respectively. The reader might take delight in the remark[1] that the word "square" is square-free, while "square-free" is not.

It is worth mentioning, that the concept of powers is not only restricted to integer exponents, but can also be defined for rational exponents. For $\alpha \in \mathbb{Q}$, a word w is an α-power if there is some $p \in P(w)$ such that $\frac{|w|}{p} = \alpha$. Fractional powers will not be investigated in this thesis though.

The following well-known theorem by Lyndon and Schützenberger [66] provides a necessary and sufficient condition for two words to be powers of the same word:

Theorem 2.4 (Lyndon & Schützenberger, 1962). *Let $u, v \in \Sigma^*$. Then $uv = vu$ if and only if there exists some word $t \in \Sigma^*$ such that $u, v \in \{t\}^*$.*

---

[1] which was mentioned for instance in [53]

7

We say that the words u and v involved in the statement of the previous theorem *commute*. This theorem is a special case of a broader phenomenon called the *defect effect*, which seems to have appeared first in a paper by Skordev and Sendov [85] and is formulated as follows:

Theorem 2.5 (Skordev & Sendov, 1961). *If a set of n words satisfies a non-trivial equation, then these words can be expressed as a product of at most $n-1$ words.*

An extensive survey on different facets of the defect theorem was written by Harju and Karhumäki [46].

The solution set of another basic word equation is given in the following theorem, also originally due to Lyndon and Schützenberger [66]:

Theorem 2.6 (Lyndon & Schützenberger, 1962). *Let $u, v, w \in \Sigma^*$. Then $uv = vw$ if and only if there exist words $p, q \in \Sigma^*$, such that $u = (pq)^i, w = (qp)^i$, and $v = (pq)^j p$ for some $i, j \geqslant 0$ and pq is primitive.*

We say that u is a *conjugate* of w (and vice-versa) if they satisfy the equation in Theorem 2.6, and we denote this relationship by $u \sim w$. It is easily observed that conjugates of primitive words must be primitive themselves and furthermore that a primitive word w has $|w|$ many distinct conjugates.

The last equation we shall be concerned with here has its solution set described by the following theorem:

Theorem 2.7 (Lyndon & Schützenberger, 1962). *If $u^\ell = v^m w^n$ for some words $u, v, w \in \Sigma^*$ and $\ell, m, n \geqslant 2$, then $u, v, w \in \{t\}^*$ for some word $t \in \Sigma^*$.*

2.3 Morphisms and antimorphisms

2.3.1 Morphisms

Let Σ and Δ be two alphabets. A function $f : \Sigma^* \to \Delta^*$ is called a *morphism*, if $f(uv) = f(u)f(v)$ for all words $u, v \in \Sigma^*$. This so-called *universal property* of morphisms makes it sufficient to define the images of all letters of Σ in order to define the images of all words in Σ^*: if $w = w_1 w_2 \cdots w_n$ with $w_i \in \Sigma$ for all $1 \leqslant i \leqslant n$, then $f(w) = f(w_1)f(w_2) \cdots f(w_n)$. By the same token we can also apply morphisms to infinite words, and the image is uniquely defined.

We say that a morphism $f : \Sigma^* \to \Delta^*$ is *non-erasing*, if $f(a) \neq \varepsilon$ for all $a \in \Sigma$. Furthermore, we call a morphism $f : \Sigma^* \to \Delta^*$ *uniform*, if there exists a positive integer k such that $|f(a)| = k$ for all $a \in \Sigma$. More precisely, we say that f is *k-uniform* in this case.

One particular use of morphisms in combinatorics on words is the concept of iterating a special type of morphism in order to generate an infinite word. For this purpose, we say that a morphism f is *prolongable*, if there exists a letter $a \in \Sigma$, such that $f(a) = au$ for some non-empty word u. More specifically, we say that f is *prolongable on a* in this case. If f is prolongable on a, we can iteratively apply f to a, to obtain the sequence

$$a, \ f(a), \ f\big(f(a)\big) = f^2(a), \ f\big(f(f(a))\big) = f^3(a), \ \ldots$$

Now, since $f(a) = au$, we have

$$f^i(a) = f^{i-1}(au) = f^{i-1}(a) f^{i-1}(u),$$

for all $i \geqslant 1$. Hence, for all $i \geqslant 1$ the word $f^{i-1}(a)$ is a prefix of $f^i(a)$, and as such this sequence $a, f(a), f^2(a), f^3(a), \ldots$ converges to an infinite word $w = \lim_{i \to \infty} f^i(a)$, that is uniquely defined by those prefixes.

Example 2.8. Let $f : \Sigma_2^* \to \Sigma_2^*$ be defined by

$$f(0) = 01,$$
$$f(1) = 10.$$

Then f is prolongable on both 0 and 1, and if we iterate f on 0, we get the sequence

$$0, f(0) = 01, f^2(0) = 0110, f^3(0) = 01101001, f^4(0) = 0110100110010110, \ldots$$

that converges to the infinite word

$$t = \lim_{i \to \infty} f^i(0) = 0110100110010110100101100110100110010110 \cdots,$$

which is well-known as the *Thue-Morse word*.

Example 2.9. Let $f : \Sigma_3^* \to \Sigma_3^*$ be defined by

$$f(0) = 012,$$
$$f(1) = 02,$$
$$f(2) = 1.$$

Then we can iterate f on 0 to get the infinite word

$$\boldsymbol{h} = \lim_{i \to \infty} f^i(0) = 01202101210201202102012101202101210201210\cdots$$

The morphism from the previous example is due to Hall [44], but the word $\boldsymbol{h}$ that is obtained by iterating it was already known to Thue [86], who showed that this word is an infinite ternary square-free word. One can observe from the definition of the morphism f used to generate $\boldsymbol{h}$, that neither 010 nor 212 is a factor of $\boldsymbol{h}$.

2.3.2 Power-free morphisms

One particular class of morphisms is comprised of morphisms preserving k-power-freeness of words, that is, morphisms, whose images of k-power-free words are in turn k-power-free.

The first such family of morphisms consists of *square-free morphisms*. To be precise, a morphism f is called *square-free*, if $f(w)$ is square-free for all square-free words w. Criteria that imply the square-freeness of morphisms were studied already by Thue [86]. This line of research was later continued by Berstel [8], Bean, Ehrenfeucht, and McNulty [3], and Brandenburg [13]. A sharp and easily testable characterisation of square-free morphisms was given by Crochemore [21]:

Theorem 2.10 (Crochemore, 1982). *A morphism* $f: \Sigma^* \to \Delta^*$ *is square-free, if it preserves square-freeness of words of length*

$$\max\left\{3, \left\lceil \frac{M-3}{m} \right\rceil + 1\right\},$$

where $M = \max\{|f(a)| : a \in \Sigma\}$ *and* $m = \min\{|f(a)| : a \in \Sigma\}$.

It follows directly from Theorem 2.10 that a uniform morphism is square-free, if it preserves the square-freeness of all words of length three.

Using this result by Crochemore, we can verify that the morphism f from Example 2.9 is not a square-free morphism: the word 010 is square-free, but $f(010) = 01202012$ contains the square 2020 as a factor. In fact, Carpi [16] has shown that if $f : \Sigma_3^* \to \Sigma_3^*$ is a square-free morphism, then $\sum_{a \in \Sigma_3} |f(a)| \geqslant 18$.

Richomme and Wlazinski [80–82] and Wlazinski [88] studied conditions that imply k-power-freeness of morphisms for $k > 2$, in particular cube-freeness. We will use the following result of theirs later in Chapter 3:

Lemma 2.11 (Richomme & Wlazinski, 2007). *A uniform morphism $f : \Sigma_n \to \Sigma_\ell$ is k-power-free for an integer $k \geqslant 3$ if and only if the images by f of all k-power-free words of length at most $kn + k + 1$ are k-power-free.*

2.3.3 Antimorphisms and involutions

Let again Σ and Δ be alphabets. A function $f : \Sigma^* \to \Delta^*$ is called an *antimorphism*, if $f(uv) = f(v)f(u)$ for all words u, v. As in the case of morphisms, this universal property allows us to define antimorphisms on Σ^* just by defining the images of all letters $a \in \Sigma$.

A function f is called an *involution*, if $f^2 = $ id, where id denotes the identity function, that is $f^2(a) = a$ for all a in the domain of f.

If f is both a morphism and an involution, we will call f a *morphic involution*. *Antimorphic involutions* are defined similarly, and will play a central role in Chapter 4. We will denote antimorphic involutions with the letter θ throughout this thesis.

We already saw one example of an antimorphic involution earlier, namely the reversal function $(.)^R$: for $w = w_1 w_2 \cdots w_n$, we have $w^R = w_n^R \cdots w_2^R w_1^R$ and $(w^R)^R = w$.

As involutions are invertible and hence injective, the application of an involution preserves the primitivity of words.

Similarly to the concept of a repetition, we call a word w a θ-*repetition* (or also θ-*power*), if $w = u_1 u_2 \cdots u_k$ for some integer $k \geqslant 2$, and $u_i \in \{u, \theta(u)\}$ for all $1 \leqslant i \leqslant k$, where u is a word and θ is an antimorphic involution. Naturally, a word is called θ-*primitive*, if no such factorisation exists. Every θ-primitive word is also primitive in the ordinary sense, but the converse does not hold: for instance, $w = abba$ is primitive but $w = ab\theta(ab)$, for θ being the aforementioned reversal function.

A property similar to the synchronisation principle for primitive words also exists for θ-primitive words, as observed by Kari, Masson, and Seki [56]:

Lemma 2.12 (Kari, Masson & Seki, 2011)**.** *For a θ-primitive word $x \in \Sigma^+$, neither $x\theta(x)$ nor $\theta(x)x$ can be a proper factor of a word $x_1 x_2 x_3$ with $x_1, x_2, x_3 \in \{x, \theta(x)\}$.*

This result can be visualised in a similar way as the synchronisation property by stating that none of the situations in Figure 2.2 can appear if x is θ-primitive, where $x_1, x_2, x_3 \in \{x, \theta(x)\}$.

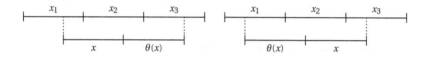

Figure 2.2. Visualisation of the impossible situations for a θ-primitive word x.

Furthermore, Czeizler, Kari, and Seki [32] showed the following result concerning a particular equation involving θ-primitive words:

Lemma 2.13 (Czeizler, Kari & Seki, 2010)**.** *Let $x \in \Sigma^+$ be a θ-primitive word, and $x_1, x_2, x_3, x_4 \in \{x, \theta(x)\}$. If $x_1 x_2 y = z x_3 x_4$ for some words $y, z \in \Sigma^+$ with $|y|, |z| < |x|$, then $x_2 \neq x_3$.*

We will make frequent use of both of these lemmas in Chapter 4. Another theorem that was generalised by Czeizler, Kari, and Seki in this setting is the Theorem of Fine and Wilf (Theorem 2.1), whose statement in terms of θ-powers is as follows:

Theorem 2.14 (Czeizler, Kari & Seki, 2010)**.** *Let $u, v \in \Sigma^+$ be words with $|u| \geq |v|$. If $\alpha \in \{u, \theta(u)\}^+$ and $\beta \in \{v, \theta(v)\}^+$ have a common prefix of length at least $2|u| + |v| - \gcd(|u|, |v|)$, then $u, v \in \{t, \theta(t)\}^+$ for some θ-primitive word $t \in \Sigma^+$.*

If the longer word involved in Theorem 2.14 is fixed by θ, then a shorter common prefix is sufficient to derive the conclusion:

Theorem 2.15 (Czeizler, Kari & Seki, 2010). *Let $u, v \in \Sigma^+$ be words with $|u| \geqslant |v|$ and $u = \theta(u)$. If $\alpha \in \{u, \theta(u)\}^+$ and $\beta \in \{v, \theta(v)\}^+$ have a common prefix of length at least $|u| + |v| - \gcd(|u|, |v|)$, then $u, v \in \{t, \theta(t)\}^+$ for some θ-primitive word $t \in \Sigma^+$.*

Kari and Seki [57] also performed a more rigorous analysis that in some other cases leads to an improved bound on the length of the common prefix which is necessary to conclude that u and v are θ-powers of a common word t. However, for our considerations the bound of $2|u| + |v| - \gcd(|u|, |v|)$ is almost always good enough. In fact, we will sometimes even use the following weaker variant of Theorem 2.14, which is also due to Czeizler, Kari, and Seki [32] (here, lcm denotes the *least common multiple* of its arguments):

Theorem 2.16 (Czeizler, Kari & Seki, 2010). *Let $u, v \in \Sigma^+$ be words with $|u| \geqslant |v|$. If $\alpha \in \{u, \theta(u)\}^+$ and $\beta \in \{v, \theta(v)\}^+$ have a common prefix of length at least $\mathrm{lcm}(|u|, |v|)$, then $u, v \in \{t, \theta(t)\}^+$ for some θ-primitive word $t \in \Sigma^+$.*

As with the ordinary Theorem of Fine and Wilf, also these extensions can be rephrased in terms of suffixes instead of prefixes, and we will also use them in that way.

Furthermore, we can generalise the notion of a palindrome, which is a word that is equal to its reverse, to words which we call θ-*palindromes*: a word w is a θ-palindrome, if $w = \theta(w)$ for some antimorphic involution θ.

If a word w is a conjugate of its image under θ, then w and $\theta(w)$ are described by the following lemma, proved by Kari and Mahalingam [55]:

Lemma 2.17 (Kari & Mahalingam, 2007). *Let $u, v \in \Sigma^*$ and θ be an antimorphic involution. Then $uv = v\theta(u)$ if and only if there exist θ-palindromes $p, q \in \Sigma^*$, such that $u = (pq)^i$, $v = (pq)^j p$ for some $i, j \geqslant 0$ and pq is primitive.*

Note that the previous lemma provides us with the additional information that p and q are θ-palindromes, which is not contained in the conclusion of Theorem 2.6.

2.4 Patterns and avoidability

Let Ξ be an alphabet of variables. We call a word in Ξ^+ a *pattern*. An instance of a pattern $p \in \Xi^+$ is the image of p under some non-erasing morphism h. We already saw instances of some simple patterns containing only a single variable in Section 2.2, namely squares, which are instances of the pattern xx, cubes (instances of xxx) and k-powers in general, which correspond to the pattern x^k.

Patterns are however a much more general concept not only limited to single variables. For instance, a well-known pattern involving two variables is $xyxyx$, instances of which are called *overlaps*. Thue [86] showed, that the Thue-Morse word t contains no factor that is an instance of this pattern.

We say that a word w *avoids* a pattern p, if none of its factors is an instance of p, so for instance the Thue-Morse word t avoids $xyxyx$ and the word h from Section 2.3 avoids xx. In general we say that a pattern p is *avoidable*, if there exists an infinite word that avoids p, otherwise p is *unavoidable*. Whether a pattern is avoidable or not is decidable using Zimin's algorithm [91], for a detailed description see Section 3.2. in [63].

However, if a pattern is avoidable, the obvious question concerns the minimal size of the alphabet on which a word avoiding the pattern exists. For example, it is quickly checked that every word of length at least four in Σ_2^* contains a factor that is an instance of xx. Hence, there is no infinite word in Σ_2^ω that avoids xx. We say that xx is *unavoidable in* Σ_2, but, as mentioned before, the word $h \in \Sigma_3^\omega$ avoids xx, so xx is *avoidable in* Σ_3. For an avoidable pattern p, the minimal integer m, such that p is avoidable in Σ_m is called the *avoidability index* of p.

## CHAPTER 3

Cubic patterns with permutations

*"A mathematician, like a painter or
a poet, is a maker of patterns."*

GODFREY HAROLD HARDY

3.1   Introduction

Avoidability of patterns in infinite words is an old area of interest with a first systematic study going back to Thue [86, 87]. The main focus of this domain lies on the existence of infinite words whose factors do not have a given form, or in other words, are not instances of some particular patterns. This field has been studied by many authors over the last one hundred years. Some known results, as well as their applications, are surveyed in [63] and [24].

The very first results, obtained by Thue at the beginning of the last century, concerned the existence of infinite words avoiding very specific patterns, namely repetitions. Recall that a repetition is a word of the form x^k for some non-empty word x and an exponent $k \geqslant 2$. The study of repetitions lies at the very centre of combinatorics on words. This notion has been generalised recently to the so-called *pseudorepetitions* [30], which are elements of $\{x, f(x)\}^+$, where x is a word and f is some function. As an example, the set of θ-powers mentioned in Chapter 2 forms a class of pseudorepetitions. The idea behind this notion is that some words might not be repetitions but nevertheless have some intrinsic repetitive structure, which is not so obvious. For example, the word $acgttgca$ is not a repetition, but it is a pseudorepetition of the form $xf(x)$ for the non-empty word $x = acgt$ and the morphic involution f with $f(a) = t, f(t) = a, f(c) = g,$

and $f(g) = c$ or the antimorphic identity function, also known as reversal. Various aspects of the combinatorial properties of these pseudorepetitions have been investigated [12, 30, 32, 68], and efficient algorithms to detect such pseudorepetitive structures in words were developed as well [39–41, 89]. See [30, 32] for a discussion about the biological motivation of introducing pseudorepetitions, and their possible applications in bio-inspired computer science or bioinformatics.

Here, we are concerned with studying avoidability questions considering patterns with functional dependencies between variables. In particular, we introduce and thoroughly investigate the case when these functions are permutations. More precisely, we allow function variables in the pattern, that are substituted by either morphic or antimorphic extensions of permutations on the alphabet. For example, consider the following pattern involving the function variable π:

$$x\,\pi(x)\,x$$

An instance of this pattern is a word uvu that consists of three parts of equal length, i.e., $|u| = |v|$, and v is the image of u under any permutation on the alphabet. For example, *aabbbaaab* (*aababbbaab*) is an instance of $x\pi(x)x$ for the morphic (respectively, antimorphic) extension of the permutation $a \mapsto b$ and $b \mapsto a$, when x is mapped to *aab*.

Recently, there has been some initial work on avoidance of patterns with involutions which is a special case of the permutation setting considered in this chapter, see [10, 19]. The original interest in investigating patterns with involutions drew its motivation from possible applications in biology, where the Watson-Crick complement corresponds to an antimorphic involution on four letters. A very restricted class of patterns, involving only permutations of the alphabet Σ_m that map the letter i to $i + 1$ (mod m), has also been studied previously [62]. Our considerations here are more general.

Since these are the first considerations on this kind of generalised pattern avoidance, we restrict ourselves to cubic patterns, following somehow the initial approach of Thue. The cube xxx is the most basic and well-investigated pattern that lends itself to nontrivial considerations on patterns with functional dependencies, as any two consecutive letters form a generalised square, and this pattern is therefore unavoidable and not very interesting in that context. Hence, we have one variable x occurring three times, and only one function variable π. The restriction to only a single function variable is justified by the same argument that makes squares bland: the number of different function variables has to be strictly less than the length of the pattern minus one, otherwise every word of the same length as the pattern is an instance thereof, and the pattern is thus trivially unavoidable. Therefore, we investigate patterns of the form:

$$\pi^i(x)\,\pi^j(x)\,\pi^k(x)$$

where $i, j, k \geqslant 0$.

It is worth noting that the notion of avoidability index plays no role in the setting of patterns involving permutations. Contrary to the classical setting, where once a pattern is avoidable for some alphabet size it remains avoidable in larger alphabets, a pattern with permutations may be avoidable in some alphabet and become unavoidable in a larger alphabet. Moreover, the set of numbers defining the sizes of the alphabets over which a pattern with permutations is avoidable is a contiguous interval of natural numbers. This is a new and somewhat unexpected phenomenon in the field of pattern avoidance. It does not occur, for example, in the involution setting, but requires permutations of higher order.

The remainder of this chapter is structured as follows: in Section 3.2 we recall the relevant definitions and introduce the problem we are concerned with. In Section 3.3 we study avoidability questions where the function variables in the patterns are replaced by morphic extensions of a permutation. The corresponding questions for the case of antimorphic extensions are investigated in Section 3.4. In some of our proofs we refer to computer programs which were used to search for occurrences of a pattern in a finite set of words. The source code for these programs can be found in Appendix B.

3.2 Preliminaries

3.2.1 Definitions

A morphism (resp. antimorphism) $f : \Sigma_m^* \to \Sigma_m^*$ is called a morphic (resp. antimorphic) permutation if the restriction of f to Σ_m, denoted $f|_{\Sigma_m}$, is a permutation on the alphabet Σ_m.

If $f : \Sigma_m \to \Sigma_m$ is a permutation, we say that the order of f, denoted $\mathrm{ord}(f)$, is the minimal positive integer such that $f^{\mathrm{ord}(f)}$ is the identity. If $a \in \Sigma_m$ is a letter, the order of a with respect to f, denoted $\mathrm{ord}_f(a)$, is the minimal positive integer such that $f^{\mathrm{ord}_f(a)}(a) = a$.

3.2.2 Avoidability of patterns under permutations

We are interested here in patterns of the form $\pi^i(x)\pi^j(x)\pi^k(x)$, where x is a word variable and π is a function symbol that stands either for morphic permutations or for antimorphic permutations over an alphabet including all letters of x. Instances of such a pattern are words $f^i(u)f^j(u)f^k(u)$, where $u \in \Sigma_m^+$ and $f : \Sigma_m^* \to \Sigma_m^*$ is a morphism permuting Σ_m, when π denotes morphic permutations, or an antimorphism that permutes Σ_m, when π stands for antimorphic permutations. Consequently, the pattern $\pi^i(x)\pi^j(x)\pi^k(x)$ is avoidable in Σ_m if there is an infinite word over Σ_m that does not contain any factor $f^i(u)f^j(u)f^k(u)$ as above.

Example 3.1. Consider the word

$$w = 002210021100221002.$$

It is not hard to check that w contains no factor that is of the form $uf(u)u$, where u is a word and f a morphic permutation (in fact, this is a consequence of Lemma 3.2, which is shown below). Hence w avoids the pattern $x\pi(x)x$, if π denotes morphic permutations. However, the situation changes if we replace π with antimorphic permutations: then the factor 022100211002210 is of the form $ug(u)u$, where $u = 02210$ and g is the antimorphic permutation defined by $g(0) = 0, g(1) = 2$, and $g(2) = 1$, since $g(02210) = 02110$. Thus, w does not avoid $x\pi(x)x$, if π denotes antimorphic permutations.

3.3 Cubes with morphic permutations

In this section, the function variable π is always substituted by a morphic permutation.

We begin this section by studying a series of basic patterns and showing that they are avoidable. These results are then used to deduce avoidability results involving more general patterns. Our first result makes use of the 5-uniform morphism $\alpha : \Sigma_2^* \to \Sigma_3^*$ that is defined by

$$\alpha(0) = 02110, \qquad\qquad \alpha(1) = 02210,$$

and the cube-free Thue-Morse word t, which was defined in Chapter 2.

Lemma 3.2. *The infinite word $t_\alpha = \alpha(t) = 02110022100221002110\cdots$ avoids the pattern $x\pi(x)x$ in Σ_m, for all $m \geqslant 3$. This pattern cannot be avoided by words over smaller alphabets.*

Proof. From the definition of α, we see that the only factors of t_α of length three that contain three distinct letters are 021 and 210. Furthermore, as t is cube-free, and so in particular it does not have 000 or 111 as a factor, every factor of t_α of length at least 17 contains both 021 and 210. Suppose now that there is an instance of $x\pi(x)x$ appearing in t_α, that is, a factor of the form $uf(u)u$ for some word u and a morphism f that permutes Σ_m. As observed before, if $|u| \geqslant 17$, then 021 is a factor of u. So the word $f(021)$ must be a factor of $f(u)$, and since f is a permutation and the only factors of length three containing three different letters in t_α are 021 and 210, we must have either $f(021) = 021$ or $f(021) = 210$.

In the first case, f is the identity on Σ_3 and thus $uf(u)u$ is a cube. However, using Lemma 2.11, we can check that α is a cube-free morphism, and since t is cube-free, so is $t_\alpha = \alpha(t)$.

Therefore we must have $f(021) = 210$, which implies that $f(210) = 102$, and as 210 is a factor of u, 102 is a factor of $f(u)$. However, 102 is not a factor of t_α, as can be observed from the definition of α.

Hence t_α has no factors of the form $uf(u)u$ where f is a permutation and u is a word of length at least 17.

It remains to be checked that t_α does not contain any factor of the form $uf(u)u$ with $|u| < 17$. This can be shown by testing whether such a word is a factor of $\alpha(v)$, for all the factors v of length 4 of the Thue-Morse word t. A simple computer program shows that indeed there are no such words.

If we consider alphabets Σ_m with $m > 3$, we observe that t_α may contain an instance of $x\pi(x)x$ that is not a cube if and only if π is mapped to a permutation

19

3. Cubic patterns with permutations

of Σ_m whose restriction to Σ_3 is also a permutation (because t_α contains no other symbols than those of Σ_3). Therefore, the other letters of the alphabet on which the function substituting π is defined can be neglected, and we can use the same reasoning as in the case when $m = 3$.

Bischoff, Currie, and Nowotka [10] showed that this pattern is not avoided by words defined on smaller alphabets. □

The following lemma is the main tool that we use to analyse the avoidability of cubes with morphic permutations. To obtain this result we apply the 9-uniform morphism $\beta : \Sigma_2^* \to \Sigma_4^*$ defined by

$$\beta(0) = 012013213, \qquad\qquad \beta(1) = 012031023.$$

Lemma 3.3. *Let $t_\beta = \beta(t) = 012013213012031023012031023012013213\cdots$ and $i, j \in \mathbb{N}$ and f, g be morphic permutations of Σ_m with $m \geqslant 4$. Then:*

- *t_β does not contain any factor of the form $uf(u)g(u)$ for any $u \in \Sigma_m^+$ with $|u| \geqslant 7$.*

- *t_β does not contain any factor $uf^i(u)f^j(u)$ with*

$$\left| \left\{ u[\ell], f^i(u)[\ell], f^j(u)[\ell] \right\} \right| \leqslant 2,$$

for all $\ell \leqslant |u|$ and $|u| \leqslant 6$.

Proof. We start by addressing the first claim. The fact that t_β contains no cube is a consequence of the well-known cube-freeness of t and Lemma 2.11. For $7 \leqslant |u| \leqslant 28$, the length of any word of the form $uf(u)g(u)$ is at most 84, and thus any such word appears as a factor of $\beta(v)$, where v is a factor of the Thue-Morse word t with $|v| = 11$. Hence, it suffices to check that there is no factor of the form $uf(u)g(u)$ in the image of the set of factors of length 11 of the Thue-Morse word. We did this using a computer program.

For $|u| \geqslant 29$, one can easily check that every factor of t_β of length at least 29 contains either the word 0120132 or the word 1231301 as a factor. We assume that 0120132 is a factor of u, the other case can be dealt with analogously. If t_β contained a factor of the form $uf(u)g(u)$, then both $f(u)$ and $g(u)$ contain a factor of the form $abcabdc$, where $a, b, c, d \in \Sigma_m$ are pairwise different letters. It is however verified that 0120132 is the only factor of the form $abcabdc$ in

t_β, hence $f(u) = g(u) = u$, and t_β contains a cube, which is a contradiction. To show the second statement, we observe that every possible occurrence of such a factor is included in the image under β of a factor of length 4 of t (by the same reasoning as above). Computer calculations show that there are only 12 different factors of the form $ug_1(u)g_2(u)$ for some $u \in \Sigma_m^+$ with $|u| \leqslant 6$ and permutations g_1, g_2 such that there is no position $1 \leqslant \ell \leqslant |u|$ with $u[l] \neq g_1(u)[\ell] \neq g_2(u)[\ell] \neq u[\ell]$. These factors are:

$$012|013|213, 013|213|012, 023|012|013, 120|132|130,$$
$$130|120|132, 132|130|120, 201|321|301, 213|012|013,$$
$$230|120|132, 301|201|321, 321|301|201, 321|301|203,$$

where the vertical lines mark the borders between $u, g_1(u)$ and $g_2(u)$. For every factor we can check that there are no $i, j \in \mathbb{N}$ and no permutation f such that $g_1 = f^i$ and $g_2 = f^j$. For instance, let us assume that there are i, j and f such that $012|013|213$ is a factor of the form $uf^i(u)f^j(u)$ (i.e., $u = 012$, $f^i(u) = 013$ and $f^j(u) = 213$). Since $u[1] = f^i(u)[1] = f^i(u[1]) = 0$, it follows that $\mathrm{ord}_f(0) \mid i$ and since $f^j(u)[1] = 2$, we conclude that the letter 2 is in the same orbit of f as 0, i.e., $\mathrm{ord}_f(2) = \mathrm{ord}_f(0)$ and $\mathrm{ord}_f(2) \mid i$. This is a contradiction with $u[3] = 2 \neq 3 = f^i(u)[3] = f^i(u[3])$. The analysis of the other factors leads to similar contradictions. $\qquad\square$

The next result exhibits two pairs of patterns that cannot be simultaneously avoided.

Lemma 3.4. *There is no $w \in \Sigma_3^\omega$ that avoids the patterns $xx\pi(x)$ and $x\pi(x)x$ simultaneously. There is no $w \in \Sigma_3^\omega$ that avoids the patterns $x\pi(x)\pi(x)$ and $x\pi(x)x$ simultaneously.*

Proof. It can be easily verified (for instance, by checking with a computer program that explores all the possibilities by backtracking) that each word of length at least nine in Σ_3^+ contains a word of the form uuu, $uuf(u)$, or $uf(u)u$, for some $u \in \Sigma_3^+$ and some morphic permutation f of Σ_3.

Similarly, any word of length at least ten in Σ_3^+ contains a word of the form uuu, $uf(u)f(u)$, or $uf(u)u$, for some word $u \in \Sigma_3^+$ and a morphic permutation f of Σ_3. $\qquad\square$

3. Cubic patterns with permutations

The following result shows the equivalence in terms of avoidability in Σ_m of several pairs of patterns with permutations.

Lemma 3.5. *Let $m \in \mathbb{N}$.*

- *A word $w \in \Sigma_m^\omega$ avoids $xx\pi(x)$ if and only if w avoids $\pi(x)\pi(x)x$.*
- *A word $w \in \Sigma_m^\omega$ avoids $x\pi(x)\pi(x)$ if and only if w avoids $\pi(x)xx$.*
- *A word $w \in \Sigma_m^\omega$ avoids $x\pi(x)x$ if and only if w avoids $\pi(x)x\pi(x)$.*

Proof. If an infinite word w has no factor $uuf(u)$, with $u \in \Sigma_m^+$ and a morphic permutation f of Σ_m, then w does not contain any factor $g(u)g(u)u$, with $u \in \Sigma_m^+$ and a morphic permutation g of Σ_m for which there exists a morphic permutation f' of Σ_m such that $g(f'(a)) = a$, for all $a \in \Sigma_m$. This clearly means that w avoids $\pi(x)\pi(x)x$ in Σ_m. The other conclusions follow by the same argument. $\square$

The following two remarks are immediate.

- The pattern $\pi^i(x)\pi^i(x)\pi^i(x)$ is avoidable in Σ_m for $m \geqslant 2$. It is avoided by the word $\boldsymbol{t}$.
- The patterns $\pi^i(x)\pi^i(x)\pi^j(x)$ and $\pi^i(x)\pi^j(x)\pi^j(x)$, $i \neq j$, are avoidable in Σ_m for $m \geqslant 3$. They are avoided by the square-free word $\boldsymbol{h}$ defined in Chapter 2.

Another set of avoidable patterns is presented in the next lemma.

Lemma 3.6. *The pattern $\pi^i(x)\pi^j(x)\pi^i(x)$, $i \neq j$, is avoidable in Σ_m, for $m \geqslant 3$.*

Proof. If $i < j$, setting $y = \pi^i(x)$ turns the pattern $\pi^i(x)\pi^j(x)\pi^i(x)$ into the pattern $y\pi^{j-i}(y)y$. We can avoid the last pattern in Σ_m if we can avoid $y\pi(y)y$ in Σ_m. This pattern is avoidable in alphabets with three or more letters, by Lemma 3.2. Also, $y\pi^{j-i}(y)y$ is avoidable in Σ_2 if and only if $j - i$ is even.

If $i > j$, we set $y = \pi^j(x)$, and $\pi^i(x)\pi^j(x)\pi^i(x)$ turns into $\pi^{i-j}(y)y\pi^{i-j}(y)$, which is avoidable if $\pi(y)y\pi(y)$ is avoidable. This latter pattern is avoidable in alphabets with three or more letters, by Lemma 3.2 and Lemma 3.5. The pattern is also avoidable in Σ_2 if and only if $i - j$ is even. $\square$

In the next lemma we study patterns of the form $x\pi^i(x)\pi^j(x)$, with $i \neq j$. For this purpose we define the following values:

$$k_1 = \inf\{t : t \nmid |i - j|, t \nmid i, t \nmid j\} \tag{3.1}$$

3.3. Cubes with morphic permutations

$$k_2 = \inf\{t : t \mid |i - j|, t \nmid i, t \nmid j\} \qquad (3.2)$$

$$k_3 = \inf\{t : t \mid i, t \nmid j\} \qquad (3.3)$$

$$k_4 = \inf\{t : t \nmid i, t \mid j\}. \qquad (3.4)$$

By definition, $\inf\varnothing = +\infty$. However, note that $\{t : t \nmid |i - j|, t \nmid i, t \nmid j\}$ is always non-empty, and that $k_1 \geqslant 3$, as either $|i - j|$ is even or one of i and j is even and thus $k_1 > 2$. Also, as $i \neq j$, at least one of the two sets $\{t : t \mid i, t \nmid j\}$ and $\{t : t \nmid i, t \mid j\}$ is non-empty as well. Further, we define

$$k = \min\{\max\{k_1, k_2\}, \max\{k_1, k_3\}, \max\{k_1, k_4\}\} \qquad (3.5)$$

According to the remarks above, it always holds that $k \neq +\infty$.

Lemma 3.7. *The pattern* $x\pi^i(x)\pi^j(x)$, $i \neq j$, *is unavoidable in* Σ_m, *for* $m \geqslant k$.

Proof. First, let us note that the fact that $m \geqslant k_1$ means that for every word $u \in \Sigma_m^+$ there exists a morphic permutation f such that $u \neq f^i(u) \neq f^j(u) \neq u$; indeed, we choose f such that the orbit of $u[1]$ is a cycle of length k_1, which means that the first letters of u, $f^i(u)$ and $f^j(u)$ are pairwise different.

Similarly, the fact that $m \geqslant k_2$ (when $k_2 \neq +\infty$) means that for every word $u \in \Sigma_m^+$ there exists a morphism f such that $u \neq f^i(u) = f^j(u)$. In this case, we choose f such that $\mathrm{ord}_f(u[1]) = k_2$, and f only changes the letters from the orbit of $u[1]$ (thus, $\mathrm{ord}(f) \mid k_2$). Clearly, the first letters of $f^i(u)$ and $f^j(u)$ are not equal to $u[1]$, but $f^i(u) = f^j(u)$ as $\mathrm{ord}(f)$ divides $|i - j|$. We get that $u \neq f^i(u) = f^j(u)$ for this choice of f.

Finally, one can show analogously that the fact that $m \geqslant k_3$ (when $k_3 \neq +\infty$) means that for every word $u \in \Sigma_m^+$ there exists a morphism f such that $u = f^i(u) \neq f^j(u)$ and the fact that $m \geqslant k_4$ (when $k_4 \neq +\infty$) means that for every word $u \in \Sigma_m^+$ there exists a morphism f such that $f^i(u) \neq u = f^j(u)$.

Further, we show that if $m \geqslant \max\{k_1, k_2\}$ (in the case when $k_2 \neq +\infty$) there is no infinite word over Σ_m that avoids $x\pi^i(x)\pi^j(x)$. As $k_1 \geqslant 3$ it follows that $m \geqslant 3$. One can quickly check that the longest word that does not contain an instance of this pattern has length six and is 001010 by trying to construct such a word letter by letter. This means that there is no infinite word over Σ_m that avoids this pattern in this case.

By similar arguments, we can show that if $m \geqslant \max\{k_1, k_3\}$ (in the case when

23

3. Cubic patterns with permutations

$k_3 \neq +\infty$) there is no infinite word over Σ_m that avoids $x\pi^i(x)\pi^j(x)$. In this case, the longest word that avoids the pattern is 01010.

If $m \geqslant \max\{k_1, k_4\}$ (in the case when $k_4 \neq +\infty$) we also get that there is no infinite word over Σ_m that avoids $x\pi^i(x)\pi^j(x)$. Here, the construction necessarily ends at length six, the longest words without an instance of the pattern are 011001, 011002, 011221, 011223 and 011220.

These last remarks show that the pattern $x\pi^i(x)\pi^j(x)$ is unavoidable by infinite words over Σ_m, for all $m \geqslant k$. $\qquad\qquad\square$

The next result represents the main step towards a characterisation of the avoidability of cubic patterns with morphic permutations.

Proposition 3.8. *For any pattern $x\pi^i(x)\pi^j(x)$ we can effectively determine all values m, such that the pattern is avoidable in Σ_m.*

Proof. Since we already examined the case $m \geqslant k$ in Lemma 3.7, we can focus on alphabets Σ_m with $m < k$.

The cases for $m = 2$ and $m = 3$ were investigated manually and the results are depicted in Figure 3.1. We can consider the exponents i and j modulo 6 here, as the order of each permutation of Σ_2 and Σ_3 is at most 6. Note that in the table marked with Σ_m for $m \in \{2, 3\}$, an entry "$\checkmark$" in line i and column j means that the pattern $xf^i(x)f^j(x)$ is avoidable in Σ_m, whereas "$\times$" means that this pattern in unavoidable in Σ_m. To build these tables we used the results from Lemma 3.4 to Lemma 3.6 and the fact that the pattern $x\pi^i(x)\pi^j(x)$ is avoidable in Σ_2 if and only if $i \equiv j \equiv 0 \pmod 2$, in which case it is avoided by the Thue-Morse word t. Furthermore, for $j \neq 0$, the avoidability of the pattern in Σ_3 follows from the fact that every instance of the pattern contains cubes or squares, so it can be avoided by the infinite words t (regarded as a word over three letters, that just does not contain one of the letters) or h, respectively. When $j = 0$, we use the word defined in Lemma 3.3 to show the avoidability of the respective patterns.

We move on to the case $m \geqslant 4$ and split the discussion further, depending on which value is the minimum of k_1, k_2, k_3, and k_4.

If $k_1 = \min\{k_1, k_2, k_3, k_4\}$, then $k > k_1$. If $m < k_1$, then $m \mid i$ and $m \mid j$ must hold, since $k_3, k_4 > k_1$. For every letter $a \in \Sigma_m$ and every morphic permutation f of Σ_m, since $\mathrm{ord}_f(a) \leqslant m$, we get that $\mathrm{ord}_f(a) \mid i$ and $\mathrm{ord}_f(a) \mid j$. So in this case an instance of the pattern $x\pi^i(x)\pi^j(x)$ is a cube, which can be avoided by the Thue-Morse word t. If $k_1 \leqslant m < k$, then for every $a \in \Sigma_m$ and every morphic permutation f of Σ_m we either have that $\mathrm{ord}_f(a)$ divides both i and j or that $\mathrm{ord}_f(a)$ divides neither i nor j nor $|i - j|$. If we have a letter a occurring in a word u such that the latter holds, it means that we must have at least 3 different letters in the word $u f^i(u) f^j(u)$. If there is no such letter in u, then $u f^i(u) f^j(u)$ is a cube. In both cases, the Thue-Morse word t avoids the pattern $x\pi^i(x)\pi^j(x)$.

If $k_2 = \min\{k_1, k_2, k_3, k_4\}$, then $k = k_1$. If $4 \leqslant m < k_2$, we get for every $a \in \Sigma_m$ and every morphic permutation f of Σ_m that $\mathrm{ord}_f(a) \mid i$ and $\mathrm{ord}_f(a) \mid j$, since $k_3, k_4 > k_2$. This means that in this case every instance of the pattern $x\pi^i(x)\pi^j(x)$ is a cube, which can be avoided by the Thue-Morse word. If $k_2 \leqslant m < k$, we have for each letter $a \in \Sigma_m$ and every morphic permutation f of Σ_m that either $\mathrm{ord}_f(a)$ divides at least one of i and j or $\mathrm{ord}_f(a) \mid |i - j|$. In all cases, this implies for each position ℓ of a word u, that at least two of the letters $u[\ell], f^i(u)[\ell]$ and $f^j(u)[\ell]$ are equal, and so the word defined in Lemma 3.3 avoids the pattern.

If $k_3 = \min\{k_1, k_2, k_3, k_4\}$, then $k = k_1$, as in the previous case. If $4 \leqslant m < k_3$, then for every letter $a \in \Sigma_m$ and every morphic permutation f, $\mathrm{ord}_f(a) \mid i$ and $\mathrm{ord}_f(a) \mid j$ must hold. Again, every instance of $x\pi^i(x)\pi^j(x)$ is a cube, and so this pattern is avoided by the Thue-Morse word t. If $k_3 \leqslant m < k = k_1$, we can observe that for every letter $a \in \Sigma_m$ and every morphic permutation f, $\mathrm{ord}_f(a)$ divides i or j or both of them. This means that for every factor of the form $u f^i(u) f^j(u)$ and every position ℓ in u we have that $u[\ell] = f^i(u)[\ell]$ or $u[\ell] = f^j(u)[\ell]$. Therefore, the word of Lemma 3.3 avoids the pattern.

If $k_4 = \min\{k_1, k_2, k_3, k_4\}$, we have a symmetric situation to the previous case, so the pattern $x\pi^i(x)\pi^j(x)$ is avoided by the Thue-Morse word t for $4 \leqslant m < k_4$

Σ_2		j (mod 6)					
		0	1	2	3	4	5
i (mod 6)	0	✓	×	✓	×	✓	×
	1	×	×	×	×	×	×
	2	✓	×	✓	×	✓	×
	3	×	×	×	×	×	×
	4	✓	×	✓	×	✓	×
	5	×	×	×	×	×	×

Σ_3		j (mod 6)					
		0	1	2	3	4	5
i (mod 6)	0	✓	✓	✓	✓	✓	✓
	1	✓	✓	×	×	×	×
	2	✓	×	✓	×	✓	✓
	3	✓	✓	×	✓	×	✓
	4	✓	✓	✓	×	✓	×
	5	✓	×	×	×	×	✓

Figure 3.1. Avoidability of $x\pi^i(x)\pi^j(x)$ in Σ_2 and Σ_3 for morphic π

3. Cubic patterns with permutations

and by the word of Lemma 3.3 for $k_4 \leqslant m < k$.

Now we can conclude the characterisation of patterns $x\pi^i(x)\pi^j(x)$. Such a pattern is always avoidable in Σ_m for all $4 \leqslant m < k$. Moreover, it might also be avoidable in Σ_2 and Σ_3, or only Σ_3 but not in Σ_2, or neither in Σ_2 nor in Σ_3 (according to Figure 3.1). Therefore, for each pair (i, j) of natural numbers defining a pattern $x\pi^i(x)\pi^j(x)$, we can effectively compute all values m such that this pattern is avoidable in Σ_m. $\square$

The following result complements the previous one.

Proposition 3.9. *For any pattern $\pi^i(x)\pi^j(x)x$ we can effectively determine all values m, such that the pattern is avoidable in Σ_m.*

Proof. Let m be a natural number. We want to check whether $\pi^i(x)\pi^j(x)x$ is avoidable in Σ_m or not. Let $M = \max\{i+1, j+1, m\}$. It is not hard to see that $f^{M!}$ is the identity for all morphic permutations f of the alphabet Σ_m. Let furthermore $y = \pi^i(x)$. As the functions substituting π are permutations, we obtain that $\pi^i(x)\pi^j(x)x$ is avoidable in Σ_m, if and only if $y\pi^{M!-i+j}(y)\pi^{M!-i}(y)$ is avoidable in Σ_m. Moreover, note that:

$$\inf\{t : t \nmid j, t \nmid M! - i, t \nmid M! - i + j\} = \inf\{t : t \nmid |i - j|, t \nmid i, t \nmid j\}$$
$$\inf\{t : t \mid j, t \nmid M! - i, t \nmid M! - i + j\} = \inf\{t : t \nmid i, t \mid j\}$$
$$\inf\{t : t \mid M! - i, t \nmid M! - i + j\} = \inf\{t : t \mid i, t \nmid j\}$$
$$\inf\{t : t \nmid M! - i, t \mid M! - i + j\} = \inf\{t : t \mid |i - j|, t \nmid i, t \nmid j\}$$

Therefore, $y\pi^{M!-i+j}(y)\pi^{M!-i}(y)$ is avoidable in Σ_m if $4 \leqslant m < k$, where k is defined using (3.5) for the given i and j. $\square$

In the exact same manner we derive the following proposition.

Proposition 3.10. *For any pattern $\pi^i(x)x\pi^j(x)$ we can effectively determine all values m, such that the pattern is avoidable in Σ_m.*

We can now summarise the results of this section in the following theorem:

Theorem 3.11. *For any pattern $\pi^i(x)\pi^j(x)\pi^k(x)$, where π is substituted by morphic permutations, we can effectively determine all values m such that the pattern is avoidable in Σ_m.*

Proof. Let us assume that $i \leqslant j, k$ first. Let $y = \pi^i(x)$, which turns the given pattern into $y\pi^{j-i}(y)\pi^{k-i}(y)$, and we can identify all alphabets where this pattern is avoidable using Proposition 3.8.

If $j \leqslant i, k$, we use Proposition 3.10 to identify the alphabets where this pattern is avoidable. Finally, if $k \leqslant i, j$, we use Proposition 3.9 to determine all alphabets where this pattern is avoidable. $\qquad\square$

Example 3.12. Using our results we can now decide if the pattern

$$x\pi^5(x)\pi^{12}(x)$$

is avoidable in a given alphabet. The calculated value for k as defined in (3.5) in this case is 8. Therefore, the pattern $x\pi^5(x)\pi^{12}(x)$ is unavoidable in Σ_2 (by Figure 3.1), avoidable in Σ_3 (also by Figure 3.1) as well as in $\Sigma_4, \ldots, \Sigma_7$ (by Proposition 3.8), and unavoidable in Σ_8 and larger alphabets (by Lemma 3.7).

3.4 Cubes with antimorphic permutations

In this section, the function variable π is always replaced by an antimorphic permutation.

As in the morphic case, we first establish a series of results regarding basic patterns. To begin with, we introduce the 7-uniform morphism $\gamma : \Sigma_2^* \to \Sigma_3^*$ defined by

$$\gamma(0) = 0011022, \qquad\qquad \gamma(1) = 1100122.$$

Lemma 3.13. *The word* $t_\gamma = \gamma(t) = 0011022110012211001220011022\cdots$ *avoids the pattern* $x\pi(x)x$ *in* Σ_m *for* $m \geqslant 3$.

Proof. We can easily check that t_γ contains no factor of the form $uf(u)u$ for some antimorphic permutation f with $|u| < 22$ using a computer program.

From the definition of t_γ it can be observed that every factor of length at least 22 of t_γ contains both 102 and 012 as a factor. We assume that t_γ contains a factor of the form $uf(u)u$ for some u of length at least 22 and an antimorphic permutation of the alphabet f. Hence, since u contains the words 102 and 012,

27

3. Cubic patterns with permutations

there must be $f(102)$ and $f(012)$ appearing in t_γ. There are only two possible choices for $f(102)$ in t_γ: either $f(102) = 102$ or $f(102) = 012$.

In the first case, we would have $f(012) = 120$, which does not appear as a factor in t_γ, and in the second case $f(012) = 021$, which does also not appear in t_γ. Hence, t_γ does not contain a factor of the form $uf(u)u$ for some word u and an antimorphic permutation f. □

Rampersad and Shallit [76] showed that every infinite square-free word $w \in \Sigma_4^\omega$ contains a factor u of length two, such that u^R is also a factor of w. We will show that for factors of length three the situation is different. For this, we define the morphism $\delta : \Sigma_3^* \to \Sigma_4^*$ by

$$\delta(0) = 0120130123013023,$$
$$\delta(1) = 0120130123023123,$$
$$\delta(2) = 0120130123120123.$$

Lemma 3.14. *There exists an infinite square-free word $w \in \Sigma_4^\omega$ such that if u is a factor of w with $|u| \geqslant 3$, then u^R is not a factor of w.*

Proof. It can be verified that the morphism δ defined above is square-free using Theorem 2.10. Hence, the image of any square-free word under δ is also square-free. That this image contains no u^R for any factor u of length at least three can be observed directly from the definition of δ. □

The following lemma now shows the avoidability of a particular type of patterns where the function variable is replaced by a morphism.

Lemma 3.15. *The word $h_\delta = \delta(h) = 01201301230130230120130\cdots$ contains no factor uu and $uf(u)u^R$ where $u \in \Sigma_m^+$ and f is a morphic permutation of Σ_m, for all $m \geqslant 4$.*

Proof. The square-freeness of h_δ results from the fact that δ is a square-free morphism, as mentioned in the proof of the previous lemma. Furthermore, also by the previous proof, h_δ contains no factor of the form $uf(u)u^R$ with $|u| \geqslant 3$. Therefore, we only have to show that no factor of h_δ is of the form $uf(u)u^R$ for $|u| \in \{1,2\}$. This can be straightforwardly deduced from the definition of δ. □

The previous lemma has a corollary that is of importance in the context of avoidability of cubes with antimorphic permutations.

Corollary 3.16. *There exists an infinite word that avoids the patterns xx and $x\pi(x)x^R$ in Σ_m, for all $m \geqslant 4$.*

Proof. By the previous lemma we obtain that there exist infinitely many finite words that contain no factors uu and $uf(u)u^R$ for $u \in \Sigma_m^+$ and morphic permutations f over alphabets Σ_m with $m \geqslant 4$. Reversing these words, we obtain infinitely many finite words over Σ_m that contain neither squares nor factors $uf(u)u^R$ for $u \in \Sigma_m^+$ and antimorphic permutations f on Σ_m, with $m \geqslant 4$. By the usual compactness argument[1] there exists an infinite word that contains none of these factors. $\square$

As in the case of the morphic permutations, we study the avoidability of the pattern $x\pi^i(x)\pi^j(x)$ next. However, a finer analysis must be performed here.

In the next lemma we look at the case when the exponent i is even and j is odd. For this purpose let the morphism $\zeta : \Sigma_2^* \to \Sigma_5^*$ be defined by

$$\zeta(0) = 012034, \qquad\qquad \zeta(1) = 120324.$$

Lemma 3.17. *Let $t_\zeta = \zeta(t) = 012034120324120324012034\cdots$, $i \in \mathbb{N}$ be even and $j \in \mathbb{N}$ be odd, and f and g be morphic and, respectively, antimorphic permutations of Σ_m, with $m \geqslant 5$. Then:*

- *t_ζ does not contain any factor of the form $uf(u)g(u)$ for $u \in \Sigma_m^+$ with $|u| \geqslant 6$.*
- *t_ζ does not contain any factor of the form $uf^i(u)f^j(u)$ such that*

$$\left| \left\{ u[\ell], f^i(u)[\ell], f^j(u)^R[\ell] \right\} \right| \leqslant 2,$$

for all $\ell \leqslant |u|$ and $|u| \leqslant 5$.

Proof. We start by proving the first claim of the lemma. If $|u| = 6$, the length of such a factor is 18 and hence it is completely contained in the images of factors of length four of the Thue-Morse word under ζ. We can verify that there is no such factor in this set by simple computer calculations.

---
[1] also referred to as König's lemma [60], see also Section 2.1 in [65].

3. Cubic patterns with permutations

If $|u| > 6$, we can show an even stronger statement, namely that there is no factor $uh(u)$ in t_ζ where h is an antimorphic permutation. To see this, we perform an extensive case analysis on the suffix of length seven of u. There are 22 different factors of length seven in t_ζ. We show two cases explicitly, the others use the same arguments. For example, if $0120340 \leqslant_s u$, this factor is always followed by 12034 in t_ζ. If this had the form $uh(u)$ for a word u and an antimorphic permutation h, we could deduce $h(0) = 1$ and $h(0) = 3$, a contradiction.

In most other cases we get that one letter would be mapped onto two different images as well. One case where we need a different argument is when $0324120 \leqslant_s u$. We can observe that this factor is always followed by 324 in t_ζ, which itself is followed by either 012 or 120. If it is followed by 012, we get a contradiction of the same type as before, since then 2 would be mapped to both 2 and 1 simultaneously. Thus, if this factor is of the form $uh(u)$ for some word u and antimorphic permutation h, we must have 0324120324120 as a factor in t_ζ. However, this only appears as a factor of t_ζ, if 111 is a factor of t, which is a contradiction to the cube-freeness of t.

It follows that t_ζ does not contain any factor of the form $uf(u)g(u)$ with $|u| \geqslant 6$, since

$$f(u)g(u) = f(u)g\left(f^{-1}\left(f(u)\right)\right),$$

and $h = g \circ f^{-1}$ is an antimorphic permutation.

For the proof of the second statement, it is sufficient to consider occurrences in the images of factors of length four of t, again because of the length constraint. A short computation shows that there are only two different factors of the form $ug_1(u)g_2(u)$ with $|u| \leqslant 5$ and g_1 and g_2 antimorphic permutations such that there is no position $1 \leqslant \ell \leqslant |u|$ with $u[\ell] \neq g_1(u)[\ell] \neq g_2(u)[\ell] \neq u[\ell]$ in those images: 240120341 and 340120341.

For both factors, we can quickly check that there is no permutation f and no $i, j \in \mathbb{N}$ such that $g_1 = f^i$ and $g_2 = f^j$. If we assume that 240120341 has the form $uf^i(u)f^j(u)$, for some u and f as in the statement, we obtain $u = 240$, $f^i(u) = 120$ and $f^j(u) = 341$. By looking at the second letter of each block we get $f^i(4) = 2$ and $f^j(4) = 4$, that is $\text{ord}_f(4) \mid j$ and 2 is in the same orbit of f as 4, so $\text{ord}_f(2) = \text{ord}_f(4)$. However, also $f^j(240) = f^j(0)f^j(4)f^j(2) = 341$, so $f^j(2) = 1$, contradicting the fact that $\text{ord}_f(2) \mid j$. The same reasoning applies to the factor 340120341. □

In the case when the exponent i is odd and j is even, we examine the 45-uniform morphism $\eta : \Sigma_2^* \to \Sigma_5^*$ defined by

$$\eta(0) = 012340124310243012340124310234102430124310234,$$
$$\eta(1) = 012340124310243012341023401243012341024310234.$$

Note that this morphism is equivalent to $\lambda \circ \beta$, where β is the morphism defined before Lemma 3.3 and $\lambda : \Sigma_4^* \to \Sigma_5^*$ is a 5-uniform morphism defined by

$$\lambda(0) = 01234, \qquad\qquad \lambda(1) = 01243,$$
$$\lambda(2) = 10243, \qquad\qquad \lambda(3) = 10234.$$

Lemma 3.18. *Let $t_\eta = \eta(t) = 012340124310243012340124310234102430124310243 \cdots$, $i \in \mathbb{N}$ be odd and $j \in \mathbb{N}$ be even and f and g be antimorphic and, respectively, morphic permutations of Σ_m, with $m \geqslant 5$. Then:*

- *t_η does not contain any factor of the form $uf(u)g(u)$ for $u \in \Sigma_m^+$ with $|u| \geqslant 11$.*
- *t_η does not contain any factor of the form $uf^i(u)f^j(u)$ such that*

$$\left| \left\{ u[\ell], f^i(u)^R[\ell], f^j(u)[\ell] \right\} \right| \leqslant 2,$$

for all $\ell \leqslant |u|$ and $|u| \leqslant 10$.

Proof. We first focus on the word $t_\beta = \beta(t)$ and show that it does not contain any factor of the form $uf'(u)g'(u)$ for any $u \in \Sigma_m^+$ with $|u| \geqslant 7$, where f' is an antimorphic permutation and g' is a morphic permutation. As in Lemma 3.3, we check the cases when u is short by computer calculations. To check that t_β has no factor of the form $uf'(u)g'(u)$ with $7 \leqslant |u| \leqslant 11$, it suffices to consider the images of all factors of length five of the Thue-Morse word under β.

In the case when $|u| \geqslant 12$ and f' is antimorphic, we can actually prove a stronger result. In fact, we show that t_β does not contain any factor of the form $uf'(u)$ for an antimorphic permutation f', when $|u| \geqslant 12$. For the sake of a contradiction, we assume that such a factor appears in t_β. By the shape of $\beta(0)$ and $\beta(1)$, we observe that every factor u of length at least 12 contains an occurrence of a factor s of length four that contains four different letters (this is already true for $|u| \geqslant 7$). In the following, we look at the last occurrence of such a factor in u and perform an exhaustive case analysis on its possible values and positions in u. Here, we use vertical lines to mark the border between u and $f'(u)$, while the dot marks the border between the images of two letters under β.

If $s = 0132$ it is followed by 130120 in t_β. If $0132 \leqslant_s u$, we got the following factor in t_β: 0132|1301. This means that $f'(0) = f'(2) = 1$, which contradicts the fact that f' is a permutation. If $01321 \leqslant_s u$, the factor overlapping the border is 01321|3012. This would mean that 1 is mapped to both 2 and 3 by f', a contradiction. If $013212 \leqslant_s u$, we have 2013213|0120 (recall that we assumed $|u| \geqslant 11$ and by the definition of β, 013213 is always preceded by 2 in t_β). The prefix 0120 of $f'(u)$ is followed by either 13 or 31 in t_β. In the former case, we get that f' maps 2 to both 2 and 3, and in the latter case f' maps 1 to both 1 and 3, a contradiction in both cases.

We now assume $s = 2130$. If $2130 \leqslant_s u$ held, then we would have 32130|1201 or 32130|12031 and either $f'(2) = f'(0) = 1$ or $f'(3) = f'(0) = 1$. So let $21301 \leqslant_s u$. Then we have either 21301|20132 or 21301|20310 and either $f'(2) = f'(1) = 2$ or $f'(2) = f'(0) = 0$, a contradiction in both cases.

The cases $s \in \{3012, 2013, 2031, 3102, 1023\}$ lead to similar contradictions following the same reasoning as above.

If $s = 1203$, we see that $1203 \leqslant_s u$, as otherwise s would not be the last occurrence of a factor with that shape. From the definition of β, we see that the factor on the border between u and $f'(u)$ must be 301203|102301 from which it follows that $f(1) = 3$ and $f(2) = 2$. This means that we get a contradiction as above if 301203 is preceded by a 1, since 102301 is always followed by 2 in t_β. Hence, we have the factor 102301213|1023012 and since f' is completely determined by this, we get that $102301203 \leqslant_p f'(u)$. It follows that the factor 1023.01203|1023.01203 occurs in t_β. The shape of β implies now that 111 is a factor of t, a contradiction.

If $s = 2301$, we can derive that there is a cube in the Thue-Morse word as above, as we get the following factor: 3.012031023.01|2031023.01203 (here we use the fact that $|u| \geqslant 12$).

Henceforth, we look at the word $t_\eta = \lambda(t_\beta)$.

Let us first assume that $|u| > 30$ and $uf(u)g(u)$ appears in t_η. The word u contains at least six occurrences of the letter 2 in this case, and each two consecutive such occurrences have exactly four letters between them. This means that in $g(u)$ each two consecutive occurrences of $g(2)$ have exactly four letters between them as well, and $g(2)$ occurs at least six times in $g(u)$. This implies that $g(2) = 2$ and that $|u|$ is divisible by 5. A similar argument shows that $f(2) = 2$.

Consider now the last occurrence of 2 in u. This letter is mapped to the first 2 of $f(u)$, and there are exactly four letters between these two consecutive occurrences of the letter 2 in t_η. Therefore, after the last occurrence of 2 in u there are exactly two more letters in this word and there are exactly two letters in $f(u)$ before the first occurrence of 2. As $5 \mid |u|$, there exists a factor vsw in t_β, with $v, s, w \in \Sigma_4^*$, such that $u = \lambda(v)$, $f(u) = \lambda(s)$, and $g(u) = \lambda(w)$. Since f is an antimorphic permutation, there exists an antimorphic permutation f' such that $s = f'(v)$, and as g is a morphic permutation, there exists a morphic permutation g' such that $w = g'(v)$. The assumption $|u| > 30$ implies $|v| \geqslant 7$. Thus, t_β would contain a factor $vf'(v)g'(v)$ where f' is an antimorphic permutation, g' is a morphic permutation, and $|v| \geqslant 7$, a contradiction to what we showed at the beginning of this proof.

For $11 \leqslant |u| \leqslant 30$, computer calculations verify the claim. Here we have to check all factors of length at most 90 and see whether they are of the form $vf(v)g(v)$ or not. Any factor of t_η of length at most 90 is a factor of $\eta(w)$ where w is a factor of length three of t, so our check can be done fast, and it yields that the first statement of the lemma holds.

As in the proof of Lemma 3.3, the second statement can be easily checked by computer calculation. □

We now move further to the main results regarding the avoidability of cubic patterns with antimorphic permutations.

It is not hard to see that all the results on the avoidability of the patterns $\pi^i(x)\pi^i(x)\pi^i(x)$ with $i \in \mathbb{N}$ and $\pi^i(x)\pi^i(x)\pi^j(x)$ with $i, j \in \mathbb{N}$ for morphic permutations also hold in the case of antimorphic permutations. An analogous result to Lemma 3.6 also holds in the antimorphic case:

Lemma 3.19. *The pattern $\pi^i(x)\pi^j(x)\pi^i(x)$, $i \neq j$, is avoidable in Σ_m for $m \geqslant 3$.*

Proof. If $i < j$, we set $y = \pi^i(x)$ and the pattern $\pi^i(x)\pi^j(x)\pi^i(x)$ then turns into $y\pi^{j-i}(y)y$. This latter pattern is avoidable if $y\pi(y)y$ is avoidable, where the functions replacing π are morphic permutations if $j - i$ is even and antimorphic permutations if $j - i$ is odd. Therefore, the pattern is avoidable by Lemma 3.2 or Lemma 3.13, respectively.

3. Cubic patterns with permutations

If $i > j$, we set $y = \pi^j(x)$, which turns the pattern into $\pi^{i-j}(y)y\pi^{i-j}(y)$. This pattern is avoidable if $\pi(y)y\pi(y)$ is avoidable, where the functions replacing π are morphic permutations if $i - j$ is even and antimorphic permutations if $i - j$ is odd. In both cases the pattern is avoidable by Lemma 3.5 and Lemma 3.2 or Lemma 3.13, respectively. □

We now consider patterns of the form $x\pi^i(x)\pi^j(x)$ with $i \neq j$ and antimorphic permutations replacing π. Let k_1, k_2, k_3, k_4, and k be defined as in (3.1) to (3.5).

Lemma 3.20. *The pattern* $x\pi^i(x)\pi^j(x)$, $i \neq j$, *is unavoidable in* Σ_m *for* $m \geqslant k$.

Proof. Clearly, the remarks made at the beginning of the proof of Lemma 3.7 are valid in the antimorphic case as well. We now distinguish different cases depending on the parity of i and j. If both i and j are even, then for every antimorphic permutation f there exists a morphic permutation f' such that $f^i(u) = f'^i(u)$ and $f^j(u) = f'^j(u)$ for all $u \in \Sigma_m^+$ and we can apply Lemma 3.7. So let us assume first that i is odd and j is even.

An attempt to construct an infinite word over Σ_m that avoids the pattern if $m \geqslant \max\{k_1, k_2\}$ quickly fails. In fact, the longest word without an occurrence of such a pattern is 001010101, which is of length nine.

If $m \geqslant \max\{k_1, k_3\}$ such a construction stops even earlier: in this case the longest word that avoids the pattern is of length five: 01010.

If $m \geqslant \max\{k_1, k_4\}$, we can not get a word of length larger than six without having an instance of the pattern. One of these longest words is 011002.

In all cases we have seen that the pattern $x\pi^i(x)\pi^j(x)$ is unavoidable in Σ_m with $m \geqslant k$ if i is odd and j is even. The cases when i is even while j is odd and when both i and j are odd are similar and lead to the same results. The details are therefore omitted. □

The main result regarding patterns of the form $x\pi^i(x)\pi^j(x)$ with $i \neq j$ and antimorphic permutations replacing π is given in the following.

Proposition 3.21. *For any pattern* $x\pi^i(x)\pi^j(x)$, $i \neq j$, *we can effectively determine the values* m, *such that the pattern is avoidable in* Σ_m.

Proof. The cases when $m = 2$ and $m = 3$ are exactly like those depicted in Figure 3.1 for the morphic case.

The case when $m = 4$ is based on the remark that it is sufficient to know how to decide the avoidability of the pattern $x\pi^i(x)\pi^j(x)$ for $i, j < 12$. Indeed, the order of any permutation of Σ_4 is at most 12, and hence larger exponents can be reduced modulo 12. With this in mind, one can analyse every pair (i, j) with $1 \leqslant i, j \leqslant 12$, and decide in each case the avoidability of the pattern $x\pi^i(x)\pi^j(x)$. The pattern is unavoidable whenever the value k computed for i and j in (3.5) is less than or equal to four. When $i = 0$ the pattern $x\pi^i(x)\pi^j(x)$ is avoided by the word $\boldsymbol{h}$ as any instance of the pattern contains squares, and when $j = 0$ the pattern is avoided by the word from Lemma 3.13.

Also, in the case when i and j are both even, we can decide the avoidability of the pattern using the results obtained for morphisms in the previous sections, as in this case the permutation replacing π can be regarded as a morphism instead of an antimorphism.

Moreover, when $i = j$ we can avoid the pattern $x\pi^i(x)\pi^i(x)$ by the word $\boldsymbol{h}$ that contains no squares. The same word $\boldsymbol{h}$ avoids the pattern in the cases when $(i, j) \in \{(4, 1), (9, 1), (8, 5), (9, 5), (3, 7), (4, 7), (3, 11), (8, 11)\}$. To complete the picture, we note that a word avoids the pattern $x\pi(x^R)x^R$ if and only if it avoids the pattern $x\pi'(x)x^R$ where π' is mapped to a morphic permutation. Therefore, by Lemma 3.15 we obtain that the pattern $x\pi^i(x)\pi^j(x)$ is avoided by the infinite word $\boldsymbol{h}_\delta$ for $(i, j) \in \{(4, 3), (8, 3), (4, 9), (8, 9)\}$ and by Corollary 3.16 we obtain that it is avoidable for $(i, j) \in \{(7, 3), (11, 3), (1, 9), (5, 9)\}$.

Further, the discussion is split in four cases. If both i and j are even, we can decide the avoidability of the pattern just as in the case of morphisms (as the instance of π can be regarded as a morphism). If both i and j are odd, we compute the value k defined in (3.5) and define $M = \max\{k, j + 1, i + 1\}$. Now, $x\pi^i(x)\pi^j(x)$ is avoidable in Σ_m if and only if $(x\pi^i(x)\pi^j(x))^R = \pi^j(x^R)\pi^i(x^R)x^R$ is avoidable in Σ_m. The last condition is equivalent to the avoidability of the pattern $\pi^j(y)\pi^i(y)y$ in Σ_m. Let $z = \pi^j(y)$, then $\pi^j(y)\pi^i(y)y$ is avoidable in Σ_m if and only if $z\pi^{M!-j+i}(z)\pi^{M!-j}(z)$ is avoidable in Σ_m. However, $M! - j + i$ is even and $M! - j$ is odd, as $M!$ is always even. Therefore, the case when i and j are odd can be reduced to the case when i is even and j is odd.

So there are only two cases remaining: the case when i is even and j is odd, and the case when i is odd and j is even. As in the morphic case, we look at the minimum among k_1, k_2, k_3 and k_4.

If $k_1 = \min\{k_1, k_2, k_3, k_4\}$, this means that $k > k_1$ and for $m < k_1$ we get that

3. Cubic patterns with permutations

m divides both i and j. For every letter $a \in \Sigma_m$ and antimorphic permutation f of Σ_m, since $\mathrm{ord}_f(a) \leqslant m$, we get that $\mathrm{ord}_f(a)$ divides both i and j. Thus, every instance of $x\pi^i(x)\pi^j(x)$ is in fact an instance of $xx^R x$ when i is odd and j is even or an instance of xxx^R when i is even and j is odd. Those patterns are avoided by the word t_γ of Lemma 3.13 or the word h, respectively. If $k_1 \leqslant m < k$, then for every $a \in \Sigma_m$ and antimorphic permutation f of Σ_m we either have that $\mathrm{ord}_f(a)$ divides both i and j or it divides neither i nor j nor $|i-j|$. If there is no letter that fulfils the latter case, then the pattern turns into xxx^R (resp. $xx^R x$) if i is odd (resp. even) and j is even (resp. odd) and we can avoid it by the word h (resp. the word t_γ from Lemma 3.13). Otherwise we get that there have to be at least three different letters in an instance of this pattern and this is obviously avoided by the Thue-Morse word.

If $k_2 = \min\{k_1, k_2, k_3, k_4\}$, then $k = k_1$. If $4 \leqslant m < k_2$, then for every $a \in \Sigma_m$ and antimorphic permutation f of Σ_m we get that $\mathrm{ord}_f(a)$ divides both i and j (since $k_3, k_4 > k_2$). Again the pattern turns into $xx^R x$ (resp. xxx^R) when i is odd (resp. even) and j is even (resp. odd), which is avoided by the word h (resp. the word t_γ from Lemma 3.13). If $k_2 \leqslant m < k$, then for each $a \in \Sigma_m$ and antimorphic permutation f of Σ_m it holds that $\mathrm{ord}_f(a)$ divides at least one of i, j and $|i-j|$. Thus, for a factor $u f^i(u) f^j(u)$, at every position $\ell \leqslant |u|$ there are at most two different letters appearing in $u, f^i(u), f^j(u)^R$ if i is even and j is odd (resp. in $u, f^i(u)^R, f^j(u)$ if i is odd and j is even). None of these factors appear in the words of Lemma 3.17 and Lemma 3.18.

If $k_3 = \min\{k_1, k_2, k_3, k_4\}$, we get again $k = k_1$. If $4 \leqslant m < k_3$, then $\mathrm{ord}_f(a)$ divides both i and j for every letter $a \in \Sigma_m$ and every antimorphic permutation f of Σ_m. Hence every instance of $x\pi^i(x)\pi^j(x)$ is in fact an instance of xxx^R (resp. $xx^R x$) if i is even (resp. odd) and j is odd (resp. even) and thus avoided by the word h (resp. the word t_γ from Lemma 3.13). If $k_3 \leqslant m < k$, we observe that $\mathrm{ord}_f(a)$ divides at least one of i and j for every letter $a \in \Sigma_m$ and every antimorphic permutation f of Σ_m. This implies that for a factor $u f^i(u) f^j(u)$, at every position $\ell \leqslant |u|$ there are at most two different letters appearing in $u, f^i(u), f^j(u)^R$ if i is even and j is odd (resp. in $u, f^i(u)^R, f^j(u)$ if i is odd and j is even) and such factors do not appear in the words of Lemma 3.17 and Lemma 3.18.

As in the morphic case, the situation when $k_4 = \min\{k_1, k_2, k_3, k_4\}$ is symmetric to the previous case and therefore the same results hold. $\qquad\square$

We can now derive the following two results from the previous one:

Proposition 3.22. *For any pattern $\pi^i(x)\pi^j(x)x$ we can effectively determine all values m such that the pattern is avoidable in Σ_m.*

Proposition 3.23. *For any pattern $\pi^i(x)x\pi^j(x)$ we can effectively determine all values m such that the pattern is avoidable in Σ_m.*

Finally, as a consequence of the last three propositions, we state the main result of this section in the following theorem:

Theorem 3.24. *For any pattern $\pi^i(x)\pi^j(x)\pi^k(x)$, where π is substituted by antimorphic permutations, we can effectively determine all values m such that the pattern is avoidable in Σ_m.*

3.5 Conclusions and open questions

In this chapter, we have extended the concept of avoidability of patterns to avoidability of patterns with permutations. We have characterised for all m whether a cubic pattern, that is, a pattern of the form $\pi^i(x)\pi^j(x)\pi^k(x)$, is avoidable in Σ_m for all $i, j, k \geqslant 0$. We have given these characterisations for both the morphic and antimorphic case.

The next natural question concerns the avoidability of longer patterns. Note that a very partial answer to that question is given in Lemma 3.3 (morphic case) and Lemma 3.17 (antimorphic case). Both these results provide a word over four letters or five letters, respectively, that avoids sequences of permutations of length three or more for all factors of length seven or more.

Once longer patterns are considered, one might also study patterns with more than just one word variable and one function variable.

## CHAPTER 4

Extended Lyndon-Schützenberger equations

> "One must divide one's time between politics and equations. But our equations are much more important to me, because politics is for the present, while our equations are for eternity."
>
> ALBERT EINSTEIN

4.1 Introduction

The study of the classical word equations $u^\ell = v^m w^n$ dates back to the year 1962. Lyndon and Schützenberger [66] showed that for $l, m, n \geqslant 2$, in all solutions of this equation in a free group, u, v, w are powers of a common element, or in other words, they are elements of the subgroup generated by some element of this free group. Such solutions are also referred to as *periodic* solutions. Their result extends canonically to the case when u, v and w are elements of a free semigroup. In this case however, significantly simpler proofs have been established over the years [20, 33, 50, 65].

Lentin [61] studied generalisations of the form $u^\ell = v^m w^n x^p$, while Appel and Djorup [2] looked at equations of the form $u^\ell = v_1^\ell v_2^\ell \cdots v_n^\ell$. Finally, the most general form of these equations, namely $u^\ell = v_1^{k_1} v_2^{k_2} \cdots v_n^{k_n}$ was investigated by Harju and Nowotka [49].

4. Extended Lyndon-Schützenberger equations

Czeizler et al. [31] introduced a generalisation of Lyndon and Schützenberger's equations of a different kind. They considered equations of the form $u_1 u_2 \cdots u_\ell = v_1 v_2 \cdots v_m w_1 w_2 \cdots w_n$, where $u_i \in \{u, \theta(u)\}$ for all $1 \leqslant i \leqslant \ell$, $v_j \in \{v, \theta(v)\}$ for all $1 \leqslant j \leqslant m$, and $w_k \in \{w, \theta(w)\}$ for all $1 \leqslant k \leqslant n$, and studied under which conditions $u, v, w \in \{t, \theta(t)\}^+$ for some word t. In other words, they studied the case when u, v, w are generalised powers (more precisely, θ-powers), and thus the solution is what is called θ-*periodic*. Here, θ is a function on the letters of the alphabet, which acts as an antimorphism (i.e., $\theta(uv) = \theta(v)\theta(u)$ for all words u, v) and as an involution (i.e., $\theta(\theta(u)) = u$ for all words u). These so-called *antimorphic involutions* are commonly used to formally model the Watson-Crick complementarity arising in DNA strands. It was this connection that made a systematic study of the combinatorial properties of words that can be expressed as a product of factors and their image under such antimorphic involutions appealing (see, [31]). Apart from this initial bio-inspired motivation, there is a strong intrinsic mathematical motivation behind the study of such words. Indeed, one of the simplest and most studied operations on words is the reversal, the very basic antimorphic involution. It is thus natural to study equations on words in which not only powers of variables, but also repeated products of a variable and its mirror image appear.

The previous results obtained on this kind of equations, which were established by Czeizler et al. [31] and Kari, Masson, and Seki [56] are summarised in Table 4.1. One can observe directly from this table that the more interesting cases in this generalised setting are those in which $\ell, m, n \geqslant 3$. Moreover, when $\ell = 3$ only several "negative" results have been found so far. By this we mean that there is a series of equations which have non-θ-periodic solutions, but very little is known about those cases of such equations where the θ-periodicity of the solutions is forced, similarly to the classical Lyndon-Schützenberger equations (the only exception was the particular Lemma 4.23, see Proposition 51 in [56]). Finally, the case $\ell = 3$ seems to be especially intricate and particularly interesting, as it separates the cases when the equation has only θ-periodic solutions ($\ell \geqslant 4$) from the cases when it may have other solutions as well ($\ell \leqslant 2$). In this chapter, the remaining open cases are solved.

As expected (see the final remarks of [56]), we applied some arguments that have not been used in this context before, but an exhaustive case analysis on the alignments of parts of the equation seems unavoidable and these arguments

40

Table 4.1. Known results about the equations $u_1 u_2 \cdots u_\ell = v_1 v_2 \cdots v_m w_1 w_2 \cdots w_n$.

ℓ	m	n	$u, v, w \in \{t, \theta(t)\}^+$?
$\geqslant 4$	$\geqslant 3$	$\geqslant 3$	Yes [31, 56]
3	$\geqslant 5$	$\geqslant 5$	Open
3	4	$\geqslant 3$ and odd	Open
3	4	$\geqslant 4$ and even	No [56]
3	3	$\geqslant 3$	No [56]
	one of $\{\ell, m, n\}$ equals 2		No [31, 56]

must be adapted to every case separately.

4.2 Preliminaries

In this chapter we will make extensive use of the concepts and results that are presented in Section 2.3.3. We recall Lentin's theorem [61], which was mentioned in the introduction, as we will use it in our proofs:

Theorem 4.1 (Lentin, 1965). *If $u^\ell = v^m w^n x^p$ for some words $u, v, w, x \in \Sigma^*$ and $\ell, m, n, p \geqslant 3$, then $u, v, w, x \in \{t\}^*$ for some word $t \in \Sigma^*$.*

We will also make frequent use of the following results from [31] (they are labelled Proposition 20 and Proposition 21 there):

Proposition 4.2 (Czeizler et al., 2011). *Let $u, v \in \Sigma^+$ so that v is θ-primitive, $u_1, u_2, u_3 \in \{u, \theta(u)\}$ and $v_1, v_2, \ldots, v_m \in \{v, \theta(v)\}$ for some odd $m \geqslant 3$.*
If $v_1 v_2 \cdots v_m <_p u_1 u_2 u_3$ and $2|u| < m|v| < 2|u| + |v|$, then $u_2 \neq u_1$ and $v_1 = v_2 = \ldots = v_m = z\theta(z)p$ for some words z, p, where $p = \theta(p)$.

Proposition 4.3 (Czeizler et al., 2011). *Let $u, v \in \Sigma^+$ so that v is θ-primitive, $u_1, u_2, u_3 \in \{u, \theta(u)\}$ and $v_1, v_2, \ldots, v_m \in \{v, \theta(v)\}$ for some even $m \geqslant 4$.*
If $v_1 v_2 \cdots v_m <_p u_1 u_2 u_3$ and $2|u| < m|v| < 2|u| + |v|$, then one of the following holds:

1. $u_1 \neq u_2$ and $v_1 = v_2 = \ldots = v_m = xz\theta(z)$ for some words x, z, where $x = \theta(x)$

41

2. $u_1 = u_2$, $v_1 = v_2 = \ldots = v_{m/2}$ and $v_{m/2+1} = v_{m/2+2} = \ldots = v_m = \theta(v_1)$.
   Furthermore, $v = rpr$ with $r = (\alpha\beta)^i \alpha$ and $p = (\alpha\beta)^j$ for θ-palindromes α and
   β such that $\alpha\beta$ is primitive and integers $i \geqslant 0$ and $j \geqslant 1$.
   It follows that $pr = r\theta(p)$, $u_1 = v_1^{m/2-1} rp$, and $v_1^{m/2}\theta(v_1)^{m/2} = u^2 r^2$.

Symmetrical results to these (i.e., $v_1 v_2 \cdots v_m <_s u_1 u_2 u_3$ in the hypotheses and u_1 and u_2 replaced by u_2 and u_3, respectively, in the conclusions) can be easily derived, and will be used in some parts of the proof.

4.3 Overview and general assumptions

As mentioned in the introduction, we are interested in the solutions of equations of the form

$$u_1 u_2 u_3 = v_1 v_2 \cdots v_m w_1 w_2 \cdots w_n, \tag{4.1}$$

where $u_1, u_2, u_3 \in \{u, \theta(u)\}$, $v_j \in \{v, \theta(v)\}$ for all $1 \leqslant j \leqslant m$ and $w_k \in \{w, \theta(w)\}$ for all $1 \leqslant k \leqslant n$ and θ is an antimorphic involution, in the cases where $m, n \geqslant 5$ as well as when $m = 4$ and $n \geqslant 3$ is odd.

Both of these open cases are addressed separately in the following. There are some premises appearing throughout the proofs in both cases, which we want to state explicitly here:

- We will always assume that $u_1 = u$, $v_1 = v$ and $w_1 = w$ in this chapter: as θ is an involution, the other cases can be reduced to this one by a simple renaming of u to $\theta(u)$, v to $\theta(v)$ and w to $\theta(w)$ if necessary.

- As it is already remarked in [31], if we show that two of the words u, v, and w are θ-powers of a word t, then so is the third. Hence, we will conclude whenever we established that two of u, v, w are θ-powers of the same word.

4.4 The first open case: $\ell = 3$ and $m, n \geqslant 5$

In this section we study (4.1) in the case when $m, n \geqslant 5$. For this purpose we will make a few more assumptions and justify them:

- We assume that u, v, and w are all θ-primitive words. Otherwise, if for instance $v \in \{v', \theta(v')\}^+$ for some θ-primitive word v' with $|v'| < |v|$, we will consider the equation $u_1 u_2 u_3 = v'_1 v'_2 \cdots v'_{m'} w_1 w_2 \cdots w_n$ instead, where $v'_i \in \{v', \theta(v')\}$ for all $1 \leqslant i \leqslant m'$, with $m' > m$, and similarly if $w \in \{w', \theta(w')\}^+$ for some word w' or $u \in \{u', \theta(u')\}^+$ for some word u'. In this way we end up with an equation of the same kind ($\ell = 3$ and $m', n' \geqslant 5$) if v or w are not θ-primitive, whereas we get an equation that is already covered by the known results presented in Table 4.1, if u is not θ-primitive.

This lets us directly conclude that neither $|v|$ nor $|w|$ divides $|u|$, as otherwise $u \in \{v, \theta(v)\}^+$ or $u \in \{w, \theta(w)\}^+$ and hence u would not be θ-primitive.

- The symmetric roles of the factors $v_1 v_2 \cdots v_m$ and $w_1 w_2 \cdots w_n$ allow us to assume that $|v_1 v_2 \cdots v_m| \geqslant |w_1 w_2 \cdots w_n|$ holds.

These two assumptions will be implicitly used throughout this section, so whenever we refer to one of the words u, v or w, it is always assumed to be θ-primitive, and we can apply tools like Lemma 2.12 and Lemma 2.13 to these words, as the θ-primitivity premises for these results are met when we apply them to u, v or w.

We split the discussion into different subsections depending on values of u_1, u_2, and u_3 and for each of these values, we analyse (4.1) for all possible lengths of $v_1 v_2 \cdots v_m$. By our general assumption that $u_1 = u$, we have $u_1 u_2 u_3 \in \{uuu, uu\theta(u), u\theta(u)u, u\theta(u)\theta(u)\}$.

The case when $m|v| \geqslant 2|u| + |v|$ is particularly easy to solve, and the following lemma applies for all values of u_1, u_2, and u_3:

Lemma 4.4. *If $m|v| \geqslant 2|u| + |v|$ and (4.1) holds, then $u, v, w \in \{t, \theta(t)\}^+$ for some word t.*

Proof. Using Theorem 2.14, we instantly get that $u, v \in \{t, \theta(t)\}^+$ for some θ-primitive word t. $\qquad \square$

As a consequence, we will not deal with the case $m|v| \geqslant 2|u| + |v|$ anymore in this section.

4.4.1 The case $u_1 u_2 u_3 = uuu$

In this subsection we will fix $u_1 = u_2 = u_3 = u$ and thus we focus on the equation

$$u^3 = v_1 v_2 \cdots v_m w_1 w_2 \cdots w_n. \tag{4.2}$$

4. Extended Lyndon-Schützenberger equations

We start analysing (4.2) in the case when the border between $v_1 v_2 \cdots v_m$ and $w_1 w_2 \cdots w_n$ falls inside u_3:

Lemma 4.5. *If $2|u| < m|v| < 2|u| + |v|$, then (4.2) implies $u, v, w \in \{t, \theta(t)\}^+$ for some word t.*

Proof. As v and w are generally assumed to be θ-primitive and $u_1 = u_2$ here, we can apply Proposition 4.2 and Proposition 4.3 to get that m must be even, and $v_1 = v_2 = \ldots = v_k = v$, while $v_{k+1} = v_{k+2} = \ldots = v_m = \theta(v)$, where k is such that $(k-1)|v| < |u| < k|v|$. Furthermore, as $m|v| < 2|u| + |v|$, the prefix of v_k occurring as a suffix of u is longer than $|v|/2$. Additionally, Proposition 4.3 states that $v = rpr$ with $r = \theta(r)$ and $pr = r\theta(p)$, with $r = (\alpha\beta)^i \alpha, p = (\alpha\beta)^j, \theta(p) = (\beta\alpha)^j$ for some θ-palindromes α and β, $i \geq 0, j \geq 1$, and $\alpha\beta$ primitive.

Moreover, if $w = \theta(w)$, then (4.1) turns into the equation

$$u^3 = v^{m/2}\theta(v)^{m/2}w^n.$$

As $m, n \geq 5$ and m is even, we can apply Theorem 4.1 to get that $u, v, \theta(v), w \in \{t\}^+$ for some word t, and the statement of this lemma holds. Therefore, we also assume $w \neq \theta(w)$ in the following.

By Proposition 4.3, we have

$$u_1 = v^{m/2-1}rp,$$

and furthermore

$$u_2 = r\theta(v)^{m/2-1}v',$$

where $v' \leq_p \theta(v)$ and $|v'| = |p|$. Since $v = rpr$, the suffix of $v_m = \theta(v)$ that is a prefix of u_3 is of length $|rr|$. Additionally, since $u_3 = u$ has the prefix $v = rpr = rr\theta(p)$ (as $pr = r\theta(p)$), we get that

$$w_1 w_2 \cdots w_n = \tilde{v}^{m/2-2}\theta(p)rp,$$

where $\tilde{v} = \theta(p)rr \sim v$. We will show that for $m \geq 8$, this equation leads to a contradiction with one of the assumptions we made. First of all, since we have $\theta(p)rp \leq_p \theta(p)rpr = \theta(p)rr\theta(p) \leq_p \tilde{v}^2$, it follows that $w_1 w_2 \cdots w_n \leq_p \tilde{v}^{m/2}$.

If $|r| < |p|$, then

$$w_1 w_2 \cdots w_n = \tilde{v}^{m/2-2}\theta(p)rp = \tilde{v}^{m/2-1}p',$$

for some $p' \leqslant_s p$. Since $m \geqslant 8$, this word is of length at least $3|v|$. Furthermore, $w_1 w_2 \cdots w_n$ is of length $n|w| \geqslant 5|w|$. Thus, Theorem 2.14 is applicable and yields $\tilde{v}, w \in \{t, \theta(t)\}^+$ for some word t. Since w is θ-primitive, this means that $|\tilde{v}| \geqslant |w|$ and hence $\tilde{v} \in \{w, \theta(w)\}^+$ must hold. By the assumption that $|r| < |p|$, and because of $pr = r\theta(p)$, we can write $p = rs$ for some word s. Then, since $\tilde{v} = \theta(p)rr \in \{w, \theta(w)\}^+$ and

$$w_1 w_2 \cdots w_n = (\theta(p)rr)^{m/2-2}\theta(p)rp,$$

also $\theta(p)rp = \theta(p)rrs \in \{w, \theta(w)\}^+$ holds. Combining these two results, we see that $s \in \{w, \theta(w)\}^+$ and thus also $\theta(s) \in \{w, \theta(w)\}^+$. However, as $\theta(p)rr = \theta(s)rrr \in \{w, \theta(w)\}^+$, also $rrr \in \{w, \theta(w)\}^+$ and by Theorem 2.16 furthermore $r \in \{w, \theta(w)\}^+$ holds. As a consequence, $p = rs \in \{w, \theta(w)\}^+$, and so $v = rpr \in \{w, \theta(w)\}^+$ as well, contradicting the θ-primitivity of v.

If $|r| \geqslant |p|$, then $\theta(p)rp \leqslant_p \theta(p)rr$, so the words $w_1 w_2 \cdots w_n$ and $\tilde{v}^\omega$ have a common prefix of length at least $\max\{(m/2-2)|v|, 5|w|\}$. If $m \geqslant 10$, this is at least $\max\{3|v|, 5|w|\}$ which is always long enough to apply Theorem 2.14 to get that $\tilde{v}, w \in \{w, \theta(w)\}^+$. In the case $m = 8$, we have

$$w_1 w_2 \cdots w_n = \tilde{v}^2\theta(p)rp.$$

If $|w| > |\theta(p)rp|$, then $n|w| > |\tilde{v}^2\theta(p)rp|$, as $|\theta(p)rp| > |v|/2$, which is a contradiction. Thus, $|w| \leqslant |\theta(p)rp|$, and so we have a common prefix of $\tilde{v}^\omega$ and $w_1 w_2 \cdots w_n$ of length $2|v| + |w|$. By Theorem 2.14, once again, we get $\tilde{v}, w \in \{t, \theta t\}^+$ for some word t, which means that $\tilde{v} \in \{w, \theta w\}^+$, as w is θ-primitive. Now, dually to the previous case, we write $r = ps'$. As $\theta(p)rr = \theta(p)rps'$ and $\theta(p)rp$ are both in $\{w, \theta(w)\}^+$, so is s'. Furthermore, as $\theta(p)rp = \theta(p)ps'p \in \{w, \theta(w)\}^+$, if $\theta(p)p \in \{w, \theta(w)\}^+$, then by Theorem 2.16, also $p \in \{w, \theta(w)\}^+$, and so $r = ps' \in \{w, \theta(w)\}^+$. This is a contradiction, as $v = rpr$ is θ-primitive. Therefore, $p\theta(p) \notin \{w, \theta(w)\}^+$, which means that $s' \in \{w, \theta(w)\}^+$ is a proper factor of some word in $\{w, \theta(w)\}^+$ of length $|s'| + |w|$. By Lemma 2.12, we must have that $s' \in \{w\}^+$ or $s' \in \{\theta(w)\}^+$, as w is θ-primitive. However, $pps' = pr =$

4. Extended Lyndon-Schützenberger equations

$r\theta(p) = ps'\theta(p)$, so $ps' = s'\theta(p)$, and we saw before that this means that s' is a θ-palindrome. In conclusion, $w = \theta(w)$ in both cases, and we get a contradiction.

Therefore, as $m \geqslant 5$ must be even, the only case left is when $m = 6$, in which (4.1) is of the form

$$uuu = vvv\theta(v)\theta(v)\theta(v)w_1w_2\cdots w_n.$$

We shift our attention to the factor $w_1w_2\cdots w_n$. As $m = 6$, we know that

$$u = rpr^2pr^2p = r^2\theta(p)rpr^2p,$$

and $w_1w_2\cdots w_n$ starts after a prefix of length $2|r|$ in u, so

$$w_1w_2\cdots w_n = \theta(p)rpr^2p = (\beta\alpha)^j(\alpha\beta)^i\alpha(\alpha\beta)^{i+j}\alpha\alpha(\beta\alpha)^i(\alpha\beta)^j.$$

Since α and β are θ-palindromes, so is $w_1w_2\cdots w_n$.

If n is odd, then $w_1w_2\cdots w_n = \theta(w_1\cdots w_n)$ implies $w_{(n+1)/2} = \theta(w_{(n+1)/2})$. It follows that $w = \theta(w)$, which contradicts the assumption $w \neq \theta(w)$ we made at the beginning of the proof.

So we can further assume n to be even and therefore $n \geqslant 6$.

If $(\beta\alpha)^j(\alpha\beta)^i\alpha(\alpha\beta)^j \in \{w,\theta(w)\}^+$, then $(\beta\alpha)^j(\alpha\beta)^i\alpha(\alpha\beta)^i\alpha \in \{w,\theta(w)\}^+$ as well. Therefore, if $i \geqslant j$, then $(\alpha\beta)^{i-j}\alpha \in \{w,\theta(w)\}^+$, and on the other hand if $i < j$, then $(\beta\alpha)^{j-i-1}\beta \in \{w,\theta(w)\}^+$. In both cases, those words, that are θ-powers of w, are θ-palindromes. Therefore, since $w \neq \theta(w)$, either $w\theta(w)$ or $\theta(w)w$ occurs as a factor in them.

If $i \geqslant j$, the factor $(\alpha\beta)^{i-j}\alpha$ appears in $w_1w_2\cdots w_n$ after the prefix $(\beta\alpha)^j$. By Lemma 2.12, we must have $(\beta\alpha)^j \in \{w,\theta(w)\}^+$ and by Theorem 2.16 thus $\beta\alpha \in \{w,\theta(w)\}^+$. If we combine this with $(\alpha\beta)^{i-j}\alpha \in \{w,\theta(w)\}^+$, we can conclude that $\alpha,\beta \in \{w,\theta(w)\}^+$ holds, which contradicts the θ-primitivity of v.

If $j > i$ and $i > 0$, then $(\beta\alpha)^{j-i-1}\beta$ appears inside the factor $(\beta\alpha)^{i+j}$ both as a prefix and after the prefix $\beta\alpha$. Thus, in this case $\beta\alpha \in \{w,\theta(w)\}^+$ as well, which again leads to $\alpha,\beta \in \{w,\theta(w)\}^+$. If $j > i$ and $i = 0$, then

$$(\beta\alpha)^j(\alpha\beta)^i\alpha(\alpha\beta)^j = (\beta\alpha)^j\alpha(\alpha\beta)^j,$$

and

$$(\beta\alpha)^j (\alpha\beta)^i \alpha (\alpha\beta)^i \alpha = (\beta\alpha)^j \alpha\alpha.$$

Hence, we immediately get that $(\beta\alpha)^j \in \{w, \theta(w)\}^+$, which leads to the same contradiction as above.

By the previous paragraphs, we can assume that

$$(\beta\alpha)^j (\alpha\beta)^i \alpha (\alpha\beta)^j = w_1 w_2 \cdots w_\ell w',$$

for some ℓ, and some nonempty $w' \leqslant_p w_{\ell+1}$. As $(\beta\alpha)^j (\alpha\beta)^i \alpha (\alpha\beta)^j$ appears also as a suffix of $w_1 w_2 \cdots w_n$, we have $w_1 = w_2 = \ldots = w_\ell$ by Lemma 2.12. Since $|(\beta\alpha)^j (\alpha\beta)^i \alpha| = n|w|/3$, and $n \geqslant 6$, we get that $ww \leqslant_p (\beta\alpha)^j (\alpha\beta)^i \alpha$.

Now, if $i \geqslant j$, we can write

$$w^\ell w' = (\beta\alpha)^j (\alpha\beta)^j (\alpha\beta)^{i-j} \alpha (\alpha\beta)^j.$$

We observe that $w \leqslant_p (\beta\alpha)^j (\alpha\beta)^j$ must hold: assume towards a contradiction, that $|w| > 2j|\alpha\beta|$. In this case, the second w of the prefix ww of $(\beta\alpha)^j (\alpha\beta)^i \alpha$ begins inside the factor $(\alpha\beta)^{i-j} \alpha$. Since w has the prefix $\beta\alpha$ and this is primitive, we deduce that $w = (\beta\alpha)^j (\alpha\beta)^j (\alpha\beta)^k$ for some k. However, this means that the second occurrence of w that follows immediately afterwards is a prefix of $(\beta\alpha)^{i-j-k} (\alpha\beta)^j$. This implies $\alpha\beta = \beta\alpha$, which is a contradiction to the primitivity of $\alpha\beta$. Thus we can safely assume that $w \leqslant_p (\beta\alpha)^j (\alpha\beta)^j$. This word $(\beta\alpha)^j (\alpha\beta)^j$ is a suffix of $w^\ell w' = (\beta\alpha)^j (\alpha\beta)^{i-j} (\alpha\beta)^j \alpha (\alpha\beta)^j$. Since w is assumed to be primitive, by Proposition 2.3, we must have $(\beta\alpha)^j \alpha (\alpha\beta)^{i-j} \in \{w\}^+$. Let $y = (\beta\alpha)^j \alpha (\alpha\beta)^{i-j}$. Then

$$w_1 w_2 \cdots w_n = yy(\beta\alpha)^{2j} (\alpha\beta)^j \theta(y),$$

from which we conclude that $(\beta\alpha)^{2j} (\alpha\beta)^j \in \{w, \theta(w)\}^+$. An application of Theorem 2.16 now gives us $\alpha\beta \in \{w, \theta(w)\}^+$, which yields the contradiction $\alpha, \beta \in \{w, \theta(w)\}^+$ as before.

On the other hand, if $i < j$, then $|w| < |(\beta\alpha)^j|$ must hold, since $n \geqslant 6$. Furthermore, the word $w_1 w_2 \cdots w_\ell w' = (\beta\alpha)^j (\alpha\beta)^i \alpha (\alpha\beta)^j$ is in this case longer than $|w_1 w_2 \cdots w_n|/2$, so $\ell \geqslant n/2$. Therefore, we got $w_1 w_2 \cdots w_n = w^{n/2} \theta(w)^{n/2}$. If $|w| < |(\beta\alpha)^{j-1}|$, we would have $|w|$ occurring as a prefix of $w_1 w_2 \cdots w_n$ and after

47

the prefix $\beta\alpha$. Thus $w = \beta\alpha$ by Proposition 2.3. However, then $w_{j+1} = w = \alpha\beta$, contradicting the primitivity of $\alpha\beta$. Hence, $|(\beta\alpha)^{j-1}| < |w| < |(\beta\alpha)^j|$ can be assumed.

If $j \geqslant 2$, then $(\beta\alpha)^{j-1} < |w|$ and $i < j$ imply that $|(\beta\alpha)^j(\alpha\beta)^i\alpha| < 3|w|$. Thus $n < 9$, and as n is even, either $n = 8$ or $n = 6$.

If $n = 8$, then $w_4 w_5$ must be a factor of $(\alpha\beta)^{i+j}\alpha$, and since $j \geqslant 2$, the word $\beta\alpha$ is a prefix of $w_4 = w$. Using Proposition 2.3, this $\beta\alpha$ must be aligned with some $\beta\alpha$ inside $(\alpha\beta)^{i+j}\alpha$. This allows us to deduce that $j = i + 1$, and that $w_4 = w = (\beta\alpha)^{j-1}\beta'$, where $\beta = \beta'\theta(\beta')$. Then, $w_2 = w \leqslant_p \theta(\beta')\alpha(\alpha\beta)^{j-1}$. Now if $j \geqslant 3$, the word $\alpha\beta$ appears as a proper factor inside $(\alpha\beta)^2$, unless $\beta = \theta(\beta')\alpha$. However, if $\beta = \theta(\beta')\alpha$, then $\alpha = \theta(\beta')$, and thus $\alpha\beta$ is not θ-primitive. Therefore $j = 2$ must hold, in which case we get that $\beta\alpha\beta' \leqslant_p \theta(\beta')\alpha\alpha\beta$. From this it immediately follows that α is not primitive, and furthermore that $\alpha \in \{\theta(\beta')\}^+$, again a contradiction to $\alpha\beta$ being θ-primitive.

If $n = 6$, then $w_1 w_2 = w^2 = (\beta\alpha)^j(\alpha\beta)^i\alpha$ and $w_3 w_4 = w\theta(w) = (\alpha\beta)^{i+j}\alpha$. As $|w| \geqslant |\beta\alpha|$, we get the contradiction $\beta\alpha = \alpha\beta$.

Thus the only possibility that remains is $j = 1$ and thus $i = 0$. This means that

$$w^{n/2}\theta(w)^{n/2} = \beta\alpha^3\beta\alpha^3\beta.$$

By concatenating α^3 to both sides of the equation, we get

$$w^{n/2}\theta(w)^{n/2}\alpha^3 = (\beta\alpha^3)^3,$$

to which we can apply Theorem 4.1 to get $w = \theta(w)$, a contradiction. $\qquad\square$

The case when the border between $v_1 v_2 \cdots v_m$ and $w_1 w_2 \cdots w_n$ falls inside u_2 turns out to be more intricate. We will deal with large number of subcases separately. The first result in this series will show that the solution set of (4.2) consists of θ-periodic solutions only, if at least one of the values m and n is odd. Then we will show that (4.2) also only admits θ-periodic solutions, if both m and n are at least 12. This bound will then be further lowered to 10. In the two subsections that follow, we will address the remaining cases. First, we will look at (4.2) assuming that $m \leqslant n$. Having established that it admits only θ-periodic solutions if m and n are at least 10, we only have two cases to consider here: The first is $m = 6$ and $n \geqslant 6$, and the second case is $m = 8$ and $n \geqslant 8$. Afterwards we will have a look at (4.2) under the assumption $m > n$. As in the case $m \leqslant n$, there are only two possible values for n in that case: $n = 6$ and $n = 8$. We will address both possibilities independently.

Before we start addressing the aforementioned first case, we will prove a series of auxiliary lemmas, which will be made extensive use of in the remainder of this section. For this we give a name to two specific factors appearing in (4.2): we define ① as the prefix of u of length $m|v| - |u|$ and ② as the remaining suffix, which means that ② is the suffix of u of length $n|w| - |u|$. Consult Figure 4.1 for a visual presentation of these definitions. As shown there, let i be the minimal integer such that ① is a proper prefix of $v_1 v_2 \cdots v_i$, and p be the maximal integer such that ② is a proper suffix of $w_p w_{p+1} \cdots w_n$. Let $v_i = v_i' v_i''$ such that ① $= v_1 v_2 \cdots v_{i-1} v_i'$. Furthermore let j be minimal such that u is a proper prefix of $v_1 v_2 \cdots v_j$ and $v_1 v_2 \cdots v_j' = u$ for $v_j = v_j' v_j''$. Similarly, let k be such that $u = w_k'' w_{k+1} \cdots w_n$ and $w_k = w_k' w_k''$. Whenever we refer to i, j, p, k in the following and they are not explicitly defined otherwise, these values are always defined as stated here.

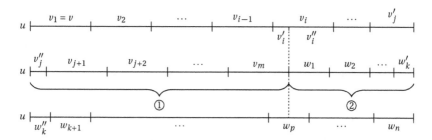

Figure 4.1. Equation (4.2) with $|u| < m|v| < 2|u|$.

We start our analysis by fixing the values of some of the factors appearing in the word $v_1 v_2 \cdots v_m$. Recall that $v_1 = v$ is generally assumed throughout this chapter.

Lemma 4.6. *Assume that $|u| < m|v| < 2|u|$ and (4.2) holds. Then $v_1 = v_2 = \ldots = v_{i-1} = v$ and $v_{j+1} = v_{j+2} = \ldots = v_m = \theta(v)$. If $|v_i'| = j|v| - |u| \geqslant |v|/2$, then also $v_i = v$ and $v_j = \theta(v)$.*

4. Extended Lyndon-Schützenberger equations

Proof. If $v = \theta(v)$ the conclusion is straightforward, so we assume $v \neq \theta(v)$. Recall that we generally assume $m, n \geq 5$ and $m|v| > n|w|$ in this section, hence $m - j \geq 1$. If $m - j \geq 2$, we have $v_1 = v_2 = \ldots = v_{i-1} = v$ and $v_{j+1} = v_{j+2} = \ldots = v_m = \theta(v)$ by repeated application of Lemma 2.12. On the other hand, if $m = j + 1$, we apply Lemma 2.13 (with $x_1 = v_j, x_2 = v_m, x_3 = v_1, x_4 = v_2$, and y and z chosen accordingly), and we get that $v_m = \theta(v)$.

We now assume that $|v_1 v_2 \cdots v_j| - |u| \geq |v|/2$ in order to show that $v_i = v$ and $v_j = \theta(v)$ in this case. Assume for the sake of a contradiction that $v_j \neq \theta(v)$, that is $v_j = v$. It follows that v has a period $p = |v_j'|$ and $p < |v|/2$. Hence $v_1 = x^2 y$ for some words x and y with $|x| = p$. Furthermore, we have $v_1 v_2 = xyv_{j+1}z$ for some word z with $|z| = |x|$. As v_2 starts with x we get that $v_{j+1} = rxs$ for some words r and s such that $|r| = |x|$. However, as v_1 has period p, also $v_{j+1} = \theta(v_1)$ has period p, therefore $r = x$ and $v_{j+1} = v_1$. Thus $v = \theta(v)$, which contradicts our assumption. This shows that in fact $v_j = \theta(v)$ holds in this case. In the exact same way we derive that $v_i = v$. $\square$

Applying the same ideas as in the proof of the previous lemma to the word $w_1 w_2 \cdots w_n$ instead, we get the following complementary information:

Lemma 4.7. *Assume that* $|u| < m|v| < 2|u|$ *and* (4.2) *holds. Then* $w_1 = w_2 = \ldots = w_{k-1} = w$ *and* $w_{p+1} = w_{p+2} = \ldots = w_n = \theta(w)$. *If* $k|w| - |u| \geq |w|/2$, *then also* $w_k = w$ *and* $w_p = \theta(w)$.

The results of the previous lemmas allow us to draw a more accurate picture of the equation we are dealing with, including this new information in Figure 4.2.

Using the previous result we can show a first fact about ①:

Lemma 4.8. *Assume that* $|u| < m|v| < 2|u|$ *and* (4.2) *holds. Then* ① $\leq_p v^i$ *and* ① $\leq_s \theta(v)^i$.

Proof. By Lemma 4.6, we have that $v_1 v_2 \cdots v_{i-1} = v^{i-1}$. As $m|v| \geq n|w|$, we either have $m \geq j + 2$ or $|v_j''| > |v|/2$. In the latter case, the claim follows using Lemma 4.6, as then $v_i = v$ and $v_j = \theta(v)$. In the other case, we have that v_i' is a suffix of $v_m = \theta(v)$ of length $|v_i'|$, and the way v_{m-1} overlaps with v_{i-1} shows that this suffix is also a prefix of v. Hence, ① $\leq_p v^i$, and the second claim follows similarly. $\square$

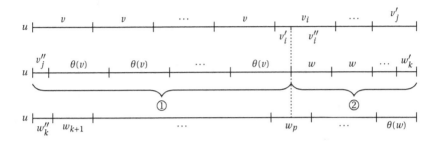

Figure 4.2. A more detailed depiction of (4.2) with $|u| < m|v| < 2|u|$.

Lemma 4.9. *Assume that* $|u| < m|v| < 2|u|$ *and* (4.2) *holds. Then* ① *and* ② *are both* θ-*palindromes, that is,* ① $= \theta($①$)$ *and* ② $= \theta($②$)$.

Proof. As mentioned before, the situation is illustrated in Figure 4.2.

The fact that ① is a θ-palindrome follows directly from its presentations established in Lemma 4.8.

If $k \geqslant 2$, we can apply the arguments used in the proofs of Lemma 4.6 and Lemma 4.8 to the word $w_1 w_2 \cdots w_n$ and draw the analogous conclusions for ②. Hence, the only special case to be explicitly considered here is when ② is shorter than $|w|$ and hence $k = 1$: if $w_1 = \theta(w_n)$, then ② is obviously a θ-palindrome. If $w_1 = w_n$, we get that $w_1 = w_1' w_1''$, where ② $= w_1'$ is the suffix of u_2 and $w_n = z w_1'$ for some word z. As ① is a θ-palindrome, it holds that $z = \theta(w_1'')$. Thus as $w_1 = w_n$, we get that $w_1' w_1'' = \theta(w_1'') w_1'$, and by Lemma 2.17 we have $w_1'' = (\alpha\beta)^i, \theta(w_1'') = (\beta\alpha)^i$, and $w_1' = (\beta\alpha)^j \beta$ for some $i, j \geqslant 0$ and θ-palindromes α and β.

Consequently, ② $= w_1'$ is a θ-palindrome as well. □

Subcase m or n odd

Lemma 4.10. *If* $|u| < m|v| < 2|u|$ *and at least one of* m, n *is odd, then* (4.2) *implies* $u, v, w \in \{t, \theta(t)\}^+$ *for some word* t.

Proof. The situation of this case is depicted in Figure 4.3 (with $v_j = v_j' v_j''$ and $w_k = w_k' w_k''$).

4. Extended Lyndon-Schützenberger equations

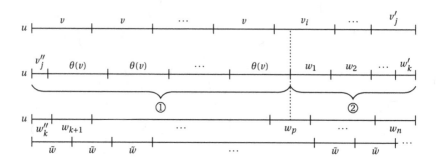

Figure 4.3. Equation (4.2) with $|u| < m|v| < 2|u|$ with m or n odd.

Lemma 4.9 tells us that the factors ① and ② are θ-palindromes, and thus $v_1 v_2 \cdots v_m =$ ①②① and $w_1 w_2 \cdots w_n =$ ②①② are θ-palindromes as well. If m is odd, we get that $v_{(m+1)/2} = \theta(v_{(m+1)/2})$ and therefore $v = \theta(v)$. Similarly, $w = \theta(w)$ if n is odd.

Hence, if both m and n are odd, we have the equation

$$u^3 = v^m w^n,$$

and as $m, n \geqslant 5$, we get that $u, v, w \in \{t\}^+$ for some word t using Theorem 2.7.

Therefore, assume that only n is odd, while m is even (for the other case see Lemma 4.11). Thus (4.1) turns into the equation

$$u^3 = v_1 v_2 \cdots v_m w^n,$$

with $m \geqslant 6$.

First we show that the claimed statement holds if $|v| > |w|$. If $|u| < 2|v| + |w|$, then $6|v| + 3|w| > 3|u|$, which is a contradiction, hence $|u| \geqslant 2|v| + |w|$ can be assumed. Since $v_1 v_2 \cdots v_m$ is a prefix of $\tilde{w}^\omega$ (where $\tilde{w} \sim w$, see Figure 4.3) of length $|u|$, and $|u| \geqslant 2|v| + |w|$, we can apply Theorem 2.14 and get that $v, \tilde{w} \in \{t, \theta(t)\}^+$ for some word t. If $|v| > |w|$ then v is not θ-primitive, a contradiction.

Thus, we assume $|v| \leqslant |w|$ in the following. Also, if $|②| \geqslant |w|$, we can apply Theorem 2.1 to the suffix w^n of u^3, which is of length at least $|u| + |w|$, to get

52

that $u, w \in \{t\}^+$ for some t and hence the claim holds.

Therefore we can assume $|v| \leqslant |w|$ and also $|\text{②}| < |w|$. As $n \geqslant 5$, we have $4|w| < |u|$ and consequently $|w| < |u|/4$ and also $|v| < |u|/4$. Since the length of $v_1 v_2 \cdots v_{i-1} = v^{i-1}$ is at least $|u| - |\text{②}| - |v|$, it follows therefore that $|v^{i-1}| \geqslant |u|/2 \geqslant |v| + |w|$. Thus we can apply Theorem 2.1 to v^{i-1} and $\bar{w}^\omega$, to get that $v, \bar{w} \in \{t\}^+$ for some word t. As we assumed v to be θ-primitive and thus primitive, we get $\bar{w} \in \{v\}^+$. Therefore, as u_1 is a prefix of $\bar{w}^\omega$, u_1 must be of the form $v^{j-1} v'_j$, where v'_j is a proper prefix of v_j. As $|v| \leqslant |w| < |u|/4$, we are facing the equation

$$u^3 = v^{j-1} v_j \theta(v)^{m-j} w^n,$$

where both $j - 1 \geqslant 3$ and $m - j \geqslant 3$. Hence, whatever value $v_j \in \{v, \theta(v)\}$ has, we can always apply Theorem 4.1 to get the claimed result. □

Consequently, we analyse (4.2) with $m, n \geqslant 5$ under the assumption that both m and n are even in the following (thus actually $m, n \geqslant 6$).

We will add another assumption, justified by the following result:

Lemma 4.11. *If* $|u| < m|v| < 2|u|$ *and* v *or* w *is a* θ-*palindrome, then* (4.2) *implies that* $u, v, w \in \{t, \theta(t)\}^+$ *for some* t.

Proof. We already showed this in the proof of Lemma 4.10 for the case of $w = \theta(w)$. Therefore, it suffices to examine the other case, namely when $v = \theta(v)$. As $|\text{①}| \geqslant |\text{②}|$, the word $v''_j v_{j+1}$ is a prefix of $v_1 v_2 = vv$, and $0 < |v''_j| < |v|$ as u is assumed to be θ-primitive. If $v = \theta(v)$, this is a contradiction with the primitivity of v by Proposition 2.3. □

In the remainder of this section we will therefore assume that neither v nor w is a θ-palindrome.

As Lemma 4.8 established that ① is a prefix of v^i, it follows that the suffix of ① that we get by omitting the prefix w''_k is a prefix of $\bar{v}^i$, where $\bar{v}$ is a conjugate of v. The alignment of this prefix of $\bar{v}^i$ with $w_{k+1} w_{k+2} \cdots w_{p-1}$ will play a central role henceforth. Our next lemma will allow us to exploit this alignment by letting us finish our proofs, whenever we showed that w and this conjugate $\bar{v}$ of v are θ-powers of a common word:

Lemma 4.12. *Assume that* (4.2) *holds with* $|u| < m|v| < 2|u|$. *If* $|v| > |w|$, *and there exists a word* $\tilde{v} \sim v$, *such that* $\tilde{v}$ *occurs in* vv *after the prefix of length* $|u|$ $\bmod |w|$, *and furthermore* $\tilde{v} \in \{w, \theta(w)\}^+$, *then* $v = \tilde{v}$.

Proof. Since $\tilde{v} \in \{w, \theta(w)\}^+$ we get that $|v| = |\tilde{v}|$ is divisible by $|w|$, and so is $3|u|$. The assumption that u is θ-primitive, implies that $|w|$ does not divide $|u|$. As $|w|$ divides $3|u|$, we have that $|w| = 3d$ where d divides $|u|$ in this case. Hence, $w_n = xyz$, with $|x| = |y| = |z| = d$. Since d divides $|u|$, but $|w|$ does not divide $|u|$, we must have $|u| \equiv d \pmod{|w|}$ or $|u| \equiv 2d \pmod{|w|}$.

We start analysing the first case, that is when $|u| \equiv d \pmod{|w|}$, which is depicted in Figure 4.4. Here, either $z \leqslant_p v$ and $xy \leqslant_s v$ (which happens if w_n is a suffix of $\tilde{v}$), or $\theta(x) \leqslant_p v$ and $\theta(z)\theta(y) \leqslant_s v$ (if $\theta(w_n)$ is a suffix of $\tilde{v}$).

As $|①| \geqslant |②|$ and $m \geqslant 5$, we have that $|①| > |v|$ must hold. By Lemma 4.6 we get $v_{j+1} = v_{j+2} = \ldots = v_m = \theta(v)$, and using Lemma 4.7 we deduce furthermore that $w_1 = w_2 = \ldots = w_k$ and $w_p = w_{p+1} = \ldots = w_n = \theta(w_1)$. Hence u has the suffix $w'_k = \theta(z)\theta(y)$, and also $w_n = xyz$ is a suffix of u, so $y = \theta(z)$.

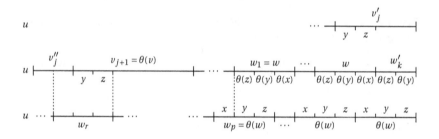

Figure 4.4. The situation in the case $|u| \equiv d \pmod{|w|}$.

We will now show that if w is θ-primitive, then $v_j = \theta(v)$ holds. For this purpose we are going to show that $x \leqslant_s v_j$. First, we observe that $x \leqslant_s v_m = \theta(v)$, so if $z \leqslant_p v$, we get that $x = \theta(z)$ and hence $\theta(w) = xyz = \theta(z)\theta(z)z$ is not θ-primitive. Hence, $\theta(x) \leqslant_p v$ and $\theta(z)\theta(y) \leqslant_s v$. Since $|v|$ is divisible by $|w|$, and $|u| \equiv d \pmod{|w|}$, there exists some w_r with $1 \leqslant r \leqslant n$ that has the prefix yz of v_{j+1} as a suffix, see again Figure 4.4. If $w_r = w = \theta(z)\theta(y)\theta(x)$, then $\theta(x) = z$ and we get the same contradiction with the θ-primitivity of w as before.

Hence $w_r = \theta(w) = xyz$ and so x is a suffix of v_j. Therefore, if $v_j = v$, then $x = \theta(y)$ which once again yields a contradiction with the θ-primitivity of w, so we conclude that $v_j = \theta(v)$ must hold.

Now, as $|u| \equiv d \pmod{|w|}$ and $|v|$ is a multiple of $|w|$, we deduce that $|v_j''| \equiv 2d \pmod{|w|}$ and thus $|v_j'| \equiv d \pmod{|w|}$. Therefore there exist s, t with $1 \leqslant s < t \leqslant n$ such that the prefix yz of v_j' appears as a factor of the word $w_s w_t$ is such a way that $y \leqslant_s w_s$ and $z \leqslant_p w_t$, see Figure 4.5.

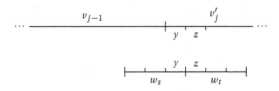

Figure 4.5. The border between v_j and v_{j-1}.

If $w_s = w = \theta(z)\theta(y)\theta(x)$, this means that $\theta(x) = y$, which leads to a contradiction with the fact that w is θ-primitive. Thus $w_s = \theta(w) = xyz$ can be assumed, which implies $y = z$, and more importantly that $xy \leqslant_s v_{j-1}$. Now, if $v_{j-1} = v$, then also $\theta(z)\theta(y) \leqslant_s v_{j-1}$ from which it follows that $x = \theta(z)$, contradicting the θ-primitivity of w. On the other hand, if $v_{j-1} = \theta(v)$, then $x \leqslant_s v_{j-1}$ and hence $x = y$, again a contradiction as before.

The analysis of the case $|u| \equiv 2d \pmod{|w|}$ is similar, hence we only provide the details for the parts where the arguments from above do not work. The main difference to the previous case is that we can not deduce that $w_k = w_1$ using Lemma 4.7 anymore. However, the possibility $w_k \neq w_1$ is ruled out easily: if $k = 1$, this is a contradiction to the assumption $w \neq \theta(w)$, hence $k > 1$ can be assumed, and by Lemma 4.7, $w_1 = w_2 = \ldots = w_{k-1}$. Now, $w_{k-1}w_k' = \theta(z)\theta(y)\theta(x)x \leqslant_s u$, and also $w_n = xyz \leqslant_s u$. Therefore $x = z$ and $\theta(x) = y$ hold, but this contradicts the θ-primitivity of w.

In the case $w_k = w_1$, we proceed as it was done for $|u| \equiv d \pmod{|w|}$ to show that $v_j = \theta(v)$, which leads to the same contradiction. $\qquad\square$

As a first application of the previous lemma, we show that all solutions of (4.2) are θ-periodic, if m and n are at least 12:

Lemma 4.13. *If $|u| < m|v| < 2|u|$ and $m \geqslant 12, n \geqslant 12$, then (4.2) implies that $u, v, w \in \{t, \theta(t)\}^+$ for some word t.*

Proof. We refer again to the notation used in Figure 4.2.

First of all, our assumption $m|v| \geqslant n|w|$ implies $|①| \geqslant |②|$. Then $|①| \geqslant 4|v|$, otherwise the pigeon hole principle implies that $|②| > 4|v|$, but this contradicts $|①| \geqslant |②|$. By the same reasoning $|①| \geqslant 4|w|$, so $p \geqslant k + 5$.

If $|w| \geqslant |v|$, then the suffix of $①$ that starts after the prefix w''_k is of length at least $3|w| \geqslant 2|w| + |v|$, hence long enough to apply Theorem 2.14. In this way we obtain $\tilde{v}, w \in \{t, \theta(t)\}^+$, where $\tilde{v}$ is the conjugate of v that appears in vv after the aforementioned prefix w''_k. Similarly if $|w| < |v|$, the suffix of $①$ starting after the prefix w''_k is of length at least $3|v| > 2|v| + |w|$, and we can again apply Theorem 2.14 to get $w, \tilde{v} \in \{t, \theta(t)\}^+$. Using Lemma 4.12 we get that $v = \tilde{v}$ and hence $v, w \in \{t, \theta(t)\}^+$. □

In the next step, we improve on the result of Lemma 4.13 by lowering the required lower bound on m and n to 10:

Subcase $m, n \geqslant 10$

Lemma 4.14. *If $|u| < m|v| < 2|u|$ and $m \geqslant 10, n \geqslant 10$, then (4.2) implies that $u, v, w \in \{t, \theta(t)\}^+$ for some word t.*

The proof of this result is composed of the following three lemmas.

Lemma 4.15. *If $|u| < m|v| < 2|u|$ and $m = 10, n \geqslant 20$ or $m \geqslant 20, n = 10$, then (4.2) implies that $u, v, w \in \{t, \theta(t)\}^+$ for some word t.*

Proof. First, we consider the case when $m = 10$ and $n \geqslant 20$. By the pigeonhole principle, $|①| > 3|v|$ must hold. As $|v_1 v_2 \cdots v_m| \geqslant |w_1 w_2 \cdots w_n|$, we have $10|v| \geqslant n|w| \geqslant 20|w|$, so $|v| \geqslant 2|w|$. Thus, $w''_k w_{k+1} \leqslant_p v$. This means that the suffix of $①$ that starts after the prefix w''_k is long enough ($|①| - |w''_k| \geqslant 2|v| + |w|$) to apply Theorem 2.14 to get $\tilde{v}, w \in \{t, \theta(t)\}^+$ for some word t, where $\tilde{v}$ is defined as stated in Lemma 4.12, and this lemma is applicable to get $v = \tilde{v}$. This however contradicts the θ-primitivity of v, as $|v| \geqslant 2|w|$.

Next, we consider the other case, namely $m \geqslant 20$ and $n = 10$. In this case we get $|v| < |w|$, as otherwise $m|v| \geqslant 2|u|$ would hold. As n is assumed to be even, this means that $p - k$ must be odd, because

$$n = 2(n - p + 1) + 2 + (p - k + 1).$$

Furthermore, $p - k \geqslant 3$ as $|①| \geqslant |②|$.

If $p - k \geqslant 5$, then $w_{k+1} w_{k+2} w_{k+3} w_{k+4}$ is a factor of $①$, so that an application of Theorem 2.14 yields $\tilde{v}, w \in \{t, \theta(t)\}^+$ for some word t and $\tilde{v}$ defined as before. As $|w| > |v|$ this is contradicting the θ-primitivity of w.

If $p - k = 3$, then

$$|①| = 2|w| + 2|w_k''|,$$

while

$$|②| = \frac{n|w| - |①|}{2}.$$

Substituting these into $|①| \geqslant |②|$ yields $|w_k''| \geqslant 2|w|/3$. We also have $|①| \geqslant 6|v|$ by the pigeon hole principle, as $m \geqslant 20$ and $|①| \geqslant |②|$. Thus, $4|w| > |①| \geqslant 6|v|$ and hence $|v| < 2|w|/3 \leqslant |w_k''|$. In summary, we get

$$|①| - |w_k''| = 2|w| + |w_k''| > 2|w| + |v|,$$

and hence Theorem 2.14 is applicable, which results in $w, \tilde{v} \in \{t, \theta(t)\}^+$ for some word t, and $\tilde{v}$ as before. As $|w| > |v|$, this again contradicts the θ-primitivity of w. □

Lemma 4.16. *If $|u| < m|v| < 2|u|$ and $m = 10, n \geqslant 10$, then (4.2) implies that $u, v, w \in \{t, \theta(t)\}^+$ for some word t.*

Proof. First of all, as $|v_1 v_2 \cdots v_m| \geqslant |w_1 w_2 \cdots w_n|$, it follows that $10|v| \geqslant n|w| \geqslant 10|w|$, so $|v| \geqslant |w|$. By Lemma 4.15, it is sufficient to examine the cases where $n \in \{10, 12, 14, 16, 18\}$. Using Lemma 4.6, we get $v_1 = v_2 = \ldots = v_{i-1} = v$ and as $m = 10$ and $|①| \geqslant |②|$ is assumed, we must have $i \geqslant 4$.

If $i \geqslant 5$, then the suffix of $①$ that starts after the prefix w_k'' has a prefix of length at least $3|v| \geqslant 2|v| + |w|$, which is a prefix of $\tilde{v}^3$ and of $w_{k+1} w_{k+2} \cdots w_n$, where $\tilde{v}$ is a conjugate of v. Therefore, Theorem 2.14 is applicable to get $\tilde{v}, w \in \{t, \theta(t)\}^+$. Also, if $i = 4$ and $|v_4'| \geqslant |v|/2$, then $v_4 = v$ by Lemma 4.6 and once again we can apply Theorem 2.14 to draw the same conclusion. Therefore, we will examine the case when $i = 4$, $3|v| < |①| < 7|v|/2$ and we can also assume that $v_4 = \theta(v)$.

When $n \geqslant 12$, $|①| \geqslant 4|w|$ holds by the pigeon hole principle. More precisely,

$$|①| = (p - k + 1)|w| + 2|w_k''|,$$

and $p-k$ must be odd, as n is even. Since $|w_k''| < |w|$, we deduce that $p-k+1 \geqslant 4$. Therefore $|①| \geqslant 4|w| + 2|w_k''|$ holds. We will now show that the suffix of $①$ that starts after the prefix w_k'' is a prefix of $w_{k+1}w_{k+2}\cdots w_n$ which is long enough to apply Theorem 2.14: being long enough in this case means being of length at least $2|v| + |w|$. Assume that this was not the case, hence $|①| - |w_k''| < 2|v| + |w|$. As $|①| = 3|v| + |v_4'|$ holds in the case we are currently analysing, we derive $|v| + |v_4'| < |w| + |w_k''|$ from this, which leads to the contradiction

$$|①| = 3|v| + |v_4'| < 3|v| + 3|v_4'| < 3|w| + 3|w_k''| < 4|w| + 2|w_k''| \leqslant |①|.$$

Thus, Theorem 2.14 is applicable and we obtain $\tilde{v}, w \in \{t, \theta(t)\}^+$ for some word t, and $\tilde{v}$ as before.

In all previous cases we concluded that $\tilde{v}, w \in \{t, \theta(t)\}^+$ for some word t, and by Lemma 4.12 also $v, w \in \{t, \theta(t)\}^+$.

The remaining case is $n = 10$, which is depicted in Figure 4.6. Employing Lemma 2.12, we deduce that $w_1 = w_2 = w_3 = w$ and $w_8 = w_9 = w_{10} = \theta(w)$ in this case. As $②$ is a θ-palindrome, it follows that $v_5 = \theta(v_6)$. We show $w_7 = \theta(w)$

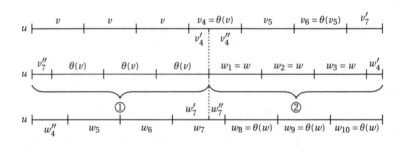

Figure 4.6. Equation (4.2) with $m = n = 10$.

holds as well. If $v_5 = v$, then $v_3 v_4 v_5 v_6 = (v\theta(v))^2$ is a θ-palindrome, and it contains the factor $w_7 \theta(w)\theta(w)$. Hence it also contains the factor $w w \theta(w_7)$, and as $w \neq \theta(w)$, we get that $w_7 = \theta(w)$ must hold. If $v_5 = \theta(v)$, we can employ similar reasoning using the θ-palindrome $v_2 v_3 v_4 v_5 = v^2 \theta(v)^2$ instead.

Now $w_7 w_8 w_9 = w_8 w_9 w_{10} = \theta(w)^3$, and the latter contains $v_5 \theta(v_5)$. Moreover, as $2|w| \geqslant |v| \geqslant |w|$ (as $m|v| < 2|u|$), this $v_5 \theta(v_5)$ appears as a proper factor inside $v_3 v_4 v_5 v_6 = v\theta(v)v_5\theta(v_5)$, and by Lemma 2.12, we get that $v = \theta(v)$, a contradiction. $\qquad\square$

Lemma 4.17. *If* $|u| < m|v| < 2|u|$ *and* $m \geqslant 10, n = 10$, *then* (4.2) *implies that* $u, v, w \in \{t, \theta(t)\}^+$ *for some word* t.

Proof. By Lemma 4.15 and Lemma 4.16, it suffices to consider the cases when $m \in \{12, 14, 16, 18\}$. Then $i \geqslant 5$ due to $|v_1 v_2 \cdots v_m| \geqslant |w_1 w_2 \cdots w_n|$ and, as before, $p - k$ must be odd, as n is assumed to be even. Now, by definition of ①, we have

$$|①| = (i - 1)|v| + |v_i'| = (p - k - 1)|w| + 2|w_k''|.$$

This implies

$$\frac{|①|}{2} = \frac{i-1}{2}|v| + \frac{1}{2}|v_i'|,$$

and

$$\frac{|①|}{2} = \frac{p-k-1}{2}|w| + |w_k''|.$$

Summing up, we get

$$|①| - |w_k''| = \frac{p-k-1}{2}|w| + \frac{i-1}{2}|v| + \frac{1}{2}|v_i'|,$$

and if $p - k \geqslant 5$, then $|①| - |w_k''| \geqslant 2|w| + 2|v|$. Thus, Theorem 2.14 is applicable to the suffix of ① that starts after the prefix w_k'', from which $\bar{v}, w \in \{t, \theta(t)\}^+$ for some word t follows, where $\bar{v}$ is defined as before. By Lemma 4.12, also $v, w \in \{t, \theta(t)\}^+$.

As $|v_1 v_2 \cdots v_m| \geqslant |w_1 w_2 \cdots w_n|$, we can not have $p - k = 1$. Hence, we are left with the case $p - k = 3$. We claim that $|v| \leqslant |w|$ holds in this case. Indeed,

4. Extended Lyndon-Schützenberger equations

$p - k = 3$ and $n = 10$ imply that $|②| \geqslant 3|u|/7$ and hence $|①| \leqslant 4|u|/7$. Then,

$$m|v| = |u| + |①| \leqslant \frac{11}{7}|u|,$$

and

$$10|w| = |u| + |②| \geqslant \frac{10}{7}|u|,$$

from which it follows that $|v| < |w|$, as $m \geqslant 12$ in our case.

Now, if $m \geqslant 14$, then $|①| > 9|v|/2$, and by Lemma 4.6 we have $v_1 = v_2 = \ldots = v_5 = v$. If $|w_7'| \geqslant |v|$, then clearly $w_5 w_6 w_7'$ is a prefix of $\tilde{v}^5$ of length at least $2|w| + |v|$, so that Theorem 2.14 is applicable to get $\tilde{v}, w \in \{t, \theta(t)\}^+$ for some word t. As before, this implies $v, w \in \{t, \theta(t)\}^+$ as well by Lemma 4.12. In the other case, that is when $|w_7'| < |v|$, this approach works, too: indeed, we have

$$|①| = (i-1)|v| + |v_i'| = 2|w| + 2|w_4''|,$$

and

$$|②| = 4|w| - |w_7'|.$$

Therefore, the inequality $|①| \geqslant |②|$ yields $|w| \leqslant 3|w_7'|/2$. For the sake of a contradiction, we assume $5|v| - |w_4''| < 2|w| + |v|$. Then

$$5|v| - |w_4''| < 2|w| + |v| \leqslant 3|w_7'| + |v|,$$

and thus

$$4|v| < 3|w_7'| + |w_4''| = 4|w_7'|,$$

since $|v_4''| = |v_7'|$. This is a contradiction, as we are in the case where $|w_7'| < |v|$. Therefore, if $m \geqslant 14$, we can apply Theorem 2.14 and Lemma 4.12 to get that $v, w \in \{t, \theta(t)\}^+$ for some word t.

The case $m = 12$ remains, see Figure 4.7.

As before, Lemma 4.6 provides us with the information $v_1 = v_2 = \ldots = v_4 = v$, and as the same reasoning as in the previous paragraph applies if $v_5 = v$, we assume henceforth that $v_5 = \theta(v)$ and $i = 5$. We shift our focus to suffixes of u.

If $w_7 = \theta(w)$, then we can apply Theorem 2.14 to the suffix of $w_7 w_8 \cdots w_{10}$ that ends before the suffix v_8' to get that $v, \bar{w} \in \{t, \theta(t)\}^+$. After reversing both sides of the equation and exchanging v and w, an application of Lemma 4.12

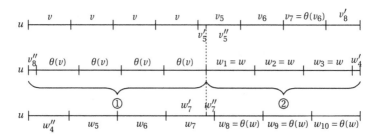

Figure 4.7. Equation (4.2) with $m = 12$ and $n = 10$.

yields the conclusion.

Hence we assume $w_7 = w$ and consider the two subcases depending on the value of v_6. If $v_6 = \theta(v)$, then $v_3 v_4 v_5 v_6 = v^2 \theta(v)^2$ is a θ-palindrome that contains $w_6 w_7 w_8 = w_6 w \theta(w)$ as its factor. As in the proof of the previous lemma, this either means that $w = \theta(w)$, or it yields a contradiction with the θ-primitivity of w using Lemma 2.12. If $v_6 = v$, then $v_7 = \theta(v)$ since ② is a θ-palindrome. Hence, $v_4 v_5 v_6 = v \theta(v) v$, and its image under θ is $v_5 v_6 v_7 = \theta(v) v \theta(v)$. The former contains $w_7 w_8 = w \theta(w)$ as a factor, whereas the latter is a proper factor of $w_7 w_8 \cdots w_{10}$. Thus Lemma 2.12 again implies $w = \theta(w)$. $\square$

We thus conclude the proof of Lemma 4.14. We will continue or study of (4.2) in the case when $m \leqslant n$ first.

Subcase $m \leqslant n$

As we solved (4.2) for $m, n \geqslant 10$ already, we will examine the equation first for $m = 6$ and $n \geqslant 6$ and then for $m = 8$ and $n \geqslant 8$.

When $m = 6$, if $|v_1 v_2 \cdots v_6| = |w_1 w_2 \cdots w_n|$, then $u = v_1 v_2 v_3 v_4$ is not θ-primitive, contradicting our assumption. As a consequence, we can assume $|v_1 v_2 \cdots v_6| > |w_1 w_2 \cdots w_n|$ henceforth. Then $2|v| < |①| < 3|v|$, so we have $v_1 = v_2 = v$ by Lemma 4.6 and thus $① = v^2 v_3'$.

We start examining (4.2), where both m and n are 6:

4. Extended Lyndon-Schützenberger equations

Lemma 4.18. *If $|u| < m|v| < 2|u|$ and $m = n = 6$, then (4.2) implies that $u, v, w \in \{t, \theta(t)\}^+$ for some word t.*

Proof. By Lemma 2.13, we have that $w_6 = \theta(w)$.

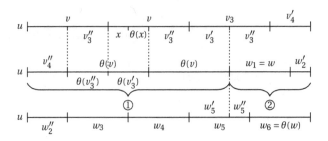

Figure 4.8. Equation (4.2) with $m = n = 6$.

We first consider the case when $v_3 = v$. This is depicted in Figure 4.8. Here, $v = v_3' v_3''$ and both v_3' and v_3'' are θ-palindromes, as can be observed easily in Figure 4.8. Furthermore, as $|①| = 2|w| + 2|w_2''|$, the length of ① is even.

This means that also $|v_3'|$ must be even, since $|①| = 3|v_3'| + 2|v_3''|$. As v_3' is centred inside the θ-palindrome ①, it follows that $v_3' = x\theta(x)$ for some word x. Then

$$w_4 w_5 \theta(w) = \theta(x) v_3'' x \theta(x) v_3'' v_3'',$$

and splitting the right-hand side into three parts of equal length yields $w_4 = \theta(x) v_3''$ and $w_5 \theta(w) = x \theta(x) v_3'' v_3''$. We will now show that v_3' and v_3'' are powers or θ-powers of the same word. Since $v = v_3' v_3''$, this is a contradiction to the θ-primitivity of v.

If $w_5 = w$, then $w_5 w_6 = w\theta(w)$ is a θ-palindrome and furthermore

$$w_5 w_6 = v_3' v_3'' \theta(v_3'') = v_3' v_3'' v_3'' = \theta(v_3' v_3'' v_3'') = v_3'' v_3'' v_3',$$

which means that v_3' and v_3'' are powers of the same word, and we reached the contradiction we aimed for.

On the other hand, if $w_5 = \theta(w)$, then we have

$$w_5 w_6 = \theta(w)^2 = x\theta(x) v_3'' v_3'',$$

which means that $x \leqslant_p \theta(w)$ and $v_3'' \leqslant_s \theta(w)$ and hence $\theta(w) = xv_3''$ by a length argument. If $w_4 = \theta(w)$, then $x = \theta(x)$, which results in the equation

$$x^2 v_3''^2 = \theta(w)^2,$$

and x and v_3'' are powers of a common word by Theorem 2.7. Otherwise, $w_4 = w = \theta(x) v_3''$, and hence we obtain the equation

$$\theta(w) = v_3'' x = x v_3'',$$

and thus x and v_3'' are powers of a common word, so in both cases $v_3' = x\theta(x)$ and v_3'' are θ-powers of the same word.

We move on to the analysis of the remaining case, that is when $v_3 = \theta(v)$. By Lemma 4.6, we can assume that $|v_3'| < |v|/2$. Let $v_3 = \theta(v) = v_3' v_3''$, and as in the previous case, we know that $v_3' = x\theta(x)$ for some word x. Then we have $\theta(v) = v_3' v_3'' = v_2'' v_3'$ and once again

$$x\theta(x) v_3'' \theta(v_3'') = w_5 \theta(w).$$

If $w_5 = w$, the right-hand side of the previous equation is a θ-palindrome, which implies

$$x\theta(x) v_3'' \theta(v_3'') = v_3'' \theta(v_3'') x\theta(x).$$

Hence $x\theta(x), v_3'' \theta(v_3'') \in \{t\}^+$ for some word t, and by Theorem 2.16 we get that $x, v_3'' \in \{t', \theta(t')\}^+$ holds for some word t'. This however contradicts the assumed θ-primitivity of $\theta(v) = v_3' v_3'' = x\theta(x) v_3''$.

Therefore we can assume $w_5 = \theta(w)$, which yields

$$x\theta(x) v_3'' \theta(v_3'') = \theta(w)^2.$$

This means that $x \leqslant_p \theta(w)$ and $\theta(v_3'') \leqslant_s \theta(w)$, hence $\theta(w) = x\theta(v_3'')$, which turns

4. Extended Lyndon-Schützenberger equations

the previous equation into

$$x\theta(x)v_3''\theta(v_3'') = x\theta(v_3'')x\theta(v_3''),$$

and that yields $\theta(x)v_3'' = \theta(v_3'')x$. As $|v_3''| > |v|/2$, this allows us to write $v_3'' = zx$ for some θ-palindrome z. Now, $v_3' = x\theta(x)$ and $v_3'' = zx$ turns the previously established equation $v_3'v_3'' = v_2''v_3'$ into

$$x\theta(x)zx = v_2''x\theta(x).$$

Comparing the suffixes of length $|x|$ of both sides implies $x = \theta(x)$ and hence $xxzx = v_2''xx$. Concatenating x to both sides of this equation results in

$$x^2zx^2 = v_2''x^3,$$

and as the left-hand side is a θ-palindrome, it follows that $v_2''x^3 = x^3v_2''$. Therefore, x and v_2'' are powers of a common word, a contradiction to the primitivity of $v = xxv_2''$. $\qquad\square$

We move on to the case when $m = 6$ and $n \geq 8$.

Lemma 4.19. *If $|u| < m|v| < 2|u|$ and $m = 6, n \geq 8$, then (4.2) implies that $u, v, w \in \{t, \theta(t)\}^+$ for some word t.*

Proof. As $m|v| \geq n|w|$ and $m = 6$ and $n \geq 8$, it follows that $|v| > |w|$. Again, as $6|v| \geq n|w|$ and $|u| < 6|v| < 2|u|$, $i = 3$ must hold and $v = x\theta(x)y$ for some words x and y as shown in the proof of Lemma 4.18, which means

$$① = v^2v_3' = x\theta(x)yx\theta(x)yx\theta(x) = w_k''w_{k+1}w_{k+2}\cdots w_{n/2}w_{n/2+1}\cdots w_{p-1}w_p',$$

where the first equality is established using Lemma 4.6. For an illustration of this situation see Figure 4.9.

If $v_3 = v$, then $v_3'' = y$ and $② = yy$, as y is a θ-palindrome. If $|②| \geq 2|w|$, then $|②| \geq |y| + |w|$, and $y, w \in \{t, \theta(t)\}^+$ for some word t by Theorem 2.15. As w is assumed to be θ-primitive, this means that $y \in \{w, \theta(w)\}^+$ and hence w_k' is empty and $u = w_kw_{k+1}\cdots w_n$, but this is a contradiction to the θ-primitivity of u. If $|②| < 2|w|$, then certainly $|①| > 4|w|$, since $|②①②| = n|w|$ and $n \geq 8$. We will show that $3|v| - |w_k''| \geq 2|v| + |w|$. Then Theorem 2.14 and Lemma 4.12 are

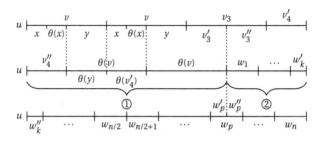

Figure 4.9. Equation (4.2) with $m = 6$ and $n \geqslant 8$.

applicable and provide the desired conclusion as before. First of all, $0 < |w_k''| < |w|$, as otherwise we would get the same contradiction with the θ-primitivity of u as in the previous case. As n is even, this means that $|①| \geqslant 4|w| + 2|w_k''|$. Assume now that $3|v| - |w_k''| < 2|v| + |w|$. Then $|v| < |w| + |w_k''|$ and consequently

$$3|v| < 3|w| + 3|w_k''| < 4|w| + 2|w_k''| < |①|,$$

which is a contradiction, as $3|v| > |①|$ in our situation.

Therefore, $v_3 = \theta(v)$ is assumed in the remainder of the proof, so $v_3'' = \theta(v_4')$. By Lemma 4.6, this implies that $|v_3'| = 2|x| < |v_3''|$. As $v_3 = v_6 = \theta(v)$ have the suffix v_3'' and the prefix $x\theta(x)$ of $\theta(v)$ is a suffix of v_3'' as well, it follows that $\theta(v)v_3''v_4'$ is a suffix of a θ-power of v_4'. Furthermore, as

$$n|w| = |②①②| = 6|v_3''| + 6|x|,$$

and $2|x| < |v_3''|$, it follows that $|w| \leqslant 6|v_3''|/8 + 6|x|/8$. Hence, as $n \geqslant 8$,

$$|\theta(v)v_3''v_4'| = 3|v_3''| + 2|x| > \frac{18}{8}|v_3''| + \frac{18}{8}|x| \geqslant 3|w|.$$

Summing up, we get that u is a suffix of $w_1 w_2 \cdots w_n$ and a suffix of u is a suffix of a θ-power of v_4'. This suffix is of length at least $3|w|$ and also at least $3|v_4'|$, hence Theorem 2.14 is applicable to conclude $v_4', w \in \{t, \theta(t)\}^+$ for some word t. As w is θ-primitive, $|w| = |t|$ must hold, which however turns $② = v_3''v_4'$ into a

θ-power of w, implying that also $u \in \{w, \theta(w)\}^+$, contradicting the θ-primitivity of u. □

Lemma 4.20. *If $|u| < m|v| < 2|u|$ and $m = 8, n \geqslant 8$, then (4.2) implies that $u, v, w \in \{t, \theta(t)\}^+$ for some word t.*

Proof. As $|\text{①}| \geqslant |\text{②}|$, we must have $|\text{①}| > 2|v|$, so there are two cases to be examined here: either $i = 4$ or $i = 3$. Furthermore, we get $|v| \geqslant |w|$.

We start analysing the case $i = 4$. In this case we have $\text{①} = v^3 v_4' = (v_4' y)^3 v_4'$, where the words v_4' and y are θ-palindromes, and $\text{②} = v_4'' v_5' = v_4'' \theta(v_4'')$, see Figure 4.10.

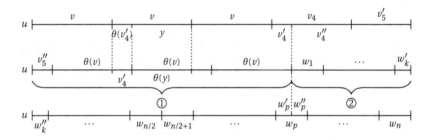

Figure 4.10. Equation (4.2) with $m = 8, n \geqslant 8$ and $i = 4$.

If $p - k \geqslant 5$, then $|w_k'' w_{k+1}| < |v_4' y v_4'|$ must hold: if $|v_4' y v_4'| \leqslant |w_k'' w_{k+1}| < 2|w|$ held, then

$$4|v_4'| + 3|y| = |\text{①}| \geqslant 2|w_k'' w_{k+1}| + 2|w| > 2(2|v_4'| + |y|) + 2|v_4'| + |y| = 6|v_4'| + 3|y|,$$

which obviously is a contradiction. Hence, the suffix of ① that starts after the prefix w_k'' is of length at least $2|v| + |w|$, and it is a prefix of $\bar{v}^3$ as ① is a prefix of v^4 by Lemma 4.8. Thus, using Theorem 2.14 and Lemma 4.12, we get that $v, w \in \{t, \theta(t)\}^+$ for some word t in this case.

We will now show, that $n \geqslant 10$ implies $p - k \geqslant 5$, so that the reasoning of the previous paragraph is applicable then. As $|w_k''| = |w_p'| < |w|$, it suffices to show that $|\text{①}| > 4|w|$ for this purpose. Now, as $|\text{①}| > 3|v|$ and consequently $|\text{②}| < 2|v|$

when $i = 4$, we observe that

$$|\text{①}| > \frac{3}{7}|\text{②①②}| = \frac{3}{7}n|w| \geqslant \frac{30}{7}|w| > 4|w|,$$

for $n \geqslant 10$, so that we can deduce that $v, w \in \{t, \theta(t)\}^+$ in this case.

Consequently, we focus on the remaining case when $i = 4$, that is $n = 8$ and $p - k = 3$, which is depicted in Figure 4.11.

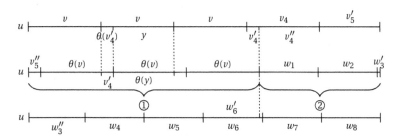

Figure 4.11. Equation (4.2) with $m = 8, n = 8, i = 4$ and $p - k = 3$.

As $|\text{②}| = 2|v_4''| > 2|w|$, the word $w_1 = w$ is a proper factor of v_4'' and hence it is also a proper factor of $v_4 = v_4' v_4''$. Furthermore, as $3|v| < |\text{①}| = 2|w_3''| + 2|w|$, both $v_1 = v$ and $v_6 = \theta(v)$ are factors of $w_3'' w_4$ and hence proper factors of $w_3 w_4$. Thus both w and $\theta(w)$ appear as proper factors inside $w_3 w_4$ and hence $w_3 \neq w_4$ and $w_3 w_4$ is a θ-palindrome. By the same argument $w_5 w_6$ contains both w and $\theta(w)$ and hence $w_5 \neq w_6$. As $w_4 = \theta(w_5)$ since ① is a θ-palindrome, we have that $w_5 w_6 = w_3 w_4$ must hold. Hence $\text{①} \leqslant_p w_3'' w_4 w_3' w_3'' w_4$ and so ① has a period of length $2|w|$ and one of length $|v|$, and

$$|\text{①}| > 3|v| > 2|w| + |v|,$$

so Theorem 2.1 is applicable to conclude that also $\gcd(|v|, 2|w|)$ is a period of ①. As v is assumed to be primitive, we must have $\gcd(|v|, 2|w|) = |v|$, but then $8|v| = 16|w|$ and hence $v_1 v_2 \cdots v_8$ is twice as long as $w_1 w_2 \cdots w_8$ and $8|v| = 2|u|$, which is a contradiction.

We have completely analysed the case when $i = 4$, so the only remaining possibility is $i = 3$, which is dealt with in the following. First of all, as $|①| \geqslant |②|$, we have that $① = vvv_3'$ with $|v_3'| > |v|/2$, and hence $v_3 = v$ by Lemma 4.6. If $v_4 = v$, then the suffix of v^4 that starts after the prefix w_k'' is a prefix of the word $w_{k+1} w_{k+2} \cdots w_n$ of length at least $3|v| > 2|v| + |w|$, so we can apply Theorem 2.14 and Lemma 4.12 to deduce $v, w \in \{t, \theta(t)\}^+$, as seen multiple times before.

Also, if $n \geqslant 12$, then $|①| \geqslant 4|w|$ by the pigeonhole principle, hence $p - k \geqslant 5$ in this case. If $p - k \geqslant 5$, then the suffix of v^3 that starts after w_k'' is once again long enough to apply Theorem 2.14 and Lemma 4.12: to see this, assume towards a contradiction that $3|v| - |w_k''| < 2|v| + |w|$. Hence $|v| < |w| + |w_k''|$ and thus

$$|①| < 3|v| < 3|w| + 3|w_k''| < 4|w| + 2|w_k''| \leqslant |①|,$$

which is a contradiction.

The remaining cases are therefore $n \in \{8, 10\}$ with $v_4 = \theta(v)$ and we can also assume that $p - k = 3$. As $②$ is a θ-palindrome, we have $v_5 = \theta(v_4) = v$.

We consider the case $n = 10$ first, which is depicted in Figure 4.12.

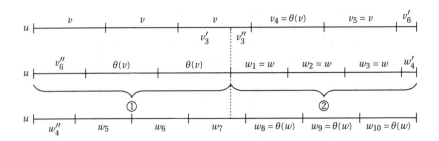

Figure 4.12. Equation (4.2) with $m = 8$, $n = 10$, $i = 3$ and $p - k = 3$.

We obtain $w_1 = w_2 = w_3 = w$ and $w_8 = w_9 = w_{10} = \theta(w)$ using Lemma 2.12 and Proposition 2.3. We will now show that w_7 is a proper factor of v_3. As $|①| = 3|v_3'| + 2|v_3''|$ and $|②| = 2|v_3'| + 4|v_3''|$ and $w_1 w_2 \cdots w_{10} = ②①②$, it follows that

$$|w| = \frac{1}{10}|②①②| = \frac{7}{10}|v_3'| + |v_3''|.$$

Therefore, we have

$$|w_8 w_9 w_{10}| = 3|w| = \frac{21}{10}|v_3'| + 3|v_3''| > 2|v_3'| + 3|v_3''| = |v_4 v_5 v_6'|,$$

and also

$$|w_7 w_8 w_9 w_{10}| = 4|w| = \frac{28}{10}|v_3'| + 4|v_3''| < 3|v_3'| + 4|v_3''| = |v_3 v_4 v_5 v_6'|,$$

and combining these two inequalities we deduce that w_7 is a proper factor of $v_3 = v$, and furthermore that $w_7 w_8$ is a proper factor of $v_3 v_4 = v\theta(v)$, and it is not centred inside $v\theta(v)$. As $v\theta(v)$ is a θ-palindrome, also the factor $\theta(w_7 w_8)$ appears inside it and is a proper factor of either $w_6 w_7 w_8$ or $w_7 w_8 w_9$. In any case Lemma 2.12 tells us that $w_7 = w_8$ must hold and hence $w_7 = \theta(w)$ as well. However, we also have that

$$|w_9 w_{10}| = 2|w| = \frac{14}{10}|v_3'| + 2|v_3''| > |v_3'| + 2|v_3''| = |v_5 v_6'|,$$

so that $v_5 = v$ is a proper factor of $w_9 w_{10}$. This implies that $w_7 = \theta(w)$ is a proper factor of v, which is a proper factor of $w_9 w_{10} = \theta(w)\theta(w)$, contradicting the primitivity of w.

We proceed to the final case, namely when $n = 8$, which is depicted in Figure 4.13.

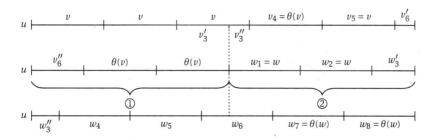

Figure 4.13. Equation (4.2) with $m = 8, n = 8$, $i = 3$ and $p - k = 3$.

By the same arguments as in the previous case (note that the lengths of

4. Extended Lyndon-Schützenberger equations

① and ② in terms of v_3' and v_3'' remained unchanged), we obtain that $|w| = 7|v_3'|/8 + 10|v_3''|/8$. We will now show that w_6 is a proper factor of $v_3 v_4 = v\theta(v)$: to see this, we observe that

$$|w_7 w_8| = \frac{14}{8}|v_3'| + \frac{20}{8}|v_3''| > |v_3'| + 2|v_3''| = |v_5 v_6'|,$$

and furthermore

$$|w_6 w_7 w_8| = \frac{21}{8}|v_3'| + \frac{30}{8}|v_3''| < 3|v_3'| + 4|v_3''| = |v_3 v_4 v_5 v_6'|.$$

Therefore, $v_3 v_4 = v\theta(v) = \alpha w_6 \beta$, where $\alpha \leqslant_s w_5$ and $\beta \leqslant_p w_7$. By calculations similar to the ones above we can determine the lengths of α and β as follows:

$$|\alpha| = 3|v| + |v_3''| - 3|w| = 3|v_3'| + 4|v_3''| - \frac{21}{8}|v_3'| - \frac{30}{8}|v_3''| = \frac{3}{8}|v_3'| + \frac{2}{8}|v_3''|,$$

and hence

$$|\beta| = 2|v| - |w| - |\alpha| = 2|v_3'| + 2|v_3''| - \frac{7}{8}|v_3'| - \frac{10}{8}|v_3''| - \frac{3}{8}|v_3'| - \frac{2}{8}|v_3''| = \frac{6}{8}|v_3'| + \frac{4}{8}|v_3''|.$$

We will use this information first to show that $w_6 = w$ must hold. For this purpose we assume that $w_6 = \theta(w)$ and will derive a contradiction from that. From the assumption that

$$3|v_3'| + 2|v_3''| = |①| \geqslant |②| = 4|v_3''| + 2|v_3'|$$

holds, we deduce that $|v_3'| \geqslant 2|v_3''|$. If $|①| = |②|$ then $|w| = |v|$, as $m = n = 8$ holds. Now $v_4 = \theta(v)$ is a factor of $\theta(w)^2$ and $v_5 = v$ is a factor of $\theta(w)^2$ anyway. The deduced equality of the lengths of w and v implies then that they occur at the same position inside $\theta(w)^2$, so that $v = \theta(v)$, which however we assumed not to be the case due to Lemma 4.11. Hence for $w_6 = \theta(w)$ to hold, $|①| > |②|$ can be assumed, from which we derive $|v_3'| > 2|v_3''|$ as above. Now, we saw above that

$$v_3 v_4 = v\theta(v) = \alpha w_6 \beta,$$

and as $v\theta(v)$ is a θ-palindrome, also

$$v_3 v_4 = \theta(\beta)\theta(w_6)\theta(\alpha) = \theta(\beta)w\theta(\alpha).$$

Thus, w occurs in $w_6 w_7 = \theta(w)^2$ twice: one occurrence is w_1, which appears after the prefix of length $|v_3'| - |\alpha| = 3|v_3'|/5 - 2|v_3''|/8$, while the other occurrence is $\theta(w_6)$ which appears inside $w_6 w_7$ after the prefix of length $|\theta(\beta)| - |\alpha|$. See Figure 4.14 for a visualisation of this situation. However, by our assumption $|v_3'| > 2|v_3''|$, it follows that $2|v_3'|/8 > 4|v_3''|/8$ holds, and consequently $|v_3'| > 4|v_3''|/8 + 6|v_3'|/8 = |\beta|$. Therefore, the two occurrences of w as a factor of $\theta(w)^2$ do not coincide, which is a contradiction to the primitivity of w.

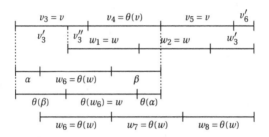

Figure 4.14. The two occurrences of w inside $w_6 w_7$ if $w_6 = \theta(w)$.

We can now assume that $w_6 = w$. If also $w_5 = w$ holds, then the word $w_5 w_6 w_7 w_8 = w^2 \theta(w)^2$ is a θ-palindrome. Thus,

$$w^2\theta(w)^2 = \alpha v\theta(v)vv_6' = \theta(v_6')\theta(v)v\theta(v)\theta(\alpha),$$

and since

$$|\alpha| = 4|w| - 3|v| - |v_3''| = \frac{4}{8}|v_3'| + |v_3''| > |v_3''| = |v_6'|,$$

it follows that $v\theta(v)$ appears as a proper factor inside $\theta(v)v\theta(v)$, which contradicts the θ-primitivity of v by Lemma 2.12.

Hence the last remaining case is when $w_5 = \theta(w)$. As ① is a θ-palindrome, we can deduce $w_4 = w$ from that. Then $w_5 w_6 w_7 = \theta(w)w\theta(w) = \gamma v\theta(v)\delta$ for

4. Extended Lyndon-Schützenberger equations

some words γ, δ. Hence

$$w_4 w_5 w_6 = w\theta(w)w = \theta(w_5 w_6 w_7) = \theta(\delta)v\theta(v)\theta(\gamma).$$

However, $w_4 w_5 w_6$ is a proper factor of $vvv\theta(v)$, which produces a contradiction with either Lemma 2.12 or the assumption that $v \neq \theta(v)$. $\qquad\square$

Subcase $m > n$

Lemma 4.21. *If* $|u| < m|v| < 2|u|$ *and* $m \geqslant 8, n = 6$, *then* (4.2) *implies that* $u, v, w \in \{t, \theta(t)\}^+$ *for some word* t.

Proof. First of all, the assumption $|①| \geqslant |②|$ implies that $|②| \leqslant 2|w|$, and hence $k = 1$ or $k = 2$.

The case $k = 1$ can be dealt with easily: The fact $|②| < |w|$ implies $|①| \geqslant 4|w|$ and $|②| < |u|/5$ which implies $|①| > 4|u|/5$.

If $m \geqslant 10$, this means that $|①| > 4|v|$ and so ① is a prefix of v^i and $i \geqslant 5$. Therefore, Theorem 2.14 and Lemma 4.12 are applicable in this case to deduce $v, w \in \{t, \theta(t)\}^+$ for some word t.

If $m = 8$, then as $8|v| < 2|u|$, we have $8|v|/5 < 2|u|/5$, which when combined with the previously established fact $|①| > 4|u|/5$ yields $|①| > 3|v|$. Thus, we can assume $i = 4$ in this case, and

$$|①| = 4|v_4'| + 3|v_4''| \geqslant 2|v_4''| = |②|.$$

From this and the fact that $|②| < |u|/5$ we deduce that $|v_4''| < |u|/10$, which in turn yields that $|v_4'| > |u|/8$, when used in the inequality $|①| > 4|u|/5$. Thus $|v_4'| > \frac{1}{2}|v|$, and Lemma 4.6 implies that $v_4 = v$, which lets us use the same argument as in the case $m \geqslant 10$.

The case when $k = 2$ is more intricate and the remainder of the proof is devoted to this.

See Figure 4.15 for a visualisation of the situation in question. Since ① is a prefix of a power of v by Lemma 4.8, if $|w_2''| = |w_5'| \geqslant |v|$, we can apply Theorem 2.14 to $w_3 w_4 w_5'$ to get that $\bar{v}, w \in \{t, \theta(t)\}^+$, for some word t, which contradicts the θ-primitivity of w, as $|w| > |v|$ here. Thus we assume that $|v| > |w_2''| = |w_5'|$ holds henceforth.

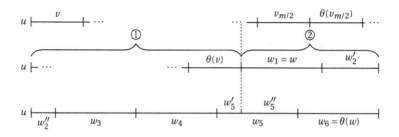

Figure 4.15. Equation (4.2) with $m \geqslant 8, n = 6$, and $k = 2$.

We will now show that $v_{m/2}$ can not be a factor of w_1, hence $|\text{①}| < 2|v|$ and the situation depicted in Figure 4.15 is actually not possible. Assume for the sake of a contradiction that $v_{m/2}$ is a factor of w_1.

If $w_2 = \theta(w)$, then $w_5 = w$ as $w_1 w_2 \cdots w_6 = \text{②①②}$ is a θ-palindrome. Hence $v_{m/2}\theta(v_{m/2})$ is a factor of $w_1 w_2'$, which is a prefix of $w_1 w_2 = w\theta(w)$ and of $w_5 w_6 = w\theta(w)$ as well. Therefore, $v_{m/2}\theta(v_{m/2})$ appears at least twice as a factor of u, and the lengths of the prefixes of u before these occurrences differ by $|w_5'|$. In order to avoid a contradiction with the θ-primitivity of v using Lemma 2.12, $|w_6'|$ must be divisible by $|v|$. This however contradicts our assumption $|v| > |w_5'|$.

Therefore we can assume that $w_2 = w$ and hence $w_5 = \theta(w)$.

If $w_4 = \theta(w)$, then $w_4 w_5 = w_5 w_6 = \theta(w)^2$ and $v_{m/2}\theta(v_{m/2})$ has another occurrence in u, namely as a factor of $w_4 w_5$. To avoid a contradiction with the θ-primitivity of v using Lemma 2.12, $|w|$ must be divisible by $|v|$. Furthermore, as $v_{\frac{m}{2}}$ is a proper factor of w_1, the occurrence inside $w_4 w_5$ that appears $|w|$ to the left is a factor of ①, which is a prefix of v^i. Therefore $v_1 = v_2 = \ldots = v_{m/2} = v$, and we can apply Theorem 2.14 to the suffix of $v_1 v_2 \cdots v_{m/2}$ that starts after w_2'' and $w_3 w_4 w_5$, to get that $\tilde{v}, w \in \{t, \theta(t)\}^+$ for some word t. This however contradicts the θ-primitivity of w, since $|w| > |v|$ by our assumption that $v_{m/2}$ is a factor of w_1.

So if $v_{m/2}$ is a factor of w_1, then $w_4 = w$. We will show that this leads to a contradiction as well. As $v_{m/2}\theta(v_{m/2})$ is a factor of $w_1 w_2'$, which is a prefix of $w\theta(w)$, it is also a factor of $w_4 w_5 = w\theta(w)$, and the lengths of the prefixes before these factors differ by $|w_4| + |w_5'|$. As before, to avoid a contradiction with

73

the θ-primitivity of v using Lemma 2.12, this difference has to be divisible by $|v|$. However, if $|w_4| + |w_5'|$ is divisible by $|v|$, then so is $|①| = 2|w_4| + 2|w_5'|$, and so $①$ is a power of v. As $①$ is a θ-palindrome, this implies $v = \theta(v)$, which is against our assumption.

In conclusion, we have proved that $v_{m/2}$ can not be a factor of w_1 without violating one of our assumptions. Therefore $|②| < 2|v|$ must hold. Now, as

$$|v_1 \cdots v_m| = |①②①| = 2(2|w| + |w_5'|) + 2|w| - |w_5'|,$$

if $m \geqslant 12$ we deduce that

$$2|v| \leqslant |w| + \frac{1}{2}|w_5'|.$$

Since we have just shown that $|②| = 2|w| - |w_5'| < 2|v|$ holds, we have

$$2|w| - |w_5'| < 2|v| \leqslant |w| + \frac{1}{2}|w_5'|,$$

and hence $|w| < 3|w_5'|/2$. Combined with the fact $2|v| \leqslant |w| + |w_5'|/2$, this however implies $|v| < |w_5'|$, which contradicts the assumption $|v| > |w_5'|$ that we made previously.

Hence, the sole remaining cases are $m = 10$ and $m = 8$. We investigate the former case first. For a visualisation consult Figure 4.16.

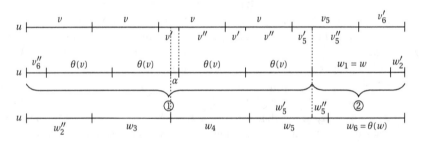

Figure 4.16. Equation (4.2) with $m = 10, n = 6$, and $k = 2$.

We have $5|w| > |u| > 5|v|$, so $|w| > |v|$. If $v_5 = v$, then we can apply Theorem 2.14 to $w_3 w_4 w_5$ and the suffix of $v_1 v_2 \cdots v_5 = v^5$ that starts after the prefix

w_2'', which results in $\bar{v}, w \in \{t, \theta(t)\}^+$ for some word t, where $\bar{v}$ is a conjugate of v. However, as $|w| > |v|$, this contradicts the θ-primitivity of w. Thus we assume $v_5 = \theta(v)$.

We have

$$w_4 w_5 = \alpha \theta(v) \theta(v) w_5'' = \alpha v'' v v_5' w_5''.$$

If $w_4 \neq w_5$, then $w_4 w_5$ is a θ-palindrome and hence we deduce that

$$w_4 w_5 = \alpha \theta(v) \theta(v) w_5'' = \theta(w_5'') \theta(v_5') \theta(v) \theta(v'') \theta(\alpha),$$

and as $|\alpha| < |v'| = |v_5'|$ and $|w_5''| < |v_5''| = |v''|$, the word $\theta(v)$ occurs as a proper factor inside $\theta(v)\theta(v)$, which contradicts its primitivity. Therefore, $w_4 = w_5$ must hold.

If $w_4 = w_5 = \theta(w)$, then $w_4 w_5 = \theta(w)^2$ has the suffix $\theta(v)\theta(v)w_5''$, whereas $w_5 w_6 = \theta(w)^2$ has the suffix $\theta(v)v_6'$ and $|v_6'| > |w_5''|$, so that $\theta(v)$ occurs as a proper factor inside $\theta(v)\theta(v)$, contradicting the primitivity of v.

However, if $w_4 = w_5 = w$, then $w_5 w_6$ is a θ-palindrome and furthermore $w_5 w_6 = \alpha v_5 v_6' = \alpha \theta(v) v_6'$, where α is a suffix of v and v_6' is a prefix of v. Since $w_5 w_6$ is a θ-palindrome, also $w_5 w_6 = \theta(v_6') v \theta(\alpha)$ holds and $\theta(v_6')$ is a suffix of $\theta(v)$ and $\theta(\alpha)$ is a prefix of $\theta(v)$. The fact that $|w| > |v|$ allows us to truncate the equation $\alpha \theta(v) v_6' = \theta(v_6') v \theta(\alpha)$ to a length of $2|v|$, to deduce that two different conjugates of $v\theta(v)$ are equal. Hence, $v\theta(v)$ is not primitive, and either $v = \theta(v)$ or we can apply Theorem 2.16 to deduce that v is not θ-primitive. In both cases, this is a contradiction.

In conclusion, the case when $m = 10$ leads to a contradiction under all circumstances, so we move on to analyse the last remaining case when $n = 6$, namely $m = 8$, which is visualised in Figure 4.17. As in the previous proofs, the two representations of ① yield that $|v_3''|$ is even, and as v_3'' is centred inside the θ-palindrome ①, it follows that $v_3'' = x\theta(x)$ for some word x. Furthermore, $v_3' = \theta(v_3')$ holds as before. Since

$$n|w| = |②①②| = 7|v_4''| + 4|v_4'|,$$

it follows that

$$|w| = \frac{7}{6}|v_4''| + \frac{4}{6}|v_4'|.$$

4. Extended Lyndon-Schützenberger equations

The previously established assumption that $|w| < |②| < 2|v|$ is still valid.

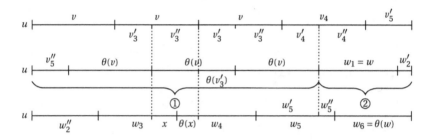

Figure 4.17. Equation (4.2) with $m = 8, n = 6$, and $k = 2$.

If $v_4 = v$ and $|v| \geqslant |w|$, then the suffix of $v_1 v_2 \cdots v_4$ after the prefix w_2'' is of length $4|v| - |w_2''| > 3|v| \geqslant 2|v| + |w|$, so that we can apply Theorem 2.14 and Lemma 4.12 to get that $v, w \in \{t, \theta(t)\}^+$ for some word t.

If $v_4 = v$ and $|v| < |w|$, then in particular $|w_6| > |v_5'|$, so that $w_3 w_4 w_5$ is a prefix of $\bar{v}^4$ and $3|w| > 2|w| + |v|$, so that we get $\bar{v}, w \in \{t, \theta(t)\}^+$ for some word t. This however contradicts the θ-primitivity of w as $|w| > |v| = |\bar{v}|$.

Thus we can assume $v_4 = \theta(v)$ in the following, which means that $v_5' \leqslant_p v$. Lemma 4.6 implies $|v_4'| < |v_4''|$ in this case.

If $w_4 = w_5 = \theta(w)$, then $v_4 v_5' = \theta(v) v_5' \leqslant_s w_5 w_6 = \theta(w)\theta(w)$ and therefore $\theta(v) v_5' \leqslant_s w_4 w_5$. However, as $|v_4'| < |v_4''| = |v_5'|$, this implies that $\theta(v)$ is a proper factor of $v_7 v_8 = \theta(v)\theta(v)$, contradicting the primitivity of v.

Before analysing the other possible values of w_4 and w_5, we first show that we can strengthen the assumption $|v_4'| < |v_4''|$ to $2|v_4'| < |v_4''|$: assume towards a contradiction that $2|v_4'| \geqslant |v_4''|$. Then the equation $v_4 = \theta(v) = v_4' v_4'' = v_3'' v_4'$ allows to conclude that $x \leqslant_p v_4'$. Furthermore, $\theta(x) \leqslant_s v_4'$, since $v_4' = v_3'$ is a θ-palindrome, which implies that $\theta(x) \leqslant_s v_4''$. Finally, $x \leqslant_p \theta(v_4'') = v_5'$. Therefore $w_4 w_5 w_6$ has the prefix $\theta(x) v \theta(v) x$, which is a θ-palindrome, and $w_4 w_5$ is a prefix thereof. Hence, $\theta(w_5)\theta(w_4)$ appears as a proper factor inside $w_4 w_5 w_6$ and by Lemma 2.12 we get $w_4 = w_5$.

We already analysed the case $w_4 = w_5 = \theta(w)$, hence we assume $w_4 = w_5 = w$. However, $\theta(x) v \theta(v) x = w_4 w_5 \gamma$ and thus $\theta(\gamma)\theta(w_5)$ is a prefix of $\theta(x) v \theta(v) x$.

Since $|w| = 4|v_4'|/6 + 7|v_4''|/6$ and

$$|\gamma| = |\theta(x)v\theta(v)x| - 2|w| = 3|v_3''| + 2|v_3'| - \frac{14}{6}|v_4''| - \frac{8}{6}|v_4'| = \frac{4}{6}|v_3''| + \frac{4}{6}|v_3'|,$$

it follows that $|\gamma| > |v_3''|/2 = |\theta(x)|$. Furthermore, since $2|v_4'| \geqslant |v_4''|$, we can deduce $|\gamma| < 3|v_3''|/6 + |v_3'| = |\theta(x)v_3'|$. This means that $\theta(w_5)$ is a factor of the θ-palindrome $v_3' v_3'' v_3'$, and so $w_5 = w$ is a factor thereof as well, which however contradicts the primitivity of w, as $v_3' v_3'' v_3'$ is a proper factor of $w_4 w_5 = ww$.

Consequently, we assume $2|v_4'| < |v_4''|$ in the remainder of this proof.

If $w_5 \neq w_6$, then $w_5 w_6$ is a θ-palindrome, and the θ-palindrome $v_4'' v_5' = v_4'' \theta(v_4'')$ is a suffix of it. Therefore, $v_4'' \theta(v_4'')$ is also a prefix of $w_5 w_6$. As $|v_4'| < |v_4''|$, the word $\theta(v)$ is a suffix of $v_4'' v_4''$. Hence $\theta(v)②$ is a suffix of $v_4''^3 \theta(v_4'')$, and $v_4'' \theta(v_4'')$ is a proper factor thereof. By Lemma 2.12 we deduce that v_4'' can not be θ-primitive in this case, hence $v_4'' \in \{z, \theta(z)\}^+$ for some word z with $|z| \leqslant |v_4''|/2$. Then the suffix $\theta(v)②$ is a suffix of a θ-power of z, and its length is

$$|v| + 2|v_4''| = 3|v_4''| + |v_4'| = \frac{18}{6}|v_4''| + |v_4'|,$$

and since $2|v_4'| < |v_4''|$, we get

$$|v| + 2|v_4''| > \frac{17}{6}|v_4''| + \frac{8}{6}|v_4'| = 2|w| + \frac{1}{2}|v_3''| \geqslant 2|w| + |z|.$$

Therefore, Theorem 2.14 can be applied to this suffix, which implies that $w, z \in \{t, \theta(t)\}^+$ for some word t. As $|w| > |v_4''| > |z|$, this means that w is not θ-primitive, a contradiction.

If $w_5 = w_6 = \theta(w)$, then $w_4 = w$, as we already showed that the other case leads to a contradiction above. See Figure 4.18 for a visualisation of this case. We observe that this implies $w_5' = \theta(w_5')$ and $w_5'' = \theta(w_5'')$. Furthermore, as $|②| = 2|v_4''| = 2|w_5''| + |w_5'|$, the length of w_5' must be even, and hence $w_5' = z\theta(z)$ for some word z. Hence $\theta(z)$ is a suffix of $v_8 = \theta(v)$, and so z is a prefix of $v_5 = v$. This prefix of v_5 appears at the same position in $②$ as the suffix $\theta(z)$ of $w_1 = w$, and hence $z = \theta(z)$. As $|v_4''| = |v_3''| = 2|x|$, we can factorise $v_4'' = y_1 y_2$ for some

4. Extended Lyndon-Schützenberger equations

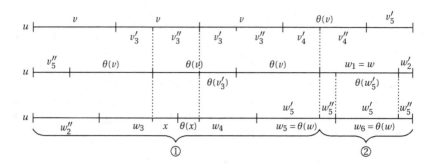

Figure 4.18. Equation (4.2) with $m = 8, n = 6, k = 2$ and $w_4 w_5 w_6 = w\theta(w)^2$.

words y_1, y_2 with $|y_1| = |y_2|$. This allows us to write

$$w\theta(w)\theta(w) = \theta(x)\theta(y_2)\theta(y_1)v_4'v_4'v_4''\theta(v_4'') = w_5''zzzzw_5''zzw_5''.$$

The fact that $|v_4''| = |w_5''| + |w_5'|/2$ follows from the equation $|②| = 2|v_4''| = 2|w_5''| + |w_5'|$. This allows us to deduce that $w_5''z = \theta(x)\theta(y_2)$ and $\theta(y_1)v_4'v_4' = zzz$ and furthermore $y_1 y_2 = w_5''z$. Hence $w_5''z = \theta(x)\theta(y_2) = y_1 y_2$, and thus $y_1 = \theta(x)$. Using these results, the equation

$$\theta(v) = v_3''v_4' = v_4'v_4''$$

can be rewritten as

$$\theta(y_1)y_1v_4' = v_4'y_1y_2.$$

This means that $\theta(y_1) \leqslant_p v_4'y_1$ and hence $y_1 \leqslant_s \theta(y_1)v_4'$. Furthermore $v_4' \leqslant_p \theta(y_1)$, since $2|v_4'| < |v_4''|$. Therefore, $v_4'y_1 = \theta(y_1)v_4'$, which turns the equation $\theta(y_1)v_4'v_4' = zzz$ into $v_4'y_1v_4' = zzz$. As z is a θ-palindrome, also $y_1 = \theta(y_1)$ holds, which together with $v_4'y_1 = \theta(y_1)v_4'$ implies that v_4' and y_1 are powers of the same word. This however contradicts the primitivity of $v = v_4'v_3'' = v_4'x\theta(x) = v_4'\theta(y_1)y_1 = x_4 y_1 y_1$. $\square$

We will now solve the final remaining case of this section: $m \geqslant 10$ and $n = 8$.

Lemma 4.22. *If $|u| < m|v| < 2|u|$ and $m \geqslant 10, n = 8$, then (4.2) implies that*

78

$u, v, w \in \{t, \theta(t)\}^+$ *for some word t.*

Proof. As we assume $10|v| \geqslant 8|w|$, and thus $|①| \geqslant |②|$, we have $|②| < 3|w|$. We will first show that the claim is true if $|②| < 2|w|$. As a first step, we show that $|v| > |w|$ in this case:

If $|②| < |w|$ and hence $② = w'_1$, for $w_1 = w'_1 w''_1$ and $|w''_1| > 0$, we have

$$|u| = \frac{1}{2}(10|v| + |②|) = 5|v| + \frac{1}{2}|w'_1| = 8|w| - |w'_1|,$$

so $8|w| = 5|v| + 3|w'_1|/2 < 5|v| + 2|w|$. It follows that $5|v| > 6|w|$, and thus $|w| < 5|v|/6 < |v|$.

If $|w| < |②| < 2|w|$, thus $② = ww'_2$, for $w_2 = w'_2 w''_2$ and $|w''_2| > 0$, then

$$|u| = 5|v| + \frac{1}{2}|ww'_2| = 8|w| - |ww'_2|,$$

and thus $8|w| = 5|v| + 3|ww'_2|/2 < 5|v| + 3|w|$, so also obtain $|w| < |v|$ in this case.

Now $2|v| > 2|w| > |②|$, so $|①| > 4|v|$. Thus we can apply Theorem 2.14 to the suffix of $①$ that starts after w''_1 or w''_2, which yields that $\bar{v} \in \{w, \theta(w)\}^+$, and using Lemma 4.12 we obtain $v \in \{w, \theta(w)\}^+$ as well.

Consequently, we assume $2|w| < |②| < 3|w|$ henceforth, thus $② = www'_3$, for $w_3 = w'_3 w''_3$ and $|w''_3| > 0$ as visualised in Figure 4.19.

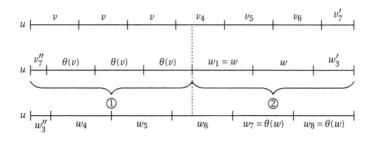

Figure 4.19. Equation (4.2) with $m = 10, n = 8$.

Now we have $|u| = 5|v| + |www'_3|/2 = 8|w| - |www'_3|$ and so $8|w| = 5|v| + 3|www'_3|/2 > 5|v| + 3|w|$. Hence in this case $|w| > |v|$ holds. We consider the possible values for w_3 and w_4 now.

If $w_3 w_4 = w w$, then $v_5 \theta(v_5)$ occurs as a factor inside $w_6 w_7 w_8 = \theta(w)^3$ and also in $w_5 w_6 w_7 = \theta(w)^3$. By Lemma 2.12, the distance between these occurrences must be a multiple $|v|$. However, the distance is exactly $|w|$, and thus we have $|w| = k|v|$ for some $k \geqslant 2$, as $|w| > |v|$. This means that $8|w| \geqslant 16|v| > 10|v|$, a contradiction to the assumption $8|w| \leqslant 10|v|$.

A similar situation appears if $w_3 w_4 = \theta(w)\theta(w)$, since $v_5 \theta(v_5)$ occurs inside $w_1 w_2 w_3 = w w \theta(w)$ and also in $w_5 w_6 w_7 = w w \theta(w)$ in this case. However, $w_5 w_6 w_7$ is shifted to the left by $|w| + |w''|$ in u. Hence, the θ-primitivity of w and Lemma 2.12 imply $|w| + |w''| = k|v|$ for some k and thus $|①| = 2|w| + 2|w''| = 2k|v|$. This means $|u| = 10|v| - 2k|v|$ is divisible by v, so $u \in \{v, \theta(v)\}^+$, contradicting the θ-primitivity.

If $w_3 w_4 = w \theta(w)$ or $w_3 w_4 = \theta(w) w$, then $w_3 w_4$ is a θ-palindrome and also $w_3 w_4 = w_5 w_6$.

We will now establish the value of v_4. As v is a prefix of $w_3'' w_4$ and $w_3 w_4 = w_5 w_6$, the word v also occurs after the prefix of length $2|w|$ in u. We show that this occurrence is a proper factor of $v_1 v_2 \cdots v_4$: Assume to the contrary that $2|w| + |v| > 4|v|$, then $2|w| > 3|v|$ and thus $8|w| > 12|v| > 10|v|$, a contradiction. Hence, if $v_4 = v$, then, by synchronisation, we get that $|v|$ divides $2|w|$, so $2|w| = k|v|$, and $k \geqslant 3$, as $|w| > |v|$. However, then we get again the contradictory statement $8|w| = 4k|v| \geqslant 12|v| > 10|v|$. Therefore we assume $v_4 = \theta(v)$ in the following, which means that $v_3 v_4 = v\theta(v)$ is a θ-palindrome.

We will now show that v_4 is a proper factor of w_6, which implies that the θ-palindrome $v_3 v_4 = v\theta(v)$ is a factor of the θ-palindrome $w_5 w_6$ that is not centred inside $w_5 w_6$. Hence $v\theta(v)$ has another occurrence inside $w_5 w_6$, which then yields a contradiction with Lemma 2.12.

For this purpose, we show that v_4 starts and ends inside w_6. Since we already established $|w| > |v|$, we can deduce that

$$3|u| = 10|v| + 8|w| > 12|v| + 6|w|,$$

from which $|u| - 2|w| > 4|v|$ follows. Furthermore,

$$3|u| = 10|v| + 8|w| < 9|v| + 9|w|,$$

so that $|u| - 3|w| < 3|v|$ holds. Hence, v_4 is a proper factor of w_6, thus $v_3 v_4$ is not centred inside $w_5 w_6$, and we reach the aforementioned contradiction. □

4.4.2 The case $u_1 u_2 u_3 = u u \theta(u)$

In this section we analyse the equation

$$u u \theta(u) = v_1 v_2 \cdots v_m w_1 w_2 \cdots w_n. \tag{4.3}$$

The case when $m|v| > 2|u|$ was the only case of an equation of the form (4.1) with $\ell = 3$ that was already investigated by Kari, Masson, and Seki [56], with the following result (Proposition 51 in [56]):

Lemma 4.23 (Kari, Masson & Seki, 2011). *If $m|v| > 2|u|$ and $m, n \geqslant 3$, then (4.3) implies that $u, v, w \in \{t, \theta(t)\}^+$ for some word t.*

Therefore, we only have to establish a similar result for the case when $|u| < m|v| < 2|u|$. We can actually show a stronger result:

Lemma 4.24. *If $|u| < m|v| < 2|u|$, $m, n \geqslant 5$ and $u_3 = \theta(u_1)$, then (4.1) implies that $u, v, w \in \{t, \theta(t)\}^+$ for some word t.*

Proof. We will assume $|v| \geqslant |w|$, otherwise we just change the roles of v and w in the following reasoning (note that we do not use the assumption $m|v| \geqslant n|w|$ in this proof). Actually, if $|v| = |w|$, we get that $v_1 = \theta(w_n)$, and that $v, w \in \{v, \theta(v)\}$, so in this case the statement holds.

Therefore we can assume that $|v| > |w|$. Now, if $|u| \geqslant 3|v|$, then we have $u \leqslant_p v_1 v_2 \cdots v_m$ and $u \leqslant_p \theta(w_n)\theta(w_{n-1})\cdots\theta(w_1)$, and $|u| \geqslant 2|v| + |w|$. Applying Theorem 2.14, we get that $v, w \in \{t, \theta(t)\}^+$ for some word t, thus the statement also holds in this case. Hence we assume $|u| < 3|v|$.

Since $m|v| < 2|u|$ and $m \geqslant 5$, it follows that $m = 5$ and $u = v_1 v_2 r$ for $v_3 = rs$. Furthermore, again from the facts that $m|v| < 2|u|$ and $m \geqslant 5$, it follows immediately that $|r| > |s|$. If $|w| \leqslant |r|$, then u would still be a prefix of $v_1 \cdots v_m$ and $\theta(w_n)\cdots\theta(w_1)$, long enough to apply Theorem 2.14, so we assume $|w| > |r|$.

As $|u| = 2|v| + |r| = 3|r| + 2|s|$, we get that

$$|w_1 w_2 \cdots w_n| = 3|u| - 5|v| = 3(3|r| + 2|s|) - 5(|r| + |s|) = 4|r| + |s|,$$

81

4. Extended Lyndon-Schützenberger equations

and so as $|r|,|s| < |w|$, this contradicts the fact that $n \geqslant 5$. □

We remark that this result is independent of the value of u_2, and hence this also gives an affirmative answer for the case $u_1 u_2 u_3 = u\theta(u)\theta(u)$, when $|u| < m|v| < 2|u|$. Therefore, this case will not be covered separately in the corresponding section.

4.4.3 The case $u_1 u_2 u_3 = u\theta(u)u$

In this section we fix $u_1 = u_3 = u$ and $u_2 = \theta(u)$, hence we analyse the equation

$$u\theta(u)u = v_1 v_2 \cdots v_m w_1 w_2 \cdots w_n. \tag{4.4}$$

We can reduce this equation to a previously analysed one, without having to distinguish between the different length cases:

Theorem 4.25. *If $m, n \geqslant 3$, then* (4.4) *implies that $u, v, w \in \{t, \theta(t)\}^+$ for some word t.*

Proof. Applying θ to the equation results in

$$\theta(u)u\theta(u) = \theta(w_n)\theta(w_{n-1})\cdots\theta(w_1)\theta(v_m)\theta(v_{m-1})\cdots\theta(v_1),$$

and we concatenate this with the original equation to obtain

$$(u\theta(u))^3 = v_1 v_2 \cdots v_m w_1 w_2 \cdots w_n \theta(w_n)\cdots\theta(w_1)\theta(v_m)\cdots\theta(v_1).$$

Cyclic shift converts this into

$$x^3 = \theta(v_m)\cdots\theta(v_1)v_1 v_2 \cdots v_m w_1 w_2 \cdots w_n \theta(w_n)\cdots\theta(w_1),$$

where x is a conjugate of $u\theta(u)$. This equation implies $v, w \in \{t, \theta(t)\}^+$ for some word t, as shown in Section 4.4.1. □

4.4.4 The case $u_1 u_2 u_3 = u\theta(u)\theta(u)$

In this section we fix $u_1 = u$ and $u_2 = u_3 = \theta(u)$, hence we analyse the equation

$$u\theta(u)\theta(u) = v_1 v_2 \cdots v_m w_1 w_2 \cdots w_n. \tag{4.5}$$

As previously remarked, the case $|u| < m|v| < 2|u|$ is already covered by Lemma 4.24. Therefore, we only analyse the other one, namely $m|v| > 2|u|$:

Lemma 4.26. *If $2|u| < m|v| < 2|u| + |v|$ and $m, n \geqslant 5$, then* (4.5) *implies that $u, v, w \in \{t, \theta(t)\}^+$ for some word t.*

Proof. By Proposition 4.2, we know that $v_1 = v_2 = \ldots = v_m = v$. We analyse first the case when m is even.

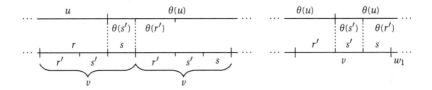

Figure 4.20. The situation at the two borders $u_1 u_2$ and $u_2 u_3$.

We start with the case when $m = 6$. We have $u_1 = vvr$, where $v = rs$ and $|r| \geqslant |s|$. As v is θ-primitive we can assume that $|r| > |s|$, as otherwise, we had $v = r\theta(r)$, contradicting the θ-primitivity. Hence, let r' be the prefix of length $|r| - |s|$ of r and s' be the remaining suffix of length $|s|$ of r such that $r = r's'$ (see Figure 4.20).

At the border between $u_1 = u$ and $u_2 = \theta(u)$, we can observe that

$$r's'sr' = r'\theta(s)\theta(s')\theta(r').$$

It follows that $\theta(s) = s'$ and $\theta(r') = r'$. Now, looking at the border between $u_2 = \theta(u)$ and $u_3 = \theta(u)$, we get that $\theta(s')r' \leqslant_p \theta(u)$ and $s's \leqslant_p \theta(u)$. It follows that $s = \theta(s) = s'$.

If $|r'| < |s|$, then $r' \leqslant_p s$. Therefore, $s = \theta(s)$ ends with $\theta(r') = r'$. As a consequence, we get that

$$w_1 w_2 \cdots w_n = r'sr'ssr',$$

and so

$$u_3 = ssr'sr'ssr'.$$

4. Extended Lyndon-Schützenberger equations

However, also

$$u_3 = sr'ssr'ssr'$$

holds, thus $r's = sr'$ and $v = r's's'$ is not primitive, a contradiction.

If $|r'| \geqslant |s|$, we have $r' = sp$ for some word p. As v is primitive, $|p| > 0$ must hold. We have

$$w_1 w_2 \cdots w_n = ps^3 ps^3 p.$$

Hence,

$$ps^3 p = w_1 w_2 \cdots w_k w' = w'' w_{n-k+1} \cdots w_n,$$

for some $k \geqslant 2$. By Lemma 2.12 we get that $w_1 = w_2 = \ldots = w_k = w$ and also $w_{n-k+1} = \ldots = w_n$ holds. Since w_1 is primitive, $w_1 \neq w_{n-k+1}$ must hold, thus $w_n = \theta(w_1) = \theta(w)$.

If $|p| \leqslant |w|$, we get that $p \leqslant_p w$, so $\theta(p) \leqslant_s w_n = \theta(w)$. However, $p \leqslant_s w_n$ holds as well, and so $p = \theta(p)$. Yet, we have

$$sp = r' = \theta(r') = \theta(p)\theta(s) = ps,$$

which shows that $p, s \in \{t\}^+$ for some word t, so $v = spss$ is not θ-primitive, a contradiction.

If $|p| > |w|$ we can apply Theorem 2.14 to $ps^3 ps^3 p$ and $w_1 w_2 \cdots w_n$ and obtain that $ps^3, p \in \{w, \theta(w)\}^+$. It follows that $s^3 \in \{w, \theta(w)\}^+$, which leads again to a contradiction with the primitivity of v or of w, as before.

In the case $m \geqslant 8$, we follow the exact same steps as we took above before splitting the discussion into the cases $|r'| < |s|$ and $|r'| \geqslant |s|$.

If $|r'| < |s|$, we get that

$$w_1 w_2 \cdots w_n = r'sr'(ssr')^k,$$

for some $k \geqslant 2$. As $r'sr'$ is a suffix of ssr' of length at least $|ssr'|/2$ and $n \geqslant 5$, we can apply Theorem 2.14 and obtain that $ssr' \in \{w, \theta(w)\}^+$, and thus also $r'sr' \in \{w, \theta(w)\}^+$. Since $|r'| < |s|$, the word ssr' is not θ-primitive, but $ssr' = \theta(v)$, and we reached a contradiction with the θ-primitivity of v.

If $|r'| \geqslant |s|$, we get that

$$w_1 w_2 \cdots w_n = p(s^3 p)^k,$$

for some $k \geqslant 3$. By Theorem 2.14, it follows that $s^3 p \in \{w, \theta(w)\}^+$ and $p \in \{w, \theta(w)\}^+$, thus $s^3 p$ is not θ-primitive. However, $s^3 p = ssr' = \theta(v)$, again a contradiction.

This concludes the analysis for even m. When m is odd, $u_1 = v^{(m-1)/2} r$, where $v = r\theta(r)s$, $|s| > 0$, and $s = \theta(s)$.

We start with the case when $|r| \geqslant |s|$.

If $|r| = |s|$, we immediately get $s = \theta(r)$, a contradiction, as then v is not θ-primitive. So, we assume that $|r| > |s|$, and we obtain easily that $\theta(s) = s$. Also, looking at the border between $u_2 = \theta(u)$ and $u_3 = \theta(u)$, we get that $s \leqslant_p \theta(r)$. Therefore, $\theta(r) = sp$ for some word p.

If $m = 5$, since $v = r\theta(r)s$, we obtain

$$w_1 w_2 \cdots w_n = psr\theta(r)sr\theta(r).$$

It follows that

$$w_1 w_2 \cdots w_n = ps\theta(p)ssps\theta(p)ssp,$$

and applying θ leads to

$$\theta(w_n)\theta(w_{n-1}) \cdots \theta(w_1) = \theta(p)ssps\theta(p)ssps\theta(p).$$

If $|p| \geqslant |w|$ we can apply Theorem 2.14 and obtain that $v = \theta(p)ssps \in \{w, \theta(w)\}^+$. Since $|p| \geqslant |w|$ implies $|v| > 2|w|$, this contradicts the θ-primitivity of v. Therefore, we assume $|p| < |w|$ henceforth.

If $ps\theta(p)ssp \in \{w, \theta(w)\}^+$, then as

$$w_1 w_2 \cdots w_n = ps\theta(p)ssps\theta(p)ssp,$$

for the suffix $s\theta(p)ssp$ it is also true that $s\theta(p)ssp \in \{w, \theta(w)\}^+$. Furthermore, as $|p| < |w|$ and $n \geqslant 5$, the word $s\theta(p)ssp$ is not θ-primitive, a contradiction since $s\theta(p)ssp = \theta(v)$ and v is assumed to be θ-primitive.

Consequently, we assume that $ps\theta(p)ssp \notin \{w, \theta(w)\}^+$. Therefore, we have

$$ps\theta(p)ssp = w_1 w_2 \cdots w_k w',$$

for some k, where $w' <_p w_{k+1}$ and similarly

4. Extended Lyndon-Schützenberger equations

$$ps\theta(p)ssp = w'' w_{n-k+1} w_{n-k+2} \cdots w_n.$$

By Lemma 2.12, we get that $w_1 = w_2 = \ldots = w_k = w$ and $w_{n-k+1} = w_{n-k+2} = \ldots = w_n$. Since w_{n-k+1} is primitive, $w_1 = \theta(w_n)$ must hold, from which $p = \theta(p)$ follows, so

$$w_1 w_2 \cdots w_n = pspssps pssp,$$

and $\theta(ps) = sp$. If $|w| \leqslant |ps|$ we get immediately that $ps, sp, s, p \in \{w, \theta(w)\}^+$ using Theorem 2.14, and this yields a contradiction. Otherwise, if $|w| > |ps|$, we have $|w_1 w_2 \cdots w_n| < 6|w|$, so $n = 5$. It is easy to see that in this case $4|ps| + |s| \geqslant 2|w| + |ps|$ holds, so we can apply Theorem 2.14 to $w_1 w_2 \cdots w_5$ and its prefix $(ps)^2 (sp)^2 s$ and get that $w \in \{ps, \theta(ps)\}^+$. This is yet another contradiction, as $|w| > |ps|$ and so w is not θ-primitive. This concludes the analysis of the case when $|r| \geqslant |s|$ and $m = 5$.

When $|r| \geqslant |s|$ and $m \geqslant 7$, we obtain

$$w_1 w_2 \cdots w_n = p(sr\theta(r))^{(m-1)/2}.$$

As $m \geqslant 7$ and $n \geqslant 5$, we can immediately apply Theorem 2.14 and reach a contradiction.

We move on to the case $|r| < |s|$. In this case we have that $\theta(r) \leqslant_p s$. Therefore, $r \leqslant_s s$ and $\theta(r)s = sr$. It follows that

$$w_1 w_2 \cdots w_n = rr\theta(r)(sr\theta(r))^{(m-1)/2-1}.$$

Furthermore $s = \theta(r)^k p$ for some $k \geqslant 1$, $p <_p \theta(r)$, and $pr = \theta(r)p$. Clearly, we get that

$$w_1 w_2 \cdots w_n = rr\theta(r)(\theta(r)^k pr\theta(r))^{(m-1)/2-1}.$$

If $m = 5$, we get

$$w_1 w_2 \cdots w_n = rr\theta(r)^{k+1} pr\theta(r) = r^2\theta(r)^{k+2} p\theta(r).$$

Note that $k \geqslant 1$ and $n \geqslant 5$. We obtain immediately that $|w| < (k+6)|r|/n$ holds.

It follows that

$$(k+4)|r| + |p| > (k+4)|r| \geqslant \frac{3(k+6)|r|}{n} > 3|w|.$$

As p is a proper prefix of $\theta(r)$ and thus $|p| < |r|$, and (as we have seen before)

$$w_1 w_2 \cdots w_n = r^2(\theta(r))^{k+2} p\theta(r)$$

holds, we can not have $|r| = |w|$.

If $|r| < |w|$, we apply Theorem 2.14 to $r^2(\theta(r))^{k+2}p$ and $w_1 w_2 \cdots w_n$ (which have a common prefix longer than $3|w| > 2|w| + |r|$, as seen before), and get that $w \in \{r, \theta(r)\}^+$, which is in contradiction with the θ-primitivity of w, as $|w| > |r|$.

If $|r| > |w|$, we apply Theorem 2.14 to $r^2(\theta(r))^{k+2}p$ and $w_1 w_2 \cdots w_n$ (which have a common prefix longer than $5|r| > 2|w| + |r|$), and get that $r \in \{w, \theta(w)\}^+$. It follows that $p \in \{w, \theta(w)\}^+$ as well. Therefore $s = (\theta(r))^k p$ is not θ-primitive, and neither is $v = r\theta(r)s$, a contradiction.

If $m = 7$, we have $k \geqslant 1$ and $n \geqslant 5$ and furthermore

$$w_1 w_2 \cdots w_n = rr\theta(r)^{k+1} pr\theta(r)\theta(r)^k pr\theta(r) = r^2\theta(r)^{k+2} p\theta(r)^{k+2} p\theta(r).$$

If $|r| \geqslant |w|$ we apply Theorem 2.14 to $r^2\theta(r)^{k+2}p$ and $w_1 w_2 \cdots w_n$, whose common prefix is of length at least $5|r| > 2|w| + |r|$, and get that $r \in \{w, \theta(w)\}^+$. Since

$$r^2\theta(r)^{k+2} p\theta(r)^{k+2} p\theta(r) = r^2\theta(r)^{k+2} r^{k+2} p^2\theta(r),$$

it follows also that $p^2 \in \{w, \theta(w)\}^+$. This leads immediately to a contradiction.

If $|r| < |w|$, we analyse two cases. First, if $|p| < |r|/2$, we have $n|w| \leqslant (2k+8)|r|$, and it follows that

$$(k+4)|r| + |p| > (k+4)|r| \geqslant 2\frac{(2k+8)|r|}{n} + |r| \geqslant 2|w| + |r|.$$

Second, if $|p| \geqslant |r|/2$ we have $n|w| \leqslant (2k+9)|r|$, and it follows that

$$(k+4)|r| + |p| > (k+4)|r| + \frac{|r|}{2} \geqslant 2\frac{(2k+9)|r|}{n} + |r| \geqslant 2|w| + |r|.$$

87

4. Extended Lyndon-Schützenberger equations

Therefore, no matter how long p is, the words $r^2\theta(r)^{k+2}p$ and $w_1 w_2 \cdots w_n$ have a common prefix that is long enough to apply Theorem 2.14. It follows that $w \in \{r, \theta(r)\}^+$, a contradiction.

In the final case to be analysed, when $m \geqslant 9$, we can directly apply Theorem 2.14 to v^m and $\theta(w_1 w_2 \cdots w_n)$, which results in a contradiction with the θ-primitivity of v or w. $\qquad\square$

4.5   The case $\ell = 3, m = 4$, and $n \geqslant 3$ odd

The other case left open in [56] concerned equations of the form

$$u_1 u_2 u_3 = v_1 v_2 v_3 v_4 w_1 w_2 \cdots w_n, \tag{4.6}$$

where $u_i \in \{u, \theta(u)\}$ for all $1 \leqslant i \leqslant 3$, $v_j \in \{v, \theta(v)\}$ for all $1 \leqslant j \leqslant 4$ and $w_k \in \{w, \theta(w)\}$ for all $1 \leqslant k \leqslant n$ and $n \geqslant 3$ is odd.

Example 50 in [56] shows that (4.6) does not enforce $u, v, w \in \{t, \theta(t)\}^+$ for some t if $n = 3$, therefore, we assume that n is odd and $n \geqslant 5$ henceforth. We make another general assumption under which we will study these equations:

- We will assume that v is θ-primitive. If this was not the case, that is $v \in \{v', \theta(v')\}^+$ for some word v' with $|v'| < |v|$, we can consider the equation $u_1 u_2 u_3 = v_1' v_2' \cdots v_{m'}' w_1 w_2 \cdots w_n$ instead, where $v_i' \in \{v', \theta(v')\}$ for all $1 \leqslant i \leqslant m'$, and $m' \geqslant 8$. This new equation is covered by the results of the previous section.

As in the previous section, we analyse all possible values of u_1, u_2, and u_3, and for all these we look at the different relations of $|v_1 v_2 \cdots v_m|$ and $|u|$ separately. Here, however, we can not assume $m|v| > |u|$, as there exists no symmetry between the values of m (= 4) and n ($\geqslant 5$).

Lemma 4.4 however still holds, and so does its dual version:

Lemma 4.27. *If* $4|v| \leqslant |u| - |w|$ *and* (4.6) *holds, then* $u, v, w \in \{t, \theta(t)\}^+$ *for some word* t.

Proof. The inequality $4|v| \leqslant |u| - |w|$ and (4.6) imply that $n|w| \geqslant 2|u| + |w|$. Thus, by an application of Theorem 2.14, we instantly get that $u, w \in \{t, \theta(t)\}^+$ for some θ-primitive word t. □

We remind the reader that the case $u_1 u_2 u_3 = u\theta(u)u$ is already covered by the very general Theorem 4.25.

4.5.1   The case $u_1 u_2 u_3 = uuu$

In this section we will fix $u_1 = u_2 = u_3 = u$, hence we analyse the equation

$$uuu = v_1 v_2 v_3 v_4 w_1 w_2 \cdots w_n. \tag{4.7}$$

4. Extended Lyndon-Schützenberger equations

We begin to analyse the case $4|v| < |u|$ first.

Lemma 4.28. *If $4|v| < |u|$ and $n \geqslant 5$ is odd, then (4.7) implies that $u, v, w \in \{t, \theta(t)\}^+$ for some word t.*

Proof. According to Proposition 4.2, the word w can not be θ-primitive in this case. Hence, $w \in \{w', \theta(w')\}^+$ for some θ-primitive word w', and we analyse the equation $uuu = v_1 v_2 v_3 v_4 w'_1 w'_2 \cdots w'_{n'}$, where $w'_i \in \{w', \theta(w')\}$ for all $1 \leqslant i \leqslant n'$ and some even $n' \geqslant 10$ instead of (4.7).

The proof now follows the lines of our proof of Lemma 4.5. In the same manner as there, we get that $w' = rpr$ for some words r and p, with $r = \theta(r)$ and $rp = \theta(p)r$. Also $w'_1 = w'_2 = \ldots = w'_{n'/2}$ and $w'_{n'/2+1} = w'_{n'/2+2} = \ldots = w_{n'} = \theta(w'_1)$. If $v = \theta(v)$, then (4.7) turns into the equation

$$u^3 = v^4 (w'_1)^{n'/2} \theta(w'_1)^{n'/2},$$

and Theorem 4.1 verifies our claim. Therefore we also assume $v \neq \theta(v)$ in the following.

Thus,

$$u = prw'^{n'/2-1} = prw'^{n'/2-2} rpr = prw'^{n'/2-2} \theta(p)rr.$$

Furthermore, $|v_1 v_2 v_3 v_4| = |u| - 2|r|$ and so

$$v_1 v_2 v_3 v_4 = prw'^{n'/2-2} \theta(p) = (prr)^{n'/2-2} pr\theta(p).$$

Let $\bar{w}' = prr$. We will show that $\bar{w}'^\omega$ and $v_1 v_2 v_3 v_4$ have a common prefix long enough to apply Theorem 2.14:

If $|w'| \geqslant |v|$, then

$$|\bar{w}'^{n'/2-2} pr| \geqslant |\bar{w}'^3 pr| > 2|w'| + |v|.$$

If $|v| > |w'|$ and $|v| \geqslant |pr\theta(p)|$, then

$$v^3 \leqslant_p \bar{w}'^{n'/2-2} pr,$$

and $3|v| > 2|v| + |w'|$. On the other hand if $|v| > |w'|$ and $|v| < |pr\theta(p)|$, then

$$|p| + 2|r| = |w'| < |v| < 2|p| + |r|,$$

so $|r| < |p|$. As $rp = \theta(p)r$, we have that $r \leqslant_p \theta(p)$, and thus

$$v_1 v_2 v_3 v_4 = \bar{w}'^{n'/2-1} \theta(p)'',$$

where $\theta(p)''$ is a suffix of $\theta(p)$. Since

$$|\theta(p)''| < |p| < |w'| < |v|,$$

we have that

$$|\bar{w}'^{n'/2-1}| > 3|v|,$$

so again $v_1 v_2 v_3 v_4$ and $\bar{w}'^\omega$ share a common prefix of length at least $3|v| > 2|v| + |w'|$ and we can apply Theorem 2.14.

In all cases, we get $v, \bar{w}' \in \{t, \theta(t)\}^+$ for some word t. However, as v is assumed to be θ-primitive, we must have $\bar{w}' \in \{v, \theta(v)\}^+$.

Now, if $|r| < |p|$, the equation $rp = \theta(p)r$ allows us to write $\theta(p) = rs$ for some word s. Then, since

$$prr \in \{v, \theta(v)\}^+,$$

and

$$v_1 v_2 v_3 v_4 = (prr)^{n'/2-2} pr\theta(p),$$

also

$$prrs = pr\theta(p) \in \{v, \theta(v)\}^+$$

holds. Combining these last two results, we see that $s \in \{v, \theta(v)\}^+$ and thus also $\theta(s) \in \{v, \theta(v)\}^+$. However, as $prr = \theta(s)rrr \in \{v, \theta(v)\}^+$, by Theorem 2.16, also $r \in \{v, \theta(v)\}^+$. As a consequence, $\theta(p) = rs \in \{v, \theta(v)\}^+$, and the same holds for p. Thus $w' = rpr \in \{v, \theta(v)\}^+$, contradicting its θ-primitivity.

If $|r| > |p|$, we write $r = \theta(p)s'$. As $prr = pr\theta(p)s'$ and $pr\theta(p)$ are both elements of $\{v, \theta(v)\}^+$, so is s'. Furthermore, as

$$pr\theta(p) = p\theta(p)s'\theta(p) \in \{v, \theta(v)\}^+,$$

4. Extended Lyndon-Schützenberger equations

if $p\theta(p) \in \{v, \theta(v)\}^+$, then by Theorem 2.16, also $p \in \{v, \theta(v)\}^+$, and consequently $r = \theta(p)s' \in \{v, \theta(v)\}^+$. This is a contradiction, since $w' = rpr$ is assumed to be θ-primitive. Therefore, $p\theta(p) \notin \{v, \theta(v)\}^+$, which means that $s' \in \{v, \theta(v)\}^+$ is a proper factor of some word in $\{v, \theta(v)\}^+$. By Lemma 2.12, we must have $s' \in \{v\}^+$ or $s' \in \{\theta(v)\}^+$, as v is θ-primitive. However,

$$\theta(p)\theta(p)s' = \theta(p)r = rp = \theta(p)s'p,$$

so $\theta(p)s' = s'p$, and we saw before that this means that s' is a θ-palindrome. In conclusion, $v = \theta(v)$ in both cases, and we get a contradiction. $\qquad\square$

We move on to the case when $|u| < 4|v| < 2|u|$:

Lemma 4.29. *If* $|u| < 4|v| < 2|u|$ *and* $n \geq 5$ *is odd, then* (4.7) *implies that* $u, v, w \in \{t, \theta(t)\}^+$ *for some word* t.

Proof. The two possible situations in this case are depicted in Figure 4.3 (with $v_j = v'_j v''_j$ for $j \in \{3, 4\}$ and $w_k = w'_k w''_k$).

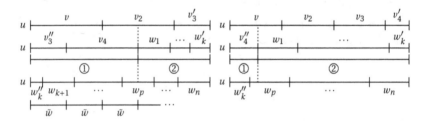

Figure 4.21. The two possible cases for (4.7) if $|u| < 4|v| < 2|u|$.

We either have $u_2 = v''_3 v_4 w_1 w_2 \cdots w'_k$ for some k (left half of Figure 4.21) or $u_2 = v''_4 w_1 w_2 \cdots w'_k$ for some k (right half of Figure 4.21). We can show that the factors ① and ② in Figure 4.21 are θ-palindromes using the same arguments as in the proof of Lemma 4.9.

This means that $w_1 w_2 \cdots w_n = ②①②$ is a θ-palindrome as well. Now, as n is odd, we get that $w_{(n+1)/2} = \theta(w_{(n+1)/2})$ and therefore $w = \theta(w)$.

Thus we have the equation $u^3 = v_1 v_2 v_3 v_4 w^n$, with $n \geq 5$.

If $|w^n| \geqslant |u| + |w|$, then Theorem 2.1 implies $u, w \in \{t\}^+$ for some t and we are done. Hence, we assume $|w^n| < |u| + |w|$, that is, $|u| > (n-1)|w|$. Then

$$|①| = 2|u| - n|w| > |u| - |w| > \frac{n-2}{n-1}|u| > \frac{1}{2}|u|.$$

This means that it suffices to consider only the case when $u = v_1 v_2 v_3'$ (Figure 4.21, left). Then Lemma 2.13 implies $v_4 = \theta(v)$. Furthermore, if $v_2 = v$, we can apply 2.1 to v^2 and $\bar{w}^\omega$, where $\bar{w}$ is a conjugate of w, to get that v is not primitive, a contradiction. Hence we also assume $v_2 = \theta(v)$. Now if $v_3 = v$, then the given equation turns into a conventional Lyndon-Schützenberger equation $u^3 = (v\theta(v))^2 w^5$, which implies $u, v\theta(v), w \in \{t\}^+$ for some word t. Otherwise, since $v_1 v_2 v_3 v_4 = ①②①$ is a θ-palindrome, we get $v = \theta(v)$, and the equation once again turns into a conventional Lyndon-Schützenberger equation $u^3 = v^4 w^5$ and the same reasoning applies. □

The last remaining case for $u_1 u_2 u_3 = uuu$ is when $4|v| > 2|u|$:

Lemma 4.30. *If* $4|v| > 2|u|$ *and* $n \geqslant 5$ *is odd, then* (4.7) *implies that* $u, v, w \in \{t, \theta(t)\}^+$ *for some word* t.

Proof. By Proposition 4.3, we have $v_1 = v_2 = v$ and $v_3 = v_4 = \theta(v)$, and furthermore $v = rpr$ for some words r, p. From the overlap between v and $\theta(v)$ inside u_2 we see that $pr = r\theta(p)$ and $r = \theta(r)$. Furthermore, $\theta(v) = prr$ and we have that $u = rprrp = rr\theta(p)rp$, where the prefix rr is a suffix of $v_4 = \theta(v)$. Therefore $w_1 w_2 \cdots w_n = \theta(p)rp$, which is a θ-palindrome, and since n is odd, we get that $w = \theta(w)$. Thus $u = rprrp$ and $u = rrw^n$, therefore $rprrp = rrw^n$. Adding r to left on both sides of this equation gives us $(rrp)^2 = r^3 w^n$, which implies $rrp, r, w \in \{t\}^+$ for some word t by Theorem 2.7. It follows that $rpr = v$ is not primitive, a contradiction. □

4.5.2 The case $u_1 u_2 u_3 = uu\theta(u)$

We continue the analysis with the case $u_1 = u_2 = u$ and $u_3 = \theta(u)$, thus we focus on the equation

$$uu\theta(u) = v_1 v_2 v_3 v_4 w_1 w_2 \cdots w_n. \tag{4.8}$$

4. Extended Lyndon-Schützenberger equations

We begin again with the case where $v_1 v_2 v_3 v_4$ is relatively short:

Lemma 4.31. *If* $4|v| < |u|$ *and* $n \geq 5$ *is odd, then* (4.8) *implies that* $u, v, w \in \{t, \theta(t)\}^+$ *for some word* t.

Proof. We assume that w is θ-primitive. If it is not, that is $w \in \{w', \theta(w')\}^+$ for some θ-primitive word w', then we would consider the equation $uu\theta(u) = v_1 v_2 v_3 v_4 w_1' w_2' \cdots w_{n'}'$, where $n' > n$. This means that in general we can not assume n to be odd anymore. However, if $n < 10$, this can still be asserted.

By Proposition 4.2, $w_1 = w_2 = \ldots = w_n = w$ holds in this case. Furthermore, we know that $w = p\theta(z)z$ where p is a θ-palindrome.

Now, as $u_3 \leq_s w^n$, we have $u_1 \leq_p \theta(w)^n$ and $v_1 v_2 v_3 v_4 \leq_p u_1$. If $|v| \geq |w|$, then $|v_1 v_2 v_3 v_4| \geq 2|v| + |w|$, and so by Theorem 2.14, we get $v, w \in \{t, \theta(t)\}^+$ for some word t. In fact, this reasoning still applies if $3|v| \geq 2|w|$, that is if $3|v|/2 \geq |w|$. As a consequence, we can assume $|w| > 3|v|/2$ in the following.

Since $4|v| + |w| > |u|$ and $|w| > 3|v|/2$, we get that $n \leq 8$, and by the remarks made at the beginning of this proof, $n = 5$ or $n = 7$.

If $n = 7$, then $w^3 \leq_s u_3 = \theta(u)$ and so $\theta(w)^3 \leq_p u_1 = u$. Since $|w| > 3|v|/2$ and $4|v| + |w| > |u| > 3|v|$, it follows that $3|v|/2 < |w| < 2|v|$. Thus, the word $u_1 = u$ has the factors depicted in Figure 4.22.

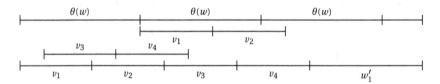

Figure 4.22. The situation inside u_1.

As $v_1 v_2$ is a prefix of $\theta(w)\theta(w)$, it appears again as a proper factor inside $v_2 v_3 v_4$. In the same manner $v_3 v_4$ appears as a proper factor inside $v_1 v_2 v_3$ (see Figure 4.22). Therefore, if $v_1 \neq v_2$ or $v_3 \neq v_4$, then v is not θ-primitive by Lemma 2.12, a contradiction.

This leaves us with two cases only: either $v_1 v_2 v_3 v_4 = v^4$ or $v_1 v_2 v_3 v_4 = vv\theta(v)\theta(v)$. In the first case v^4 is a prefix of $\theta(w)^3$ and $4|v| > 2|v| + |v| > |w| + |v|$. Thus we can apply Theorem 2.1, to get $v, \theta(w) \in \{t\}^+$ for some word t. In the other case, when $v_1 v_2 v_3 v_4 = v v \theta(v) \theta(v)$, then $v_1 v_2 v_3 v_4$ is a θ-palindrome and $\theta(w)$ is a prefix of it. This means that w is a suffix of $v_1 v_2 v_3 v_4$ and so w^{n+1} is a suffix of $u u \theta(u)$ of length $(n+1)|w| > 2|u| + |w|$. Therefore we can apply Theorem 2.14 to get that $u, w \in \{t, \theta(t)\}^+$ for some word t in this case.

If $n = 5$, we know that

$$u_1 = u = \theta(w)\theta(w)\theta(z) = \theta(z)zp\theta(z)zp\theta(z).$$

Thus u has a prefix $\alpha = \theta(z)zp\theta(z)z$, which is a θ-palindrome.

We observe that $|u| = 5|z| + 2|p|$ and also $4|v| = |u| - |p|$. It follows that

$$4|v| = 5|z| + |p| > 4|z| + |p| = |\alpha| > \frac{15}{4}|z| + \frac{3}{4}|p| = 3|v|.$$

Therefore

$$\alpha = v_1 v_2 v_3 v_4' = \theta(v_4')\theta(v_3)\theta(v_2)\theta(v_1),$$

where v_4' is a proper prefix of v_4. Using Lemma 2.12 we get $v_1 = v_2 = v_3 = v$.

If $|w| < 2|v|$, then $v_1 v_2 v_3 = v^3$ is a prefix of $\theta(w)\theta(w)$ of length at least $|w| + |v|$. Thus, Theorem 2.1 is applicable to get $v, \theta(w) \in \{t\}^+$ for some word t.

If $2|v| < |w| < 3|v|$, we have a situation in u_1 as depicted in Figure 4.23. Since

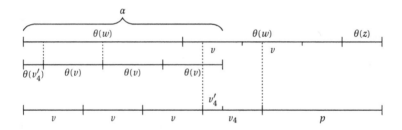

Figure 4.23. The situation inside u_1 when $2|v| < |w| < 3|v|$.

v as a prefix of $\theta(w)$ appears as a proper factor inside vv_4 and it is assumed to be primitive, $v_4 = \theta(v)$ must hold. Thus $\theta(v)$ appears as a factor inside the prefix vv of $\theta(w)$ after a prefix of length $3|v| - |w|$. However, $\theta(v)$ also appears inside vv after the prefix of length $|v_4'| = |\alpha| - 3|v|$. As v is assumed to be primitive, these occurrences must coincide and thus $3|v| - |w| = |\alpha| - 3|v|$ must hold. Using the known values

$$|\alpha| = |\theta(z)zp\theta(z)z| = 4|z| + |p|,$$

and

$$|v| = \frac{5}{4}|z| + \frac{1}{4}|p|,$$

this equation is equivalent to $3|z| = |p|$. Furthermore, $\theta(z) \leqslant_s p$ and as $p \leqslant_s \theta(w)$, we get that $p = \theta(z)^3$. This however means that

$$\theta(w) = \theta(z)zp = \theta(z)z\theta(z)^3,$$

contradicting the θ-primitivity of w.

If $3|v| < |w| < 4|v|$, then as in the previous case $\theta(z) \leqslant_s p$ and $p \leqslant_s \theta(w)$. Therefore and since p is a θ-palindrome, $p = z^k z'$ for some $k \geqslant 1$ and $z' \leqslant_p z$. Now, as v^3 is a prefix of

$$\theta(w) = \theta(z)zp = \theta(z)zz^k z',$$

and $|v| > |z|$ (recall that $|v| = 5|z|/4 + |p|/4$), we can apply Theorem 2.14 here to get $v, z \in \{t, \theta(t)\}^+$ and since $|v| > |z|$, this contradicts the θ-primitivity of v. $\quad\square$

We move on to the case where the border between the words $v_1 v_2 v_3 v_4$ and $w_1 w_2 \cdots w_n$ falls inside u_2:

Lemma 4.32. *If $|u| < 4|v| < 2|u|$ and $n \geqslant 5$ is odd, then* (4.8) *implies that $u, v, w \in \{t, \theta(t)\}^+$ for some word t.*

Proof. Once again we assume that w is a θ-primitive word, as in the proof of the previous lemma. Recall that if it was not, that is $w \in \{w', \theta(w')\}^+$ for some θ-primitive word w', then we would instead consider the equation $uu\theta(u) = v_1 v_2 v_3 v_4 w'_1 w'_2 \cdots w'_{n'}$, where $n' > n$. So, in general we can not assume n to be odd anymore, but for $n < 10$, we still can.

There are now two cases to be considered. The first is when $v''_3 v_4 \leqslant_p u_2$, where v''_3 is a suffix of $v_3 = v'_3 v''_3$.

In that case we see that $|v| > |u|/3$ and thus $4|v| > 4|u|/3$. It follows that $n|w| < 5|u|/3$ and since $n \geqslant 5$, we get $|w| < |u|/3 < |v|$. Thus, if $|v'_3| \geqslant |w|$, we can apply Theorem 2.14 to deduce $v, w \in \{t, \theta(t)\}^+$ for some word t, since u is a prefix of $\theta(w_1 w_2 \cdots w_n)$ and of $v v_2 v_3$, and $|u| = 2|v| + |v_3'| \geqslant 2|v| + |w|$ then.

Therefore we assume $|v_3'| < |w|$ in the following. Lemma 2.13 tells us that $v_4 = \theta(v)$ must hold in this case. Using the same methods that were used in the proof of Lemma 4.9 to show that the factor ① there is a θ-palindrome, we deduce that the prefix $v_3'' v_4$ here is a θ-palindrome too.

Now, $w_1 w_2 \cdots w_n$ is a suffix of $u\theta(u)$ and $u\theta(u)$ is a θ-palindrome. Hence, the word $\theta(w_n)\theta(w_{n-1}) \cdots \theta(w_1)$ is a prefix of $u\theta(u)$. Thus, we have $v_3'' v_4 = \theta(w_n)\theta(w_{n-1}) \cdots \theta(w_k'')$ for some k and $w_k = w_k' w_k''$, and since $v_3'' v_4$ is a θ-palindrome, also $v_3'' v_4 = w_k'' w_{k+1} \cdots w_n$. It follows that

$$u\theta(u) = w_k'' \cdots w_n w_1 \cdots w_n = \theta(w_n) \cdots \theta(w_1)\theta(w_n) \cdots \theta(w_k'').$$

Repeated application of Lemma 2.12 allows us to conclude that $w_1 = w_2 = \ldots = w_n = w$.

If $v_2 = v$, we can apply Theorem 2.1 to vv and the power of $\theta(w)$ that is a prefix of u to get that $v, \theta(w) \in \{t\}^+$ for some word t. Therefore $v_2 = \theta(v)$ can be assumed henceforth.

As $\theta(w) \leqslant_p v$, it follows that $w \leqslant_s v_1 v_2$ and $w \leqslant_s v_4$. However, $v_3'' v_4 \leqslant_p v_1 v_2 \leqslant_p v_3'' v_4 w$, and thus w appears as a factor inside ww, contradicting its primitivity.

We move on to the other case, namely when $v_4'' \leqslant_p u_2$, where v_4'' is a suffix of $v_4 = v_4' v_4''$. In this case $v_1 v_2 v_3 \leqslant_p u$ and $u \leqslant_p \theta(w_n)\theta(w_{n-1}) \cdots \theta(w_1)$. If $|w| \leqslant |v|$, we can thus apply Theorem 2.14 to get that $v, w \in \{t, \theta(t)\}^+$ for some word t. Therefore we can assume $|w| > |v|$. If $2|w| + |v| \leqslant |u|$ held, we could also apply Theorem 2.1 to get that same result. So $2|w| + |v| > |u|$ can be assumed as well. This means that $6|w| + 3|v| > 3|u|$. As a consequence, $n = 5$ must hold.

Now $|v| < |u|/3$ and thus $|w| > |u|/3$ must hold, which results in $|v| < |w|$. Moreover, $|u| < 4|v|$ implies $|w| < 2|u|/5$, and hence $|w| < 8|v|/5$.

Since $u_2 u_3 = u\theta(u) = v_4'' w_1 \cdots w_5$ is a θ-palindrome and $0 < |v_4''| < |w|$, we get $w_1 = w_2 = w_3 = w_4 = w$ by Lemma 2.12. If $w_5 = \theta(w)$, then $v_1 = v$ is a prefix of w. Then we find as a prefix of u_2 that $v_4'' v \leqslant_p v v_2$, but this contradicts the θ-primitivity of v by Lemma 2.13. Therefore, $w_5 = w$, and the equation turns into

$$uu\theta(u) = v v_2 v_3 v_4 w^5.$$

Now $u\theta(u) = v_4'' w^5$ implies $w = z\theta(z)p$ for some words p, z, with $p = \theta(p)$. Hence $u = (pz\theta(z))^2 pz$ and $v_4'' = p$. If $|u| \geqslant 2|w| + |v|$, that is, $|pz| \geqslant |v|$, then Theorem 2.14 is applied to $u = vv_2v_3v_4' = (pz\theta(z))^2 pz$ to obtain that $v, \theta(w) \in \{t, \theta(t)\}^+$ for some word t, but as $|w| > |v|$, this contradicts the θ-primitivity of w. Thus, $|u| < 2|w| + |v|$, which is equivalent to $|v_4'| > |z|$. With $|u| = 3|v| + |v_4'| = 3|p| + 5|z|$, this yields $3|v| < 3|p| + 4|z|$. Thus, $vv_2v_3 \leqslant_p (pz\theta(z))^2 p \leqslant_p vv_2v_3v_4$ and as $(pz\theta(z))^2 p$ is a θ-palindrome, $\theta(vv_2v_3) \leqslant_s (pz\theta(z))^2 p \leqslant_p vv_2v_3v_4$. As a result, $v = v_2 = v_3$ by Lemma 2.12. Consequently, $v^3 \leqslant_p \theta(w)^3$, to which Theorem 2.1 is applicable (recall that $|w| < 8|v|/5$, and hence $3|v| > |v| + |w|$) which gives $v, \theta(w) \in \{t\}^+$ for some word t, and since $|w| > |v|$, this contradicts the primitivity of w. $\qquad\square$

We remind the reader that the case when $u_1 u_2 u_3 = uu\theta(u)$ and $2|u| < 4|v| < 2|u| + |v|$ is already covered by Lemma 4.23, which was established by Kari, Masson, and Seki [56].

We come to the last valuation of u_1, u_2, and u_3 that is to be considered:

4.5.3 The case $u_1 u_2 u_3 = u\theta(u)\theta(u)$

In this section we study the equation

$$u\theta(u)\theta(u) = v_1 v_2 v_3 v_4 w_1 w_2 \cdots w_n. \tag{4.9}$$

The case when $4|v| < |u|$ is simple:

Lemma 4.33. If $4|v| < |u|$ and $n \geqslant 5$ is odd, then (4.9) implies that $u, v, w \in \{t, \theta(t)\}^+$ for some word t.

Proof. If $u\theta(u)\theta(u) = v_1 v_2 v_3 v_4 w_1 w_2 \cdots w_n$ and $4|v| < |u|$, then applying θ on both sides we get

$$uu\theta(u) = \theta(w_n)\theta(w_{n-1})\cdots\theta(w_1)\theta(v_4)\theta(v_3)\theta(v_2)\theta(v_1),$$

with $n|w| > 2|u|$. We can apply Lemma 4.23 to obtain the claimed statement. $\qquad\square$

Lemma 4.34. If $|u| < 4|v| < 2|u|$ and $n \geqslant 5$ is odd, then (4.9) implies that $u, v, w \in \{t, \theta(t)\}^+$ for some word t.

Proof. We consider two separate cases: the first is when $v_3'' v_4 \leqslant_p u_2$, where v_3'' is a suffix of $v_3 = v_3' v_3''$. As v is assumed to be θ-primitive, $|v_3'| \neq |v_3''|$. In this case $|v| > |u|/3$ and so $4|v| > 4|u|/3$. It follows that $n|w| < 5|u|/3$ and since $n \geqslant 5$, we get that $|w| < |u|/3 < |v|$. Furthermore we can assume that $|u| < 2|v| + |w|$, otherwise we get the claimed result by a simple application of Theorem 2.14. This means that $|w| > |v_3'|$.

We will now prove that $v_1 = v_3 = v_4 = v$ holds, as follows: For the sake of contradiction, suppose $v_4 = \theta(v)$. Since $\theta(w_n) \leqslant_p v$, this assumption implies that v_4 ends with w_n. Then $w_n w_1 \ldots w_k' \leqslant_s \theta(u)$ where $w_k = w_k' w_k''$ for some k and thus $w_n w_1 \ldots w_k' \leqslant_s w_1 w_2 \cdots w_n$. By Lemma 2.12, we get that $w_n = w_1 = \ldots = w_{k-1}$ and $w_{n-1} = w_n$ and by Proposition 2.3, $w_n \neq w_n$ must hold, a contradiction. Thus, $v_4 = v$. The word $\theta(v_4)\theta(v_3)$ appears inside the θ-palindrome $u\theta(u)$ as a factor of $v_2 v_3 v_4$ in such a way that Lemma 2.12 implies $v_3 = v_4$ (recall that $|v_3'| \neq |v_3''|$). Thus we have proved $v_1 = v_3 = v_4 = v$.

We split the discussion further, according to the relationship between $|v_3'|$ and $|v_3''|$:

If $|v_3'| > |v_3''|$, then also $|w| > |v_3''|$, as we already established $|w| > |v_3'|$. Now,

$$|v| = |v_3'| + |v_3''|,$$

and

$$|u| = 3|v_3'| + 2|v_3''|.$$

From this we get that

$$n|w| = 3|u| - 4|v| = 5|v_3'| + 2|v_3''|.$$

However, $|w| > |v_3'|$ and $|w| > |v_3''|$, so n must be 5.

Assume $3|w| \leqslant 2|v|$, that is $6|w| \leqslant 4|v|$. Now, as $|v_3'| > |v_3''|$, we have that $5|v|/2 < |u|$, and therefore $4|v| < 8|u|/5$. Since $6|w| \leqslant 4|v|$, we get $6|w| < 8|u|/5$ and hence $5|w| < 8|u|/6$. It follows that

$$4|v| + 5|w| < \frac{8}{5}|u| + \frac{8}{6}|u| = \frac{88}{30}|u| < 3|u|,$$

a contradiction. Thus $3|w| > 2|v|$ must hold, and as $\theta(w_5)\theta(w_4)\theta(w_3)$ is a prefix of $vv_2 v$, we can apply Proposition 4.2 to get $v_2 = \theta(v)$ and $w_3 = w_4 = w_5$. The

4. Extended Lyndon-Schützenberger equations

fact that $w_1 w_2'$ is a suffix of $w_3 w_4 w_5$ leads to $w_1 = w$ and $w_3 = w_4 = w_5 = \theta(w)$. Now we have that $w_5 \leqslant_p v_1$, so $w \leqslant_p v$ and thus we have two occurrences of w inside $u_2 = \theta(u)$: one (the prefix of v_4) is after the prefix of length $3|v| - |u|$ and the other one (w_1) is after the prefix of length $4|v| - |u|$. Both these occurrences fall inside $w_3 w_4 w_5 = \theta(w)^3$. As w is primitive, the difference between those two occurrences must be a multiple of $|w|$. This difference is $|v|$ though, and since $|v| > |w|$, but $2|w| > |v|$ (as $|w| > |v_3'|$ and $|w| > |v_3''|$), this is impossible.

We come to the case when $|v_3'| < |v_3''|$. By Lemma 2.12, $v_2 = v_3 = v_4$ holds.

We first establish also $v_1 = v_2$: assume towards a contradiction, that $v_1 = \theta(v_2)$. Then as $\theta(w_n) \leqslant_p v_1$, we have $w_n \leqslant_s v_4 = v_2 = \theta(v_1)$. Now, if w_1 is a factor of u_2, the word $w_n w_1 \cdots w_k'$ for some $k \geqslant 2$ is a suffix of $\theta(u)$. However, also $\theta(u) = w_k'' w_{k+1} \cdots w_n$. By Lemma 2.12, we get that $w_n = w_1 = \ldots = w_{k-1} = w$ must hold, and also that $w_{n-1} = w_n$. But then $w_{k-1} = w_n$ appears as a proper factor inside $w_{n-1} w_n = w_n w_n$, contradicting the primitivity of w. If w_1 is not a factor of u_2, that is $w_1' \leqslant_s u_2$, where $w_1 = w_1' w_1''$, then $w_n w_1'$ is a suffix of $w_{n-1} w_n$, which means that $x w_n w_1 = w_{n-1} w_n y$ where $y = w_1''$ and x is the prefix of length $|w_1''|$ of w_{n-1}. Lemma 2.13 now gives us the contradictory statement $w_n \neq w_n$. Thus $v_1 = v_2 = v_3 = v_4 = v$ must hold.

If the prefix of length $|v| + |w|$ of $\theta(w_1 w_2 \cdots w_n)$ is a prefix of a word in $\{w\}^+$ or $\{\theta(w)\}^+$, then we can apply Theorem 2.1 to get the claimed result. Thus we assume that $w\theta(w)$ or $\theta(w)w$ appears as a factor inside vv after a prefix that is strictly shorter than $|v|$. Without loss of generality we assume that it is $w\theta(w)$ that occurs there, and we focus on the first occurrence of this factor inside vv.

We first rule out the case when $w\theta(w)$ is a prefix of vv: we observe that $|u| \geqslant 2|w| + |v|$. To see this, assume that $|u| < 2|w| + |v|$. This means that $3|u| < 6|w| + 3|v| < 5|w| + 4|v|$, which is a contradiction. Therefore, if $w\theta(w)$ is a prefix of vv, it has another appearance inside u after a prefix of length $|v|$. However, as $|v|$ is not divisible by $|w|$ (otherwise $v \in \{w, \theta(w)\}^+$ and $|v| > |w|$, so v would not be θ-primitive), this other occurrence of $w\theta(w)$ is a proper factor of some word $w_i w_{i+1} w_{i+2}$ inside $u_3 = \theta(u)$. By Lemma 2.12 this is impossible if w is θ-primitive. Hence, we assume that $xw\theta(w)$ is a prefix of vv, where $x \in \{w\}^+$. As $|w| > |v_3'|$, we have an occurrence of $w\theta(w)$ in $u_2 = \theta(u)$ after a prefix of length $|x| - |v_3'|$. So in u, we have an occurrence of $w\theta(w)$ after the prefix of length $|x|$, and after the prefix of length $|u| - (|x| - |v_3'|) - 2|w|$. As $x \in \{w\}^+$, we must have $|u| - (|x| - |v_3'|) - 2|w| \geqslant |x|$. Now as u is prefix of $\theta(w_1 \cdots w_n)$, in order to avoid a contradiction with Lemma 2.12, the difference between the lengths of those two prefixes must be divisible by $|w|$. However, this difference is

$$|u| - (|x| - |v_3'|) - 2|w| - |x| = |u| - 2|x| + |v_3'| - 2|w|,$$

and as $x \in \{w\}^+$, the term $|u| + |v_3'|$ must be divisible by $|w|$. Now $|u| = 2|v| + |v_3'|$, thus $2|u| = 4|v| + 2|v_3'|$. As $|w_1 w_2 \cdots w_n| = 3|u| - 4|v|$, this means that also $|w_1 w_2 \cdots w_n| = |u| + 2|v_3'|$ holds. If now $|u| + |v_3'|$ is divisible by $|w|$, then also $|v_3'|$ must be divisible by $|w|$. This however is a contradiction, as we assumed that $|v_3'| < |w|$.

The other case to be considered is when $w_4'' \leqslant_p u_2$. In this case, we can apply Theorem 2.14 to $\theta(w_1 w_2 \cdots w_n)$ and $v_1 v_2 v_3$ if $|v| \geqslant |w|$ to get the claimed result. Thus we assume $|v| < |w|$ in the remainder of this proof. Theorem 2.14 still applies if $2|w| + |v| \leqslant |u|$, so we assume $2|w| + |v| > |u|$ as well. This means that $6|w| + 3|v| > 3|u|$, and hence n must be 5. Then we can easily observe that the border between u_2 and u_3 lies inside w_3. So, let $w_3 = w_3' w_3''$ such that $w_1 w_2 w_3'$ is a suffix of u_2 and $u_3 = w_3'' w_4 w_5$. As also $w_1 w_2 w_3' \leqslant_s \theta(u)$, by Lemma 2.12, we get that $w_1 = w_2 = w$ while $w_4 = w_5 = \theta(w)$.

Now, $\theta(v_1 v_2) \leqslant_s w_4 w_5 = \theta(w)\theta(w)$, which implies $v_1 v_2 \leqslant_p w_1 w_2 = ww$. Hence $v_4'' v_1 v_2 \leqslant_p \theta(u)$ and thus $\theta(v_2)\theta(v_1)\theta(v_4'') \leqslant_s u$. It follows that $v_1 = v_2 = v$ holds.

If $3|v| > 2|w|$, since we have $v_1 v_2 v_3 \leqslant_p \theta(w_5)\theta(w_4)\theta(w_3)$, can apply Proposition 4.2 to get a contradiction with the fact that $w_4 = w_5$. Thus we assume $3|v| < 2|w|$ (if $3|v| = 2|w|$ we can apply Theorem 2.16 to get $v, w \in \{t, \theta(t)\}^+$ directly). Then since $ww \leqslant_p u$ and $v_1 = v_2 = v$, we must have $v_3 = \theta(v)$. Now there is an occurrence of vv in $\theta(u)$ after the prefix of length $4|v| - |u|$, and an occurrence of v after the prefix of length $|u| - 3|v|$. To avoid this v to appear as a proper factor inside the factor vv, we must have either $|u| - 3|v| \leqslant 4|v| - |u|$ or $|u| - 3|v| \geqslant 5|v| - |u|$. We show that both of these possibilities lead to a contradiction: if $|u| - 3|v| \leqslant 4|v| - |u|$, we have

$$2|u| \leqslant 7|v| = 4|v| + 3|v| < 4|v| + 2|w|.$$

This however means that $3|w| < |u|$ must hold, which leads to a contradiction as we have seen before. On the other hand, if $|u| - 3|v| \geqslant 5|v| - |u|$, we have

$2|u| \geqslant 8|v|$, which is a contradiction straightaway, as $4|v| > |u|$. $\qquad\square$

Lemma 4.35. *If* $2|u| < 4|v| < 2|u| + |v|$ *and* $n \geqslant 5$ *is odd, then* (4.9) *implies that* $u, v, w \in \{t, \theta(t)\}^+$ *for some word* t.

Proof. By Proposition 4.3, we have $v_1 = v_2 = \ldots = v_4 = v$ and $v = xz\theta(z)$, for some words x and z, with $x = \theta(x)$. Furthermore,

$$u = vxz = xz\theta(z)xz.$$

Therefore, the situation in $u_3 = \theta(u)$ looks as illustrated in Figure 4.24.

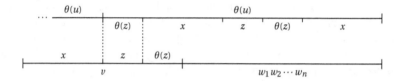

Figure 4.24. Factorisation of $\theta(u)$.

We see that $z = \theta(z)$ in this case. Now

$$\theta(u) = zxzzx = zzw_1 w_2 \cdots w_n,$$

and so

$$xz^2 x = zw_1 w_2 \cdots w_n.$$

Since both xz^2x and z are θ-palindromes and $|z| \leqslant |w_1 w_2 \cdots w_n|$, the equation implies $z \leqslant_s w_1 \cdots w_n$. Hence, there exists some positive integer k such that $z = w_k'' w_{k+1} \cdots w_n$ where $w_k = w_k' w_k''$ for some w_k', w_k''. If w_k'' is empty, that is, $z = w_{k+1} w_{k+2} \cdots w_n$, then

$$xz^2 x = xz\theta(xz) = w_{k+1} w_{k+2} \cdots w_n w_1 \cdots w_n.$$

By an application of Theorem 2.16 we obtain $xz \in \{w, \theta(w)\}^+$ because w is θ-primitive. Combining this with $z = w_{k+1} w_{k+2} \cdots w_n$ yields $x \in \{w, \theta(w)\}^+$. It follows that $v = xz^2 \in \{w, \theta(w)\}^+$ holds, but this contradicts the θ-primitivity of

v, as $|v| \geqslant 3|w|$. If, on the other hand, w_k'' is not empty, then

$$xz^2x = w_k'' w_{k+1} \cdots w_n w_1 \cdots w_n$$

implies $w_1 = \ldots = w_n = w$. Now we have $xz^2x = zw^n$ and concatenating z^2 to the left on both sides results in

$$(z^2x)^2 = z^3 w^n.$$

This is one of the equations studied by Lyndon and Schützenberger, and by Theorem 2.7 it implies $z^2x, z \in \{w\}^+$. However $|z^2x| \geqslant 3|w|$, hence z^2x is not primitive and neither is its conjugate v, a contradiction. □

4.6 Conclusions and open questions

We have solved the two open problems that remained concerning equations of the form $u_1 u_2 \cdots u_\ell = v_1 v_2 \cdots v_m w_1 w_2 \cdots w_n$, namely the cases where $\ell = 3$ and either $m, n \geqslant 5$ or $m = 4$ and $n \geqslant 5$ is odd. In both cases, these equations only admit θ-periodic solutions. The complete overview when these equations enforce the θ-periodicity of their solutions is given in Table 4.2.

Table 4.2. Full characterisation of solutions in terms of θ-periodicity.

ℓ	m	n	$u, v, w \in \{t, \theta(t)\}^+$?
$\geqslant 4$	$\geqslant 3$	$\geqslant 3$	Yes
3	$\geqslant 5$	$\geqslant 5$	Yes
3	4	$\geqslant 5$ and odd	Yes
3	4	$\geqslant 4$ and even	No
3	3	$\geqslant 3$	No
	one of $\{\ell, m, n\}$ equals 2		No

A problem that naturally arises is to study similarly generalised versions of other well-known equations, for instance the ones mentioned in the introduction: $u^\ell = v^m w^n x^p$ or $u^\ell = v_1^\ell v_2^\ell \cdots v_n^\ell$. However, as the analysis of equations of the form $u_1 u_2 \cdots u_\ell = v_1 v_2 \cdots v_m w_1 w_2 \cdots w_n$ already encompasses numerous individual cases and does not scale well, this might not be a feasible task without a substantial simplification of the arguments used in this chapter.

## CHAPTER 5

Shuffling square-free words

"And now for something completely different."

MONTY PYTHON'S FLYING CIRCUS

5.1 Introduction

In this chapter we combine the notion of repetition-freeness with the shuffle-operation, which is a classical operation on words, defined as follows:

for two words u and v over a finite alphabet Σ, the set of all *shuffles* of u and v, denoted by $u \sqcup\!\sqcup v$ is defined as

$$u \sqcup\!\sqcup v = \left\{ u_1 v_1 \cdots u_n v_n : u = u_1 u_2 \cdots u_n, \ v = v_1 v_2 \cdots v_n \ (u_i, v_i \in \Sigma^*) \right\}$$

This operations mimics the shuffling of two decks of cards, hence the name. The definition extends to infinite words in a natural way. In this chapter we consider avoidance of repetitiveness among the shuffled words. This topic was studied, e.g., by Prodinger and Urbanek [75] in 1979, who considered squares in the shuffles of two words; see also Currie and Rampersad [28] and Rampersad, Shallit, and Wang [79].

Charlier et al. [18] introduced and analysed infinite *self-shuffling words*. In this problem setting the shuffle operation is applied to an infinite word w such that $w \in w \sqcup\!\sqcup w$. More formally, an infinite word $w \in \Sigma^\omega$, defined over a finite alphabet Σ, is *self-shuffling*, if w admits factorisations: $w = \prod_{i=0}^{\infty} u_i v_i = \prod_{i=0}^{\infty} u_i = \prod_{i=0}^{\infty} v_i$ with $u_i, v_i \in \Sigma^+$. In [18] a short and elegant proof is given for the fact that the Fibonacci word, that is the infinite fixed point of the morphism $0 \mapsto 01, 1 \mapsto 0$,

105

is self-shuffling, and a longer proof is provided for the self-shuffling property of the Thue–Morse word.

Here we are mainly interested in finite and infinite square-free words w that can be obtained by shuffling a square-free word u with itself, i.e., $w \in u \sqcup u$. These words form a subset of a class of words referred to as *shuffle-squares*, which are words obtained by shuffling a (not necessarily square-free) word u with itself.

We show first that for each integer $n \geqslant 3$ there exists a square-free ternary word u of length n, such that $u \sqcup u$ contains a square-free word.

As a side-product of the proof techniques used to establish this result, we improve upon a result on palindrome positions in ternary square-free words by Currie [26].

Afterwards, we show that an infinite square-free self-shuffling word exists.

Finally, we consider the avoidability of so called *shuffle-squares*, which are elements of $w \sqcup w$ for some word w, in infinite words. We give a rather simple nonconstructive proof showing that there exists a word on an alphabet of ten letters such that none of its factors is a shuffle-square.

5.2 Preliminaries

Apart from the definitions in Chapter 2, we will make use of the following concepts in this chapter.

Let $u_0, u_1 \in \Sigma^*$ be words over an alphabet Σ and let $\beta \in \Sigma_2^*$ be a binary word of length $|\beta| = |u_0| + |u_1|$, called a *conducting sequence*, such that the number of occurrences of the letter $x \in \Sigma_2$ in β is equal to the length $|u_x|$. While forming the shuffle

$$w = u_0 \sqcup_\beta u_1$$

of u_0 and u_1 *conducted by* β, at step i we choose the first unused letter from u_0 if $\beta[i] = 0$ or the first unused letter from u_1 if $\beta[i] = 1$. That is, the i-th letter $w[i]$ of w is defined by

$$w[i] = u_{\beta[i]}[j] \quad \text{where } j = \left| \{k : \beta[k] = \beta[i] \text{ for } 1 \leqslant k \leqslant i\} \right|.$$

This definition can be extended to infinite words $u, v \in \Sigma^\omega$ in a natural way. Here,

$u \sqcup_\beta v \in \Sigma^\omega$ is an infinite word obtained by shuffling u and v conducted by the sequence $\beta \in \Sigma_2^\omega$, where we require that β contains infinitely many occurrences of both 0 and 1.

Example 5.1. Let $u = 01202$ and $v = 01102$ be two ternary words of length five, and let $\beta = 0110100110$ be a conducting sequence. Then $u \sqcup_\beta v = 0011120022$.

A morphism $h: \Sigma^* \to 2^{\Delta^*}$ from a word monoid to a power monoid of words is called a *substitution*. A substitution h is said to be *square-free*, if for every square-free word $w \in \Sigma^*$ the image $h(w)$ consists of square-free words only.

5.3 Square-free shuffles of finite words

Harju [45] raised the question whether for each $n \geqslant 3$, there exists a square-free word u of length n such that $u \sqcup_\beta u$ is square-free for some β. We give an affirmative answer to this question after a short technical lemma that will be used in our construction:

Lemma 5.2. *The substitution* $h: \Sigma_3^* \to 2^{\Sigma_3^*}$, *defined by*

$$h(0) = \{01202120102120210, 012021020102120210\}$$
$$h(1) = \{12010201210201021, 120102101210201021\}$$
$$h(2) = \{20121012021012102, 201210212021012102\}$$

is square-free.

Proof. Note that the words in $h(a)$, $a \in \Sigma_3$, have lengths 17 and 18. The substitution h has the following three properties, which are easy to check:

1. No image of a letter appears properly inside any image of a word of length two, i.e., $h(ab) \cap xh(c)y = \varnothing$ for $a, b, c \in \Sigma_3$ and $x, y \in \Sigma_3^*$, if $x, y \neq \varepsilon$.

2. No image of a letter is a prefix of an image of another letter.

3. For $a, b \in \Sigma_3$ with $a \neq b$, $a' \in h(a)$ and $b' \in h(b)$ end with different letters.

Assume towards a contradiction that w is square-free, but $w' \in h(w)$ contains a square uu. A simple inspection shows that h produces no square uu with $|u| \leqslant 52$, as this would be contained inside the image of a square-free word of

5. Shuffling square-free words

length eight, and we can check all of these[1]. Therefore, assume that $|u| > 52$, so that u contains at least two full images of a letter under h. Let now

$$u = s_1 w'_1 \cdots w'_j p_1 = s_2 w'_{j+2} \cdots w'_n p_2,$$

where $p_1 s_2 \in h(w_{j+1})$, $w'_i \in h(w_i)$ for all $1 \leqslant i \leqslant n$, and s_1 is a suffix of some $w'_0 \in h(w_0)$ and p_2 is a prefix of some $w'_{n+1} \in h(w_{n+1})$. Also, $s_1, s_2 \neq \varepsilon$.

If $|s_1| > |s_2|$, then $w'_{j+2} \in h(w_{j+2})$ appears properly inside $w'_0 w'_1 \in h(w_0 w_1)$, a contradiction to Property 1. The same situation appears if $|s_1| < |s_2|$, then w'_1 occurs properly inside $w'_{j+1} w'_{j+2}$. If $|s_1| = |s_2|$, then by iterated application of Property 2, we get that $w'_1 = w'_{j+2}, \ldots, w'_j = w'_n$. As Property 2 also shows that h is injective, we have $w_1 = w_{j+2}, \ldots, w_j = w_n$. Furthermore, by Property 3 we have $w_0 = w_{j+1}$, and thus a square $(w_0 \cdots w_j)^2$ in w. This proves the claim. $\square$

Charlier et al. [18] showed that the image of a self-shuffling word under a morphism is self-shuffling as well:

Proposition 5.3 (Charlier et al., 2013). *Let Σ and Δ be finite non-empty sets and $h : \Sigma^* \to \Delta^*$ a morphism. If $x \in \Sigma^\omega$ is self-shuffling, then so is $h(x) \in \Delta^\omega$.*

Using the ideas presented in the proof of Proposition 5.3 in [18], we can derive the following result about shuffles of images of square-free words under a substitution:

Lemma 5.4. *Let u be a square-free word that can be shuffled with itself to get a square-free word $u \sqcup_\beta u = u_1 u'_1 u_2 u'_2 \cdots u_n u'_n$, and let h be a square-free substitution, then any $x \in h(u)$ can also be shuffled with itself to get a square-free word in $h(u \sqcup_\beta u) = h(u_1) h(u'_1) h(u_2) h(u'_2) \cdots h(u_n) h(u'_n)$.*

We are now able to state the main result of this section:

Theorem 5.5. *For each $n \geqslant 3$, there exists a square-free word $w_n \in \Sigma_3^*$ of length n such that $w_n \sqcup_\beta w_n$ is square-free for some β.*

Proof. First of all, if $u \in \Sigma_3^*$ is any non-empty square-free word, then $u34 \in \Sigma_5^*$ is also square-free. Furthermore, for $\beta = 0^{|u|+1} 1^{|u|} 011$, we have $u34 \sqcup_\beta u34 =$

---

[1]for instance with the computer program listed in Appendix B.

$u3u434$, which is obviously square-free as well. Thus, there exist square-free words $v \in \Sigma_5^*$ of length n such that $v \sqcup_{\beta_n} v$ is square-free for $\beta_n = 0^{n-1}1^{n-2}011$ for each $n \geq 3$.

We map these to words in Σ_3^* of length $18n$ for all $n \geq 3$ using the following 18-uniform square-free morphism from Σ_5^* to Σ_3^* which was discovered by Brandenburg [13]:

$$h_{18}(0) = 010201202101210212$$
$$h_{18}(1) = 010201202102010212$$
$$h_{18}(2) = 010201202120121012$$
$$h_{18}(3) = 010201210201021012$$
$$h_{18}(4) = 010201210212021012$$

Applying the substitution h from Lemma 5.2 to the result, we construct words with the desired property of all integer lengths in the intervals $[18 \cdot 17 \cdot n, 18 \cdot 18 \cdot n]$ for all $n \geq 3$. We notice that for $n \geq 17$, the intervals obtained from n and $n+1$ intersect. Therefore this construction produces square-free words in Σ_3^* of all lengths $\geq 18 \cdot 17 \cdot 17 = 5202$, that can be shuffled with themselves to get a square-free word. What is more, Brandenburg [13] found also a 22-uniform square-free morphism from Σ_5^* to Σ_3^*, and there are k-uniform morphisms of that kind for $k \in \{19, 23, 24\}$ as well:

$$h_{19}(0) = 0102012021020121012 \qquad h_{23}(0) = 01020120210120102120121$$
$$h_{19}(1) = 0102012021201021012 \qquad h_{23}(1) = 02120102012021020121012$$
$$h_{19}(2) = 0102012021201210212 \qquad h_{23}(2) = 02120102012102120121012$$
$$h_{19}(3) = 0102012102120121012 \qquad h_{23}(3) = 02120102101210201021012$$
$$h_{19}(4) = 0210201202120121012 \qquad h_{23}(4) = 02120102101210212021012$$

$$h_{24}(0) = 010201202101201020120212$$
$$h_{24}(1) = 010201210120102101210212$$
$$h_{24}(2) = 010201210120210201210212$$
$$h_{24}(3) = 010201210201021201210212$$

$$h_{24}(4) = 010210120102120210120212$$

Square-freeness of these morphisms is proven using Theorem 2.10. With the construction above and these morphisms, we find square-free words $w_n \in \Sigma_3^*$ that can be shuffled with themselves to get a square-free word for each length n, where

$$n \in \bigcup_{\substack{k \in \{18,19,22,23,24\} \\ n \geqslant 3}} [k \cdot 17 \cdot n, k \cdot 18 \cdot n].$$

Furthermore, Currie [25] constructed k-uniform square-free morphisms for all $k \geqslant 11$, except for $k \in \{14, 15, 16, 20, 21, 22\}$. Using these we construct square-free words with the desired property for all n that are divisible by some $d \geqslant 11$ and $d \notin \{14, 15, 16, 20, 21, 22\}$, and $n/d \geqslant 3$ from the word $w_{n/d}$.

Combining all previous results, there are only 335 values left, for which a square-free word $w_n \in \Sigma_3^*$ of this length that can be shuffled with itself in a square-freeness preserving manner must be explicitly constructed. Such words were found by a computer search, see the table in Appendix A. □

Currie and Saari [29] also answered Harju's question and provided another proof for the previous result. Our construction appears to be significantly simpler though, and the auxiliary Lemma 5.2 might be a useful tool to generate square-free words, as illustrated in the following section.

5.4 Short palindromes in square-free words

This section is not related to shuffles of words, but it provides an improved proof for a theorem of Currie [26], which can be easily obtained as a corollary of Lemma 5.2.

For any square-free ternary word, each of its factors of length three is either a palindrome aba or of the form abc for different letters $a, b, c \in \Sigma_3$.

Brešar et al. [14] raised the following question: for a positive integer k, is there an infinite set A of positive integers with gaps of size at least k, so that whenever $v \in \Sigma_3^\omega$ is square-free, then a palindrome of length three is guaranteed to occur in v at some position $a \in A$?

Currie [26] gave a negative answer to this question in general by proving the following theorem:

Theorem 5.6 (Currie, 2008). *There exists a constant N_0 such that for any sequence (a_n) of positive integers, with $a_{n+1} - a_n \geqslant N_0$ for each n, and any function $\pi :$ $\mathbb{N} \to \{P, N\}$, there exists an infinite ternary square-free word $v = v_1 v_2 \cdots$, such that for each m, $v_{a_m} v_{a_m+1} v_{a_m+2}$ is a palindrome if and only if $\pi(m) = P$.*

For Currie's proof to work, N_0 must be chosen such that every factor of length at least N_0 of the infinite word h (which is the fixed point of the morphism f defined as $f(0) = 012, f(1) = 02$ and $f(2) = 1$) contains at least seven occurrences of the factor 121020121. As the factor of length 399 that appears after the prefix of length 728 in h contains only six occurrences of 121020121, this theorem applies only if $N_0 \geqslant 400$. We provide a simpler proof for Theorem 5.6 that applies for all $N_0 \geqslant 67$:

Proof. Let w be any infinite ternary square-free word (such as h). The substitution $g : \Sigma_3^* \to 2^{\Sigma_3^*}$, defined by

$$g(0) = \{01202120102120210, 012021020102120210\}$$
$$g(1) = \{12010201210201021, 120102101210201021\}$$
$$g(2) = \{20121012021012102, 201210212021012102\}$$

with images of lengths 17 and 18 is square-free, as we showed in Lemma 5.2. Thus the word $v \in g(w)$ which is obtained by replacing each letter of w with its image of length 17 in g is square-free. We now modify v to have palindromes and non-palindromes at the positions a_m as specified by π:

We observe that for all i, if $v_i v_{i+1} v_{i+2}$ is a palindrome, then $v_{i-1} v_i v_{i+1}$ is not, for otherwise v would not be square-free. Furthermore, we can easily check that if $v_i v_{i+1} v_{i+2}$ is not a palindrome, then there exists an integer $1 \leqslant j \leqslant 3$, such that $v_{i-j} v_{i-j+1} v_{i-j+2}$ is a palindrome, just by inspecting the images of all letters in the substitution g.

We can choose a suitable suffix of v, such that v_{a_1} is a palindrome if and only if $\pi(1) = P$.

Now, if $N_0 \geqslant 67$, there are at least three full length-17-images of letters in g between $v_{a_{m-1}}$ and v_{a_m}. Each of these can be replaced by their counterparts of length 18 in g, to get a new word that is still square-free. Such a replacement does not change any of the factors $v_{a_\ell} v_{a_\ell+1} v_{a_\ell+2}$ where $\ell < m$.

Thus, if $\pi(m) = N$ but $v_{a_m} v_{a_m+1} v_{a_m+2}$ is a palindrome, we replace one of these blocks by the longer image, which leads to a new word v' with the property that $v'_{a_m} v'_{a_m+1} v'_{a_m+2} = v_{a_m-1} v_{a_m} v_{a_m+1}$, which is not a palindrome.

On the other hand if $\pi(m) = P$ but $v_{a_m} v_{a_m+1} v_{a_m+2}$ is not a palindrome, we know that there exists a $j \leqslant 3$ such that $v_{a_m-j} v_{a_m-j+1} v_{a_m-j+2}$ is a palindrome. Therefore, replacing j of the three full images between a_m and a_{m-1} with their longer counterparts leads to a new word v' where $v'_{a_m} v'_{a_m+1} v'_{a_m+2} = v_{a_m-j} v_{a_m-j+1} v_{a_m-j+2}$ is a palindrome.

Iterating this procedure produces a ternary square-free word with the desired properties. $\qquad\square$

5.5 Infinite square-free self-shuffling words

Harju [45] also considered square-free shuffles of infinite words. His main result in this context is the following theorem:

Theorem 5.7 (Harju, 2013). *There exists an infinite square-free word $u \in \Sigma_3^\omega$ and a conducting sequence $\beta \in \Sigma_2^\omega$ such that $w = u \shuffle_\beta u$ is square-free.*

Note that the word w, that results from shuffling u with itself according to β, differs from u, in the construction that is used in the proof of this result. Hence, a question raised by Harju concerns the existence of an infinite square-free self-shuffling word. More precisely, he asked the following question: Is there an infinite square-free word $u \in \Sigma_3^\omega$ and a conducting sequence $\beta \in \Sigma_2^\omega$ such that $u = u \shuffle_\beta u$?

We will answer this question affirmatively in the following, thereby also providing another proof of Theorem 5.7.

A *prefix code* is a set of words with the property that none of its elements is a prefix of another element. Similarly, a *suffix code* is a set of words where no element is a suffix of another one. A *bifix code* is a set that is both a prefix code and a suffix code.

Let $h : \Sigma_4^* \to \Sigma_4^*$ be the morphism defined as follows:

$$h(0) = 0121,$$
$$h(1) = 032,$$
$$h(2) = 013,$$
$$h(3) = 0302.$$

We will show that the fixed point $h^\omega(0)$ is a square-free and self-shuffling word in the following. Note that h is not a square-free morphism, that is it does not preserve square-freeness, as $h(23) = 0130302$ contains the square 3030.

Lemma 5.8. *The word* $w = h^\omega(0)$ *contains no factor of the form* $3u1u3$ *for some word* $u \in \Sigma_4^*$.

Proof. We assume that there exists a factor of the form $3u1u3$ in w, for some word $u \in \Sigma_4^*$. From the definition of h, we observe that u can not be empty. Furthermore, we see that every 3 in w is preceded by either 0 or 1. If $1 \leqslant_s u$, then we had an occurrence of the factor 11 in w, which is not possible by the definition of h, hence $0 \leqslant_s u$. Now, every 3 is followed by either 0 or 2 in w and 01 is followed by either 2 or 3. Since both $3u$ and $01u$ are factors of w, we must have $2 \leqslant_p u$. This means that the factor 012 appears at the centre of $u1u$, which can only be followed by 1 in w, thus $21 \leqslant_p u$. However, this results in the factor 321 as a prefix of $3u1u3$, which does not appear in w, as seen from the definition of h. $\qquad\square$

Lemma 5.9. *The word* $w = h^\omega(0)$ *is square-free.*

Proof. We first observe that $\{h(0), h(1), h(2), h(3)\}$ is a bifix code. Furthermore, we can verify that there are no squares uu with $|u| \leqslant 3$ in w. Let us assume now, that the square uu appears in w and that u is the shortest word with this property. If $u = 02u'$, then $u' = u''03$ must hold, since 02 appears only as a factor of $h(3)$, and thus uu is a suffix of the factor $h(3)u''h(3)u''$ in w. As $w = h(w)$, also the shorter square $3h^{-1}(u'')3h^{-1}(u'')$ appears in w, a contradiction. The same desubstitution principle also leads to occurrences of shorter squares in w if $u = xu'$ and $x \in \{01, 03, 10, 12, 13, 21, 30, 32\}$.

If $u = 2u'$ then either $03 \leqslant_s u$, or $030 \leqslant_s u$, or $01 \leqslant_s u$, by the definition of h. In the last case, that is when $01 \leqslant_s u$, we must have $21 \leqslant_p u$, which is covered by the previous paragraph. If $u' = u''030$, then uu is followed by 2 in w and we can desubstitute to obtain the shorter square $h^{-1}(u'')3h^{-1}(u'')3$ in w. If $u = 2u'$ and $u' = u''03$, and uu is preceded by 03 or followed by 2 in w, we can desubstitute to $1h^{-1}(u'')1h^{-1}(u'')$ or $h^{-1}(u'')1h^{-1}(u'')1$, respectively. Therefore, assume that $u = 2u''03$ and uu is preceded by 030 and followed by 02 in w. This however means that we can desubstitute to get an occurrence of the factor $3h^{-1}(u'')1h^{-1}(u'')3$ in w, a contradiction to Lemma 5.8. □

Lemma 5.10. *The word $w = h^\omega(0)$ is self-shuffling.*

Proof. In what follows we use the notation $x = v^{-1}u$ meaning that $u = vx$ for finite words x, u, v. We claim that $w = h^\omega(0) = \prod_{i=0}^\infty u_i v_i$, where

$$
\begin{aligned}
u_0 &= h^2(0), & v_0 &= h(0)03, \\
u_1 &= 0, & v_1 &= 2h(2)0, \\
u_{6i+2} &= h^i(0^{-1}h(0)0), & v_{6i+2} &= h^i(0^{-1}h(1)0), \\
u_{6i+3} &= h^i(0^{-1}h(3)0), & v_{6i+3} &= h^i(0^{-1}h(03)0), \\
u_{6i+4} &= h^i(0^{-1}h(201)0), & v_{6i+4} &= h^i(1), \\
u_{6i+5} &= h^i(30), & v_{6i+5} &= h^i(3), \\
u_{6i+6} &= h^i(2h(03)), & v_{6i+6} &= h^{i+1}(0), \\
u_{6i+7} &= h^{i+1}(20), & v_{6i+7} &= h^{i+1}(0^{-1}h(2)0),
\end{aligned}
$$

for all $i \geqslant 0$.

Now we verify that

$$
w = \prod_{i=0}^\infty u_i v_i = \prod_{i=0}^\infty u_i = \prod_{i=0}^\infty v_i,
$$

from which it follows that w is self-shuffling. It suffices to show that each of the above products is fixed by h. Indeed, straightforward computations show that

$$
\prod_{i=0}^\infty u_i = h^2(0)h^2(121)h^3(121)\cdots
$$

which is fixed by h:

$$h(\prod_{i=0}^{\infty} u_i) = h\left(h^2(0)h^2(121)h^3(121)\cdots\right) = h^3(0)h^3(121)h^4(121)\cdots =$$

$$= h^2(0121)h^3(121)h^4(121)\cdots = h^2(0)h^2(121)h^3(121)\cdots = \prod_{i=0}^{\infty} u_i,$$

hence $\prod_{i=0}^{\infty} u_i$ is fixed by h and thus $w = \prod_{i=0}^{\infty} u_i$. In a similar way we show that $w = \prod_{i=0}^{\infty} v_i = \prod_{i=0}^{\infty} u_i v_i$. □

We can immediately produce a square-free self-shuffling word on three letters from $h^{\omega}(0)$: by Proposition 5.3, the property of being self-shuffling is preserved by the application of a morphism. Furthermore, Brandenburg [13] has shown that the morphism $f: \Sigma_4^* \to \Sigma_3^*$, defined by

$$f(0) = 010201202101210212,$$
$$f(1) = 010201202102010212,$$
$$f(2) = 010201202120121012,$$
$$f(3) = 010201210201021012,$$

is square-free. Hence, the word $f(h^{\omega}(0))$ is a ternary square-free self-shuffling word, from which we can produce a multitude of others by applying square-free morphisms from Σ_3^* to Σ_3^* (for instance the ones constructed by Currie [25]).

5.6 Avoiding shuffle-squares and shuffle-cubes

A word $w \in u \sqcup\!\sqcup u$ for some word u is also referred to as a *shuffle-square*. At the Dagstuhl meeting "Combinatorics and Algorithmics of Strings" [22], Karhumäki asked whether shuffle-squares are avoidable, that is whether there exists an infinite word over some alphabet Σ_m such that none of its factors is a shuffle-square, and if yes, which is the minimal possible alphabet size m.

Currie [27] used the Lovász Local Lemma to show that shuffle-squares are indeed avoidable in the alphabet $\Sigma_{\lceil e^{95} \rceil}$. We will provide a simple - also non-constructive - proof which shows that there exists a word over Σ_{10} that avoids

5. Shuffling square-free words

shuffle-squares based on the following criterion by Miller [72], which is a simple, yet powerful utility to show avoidability results.

Theorem 5.11 (Miller, 2012). *Let S be a set of non-empty words over a k-letter alphabet Σ. If there exists $c \in \left(\frac{1}{k}, 1\right)$ such that*

$$\sum_{s \in S} c^{|s|} \leqslant kc - 1,$$

then there is an infinite word over Σ that avoids S.

This formulation of Miller's theorem is due to Rampersad [78]. In the following, let S_k be the set of shuffle-squares in Σ_k^+, that is

$$S_k = \bigcup_{w \in \Sigma_k^+} w \sqcup\!\!\sqcup w.$$

As mentioned at the beginning of this chapter, every word $s \in S_k$ is obtained by shuffling a word $w \in \Sigma_k^+$ with itself, using a so-called *conducting sequence* β of length $2|w|$, which is a binary word instructing how to shuffle.

The canonical upper bound on the number of shuffle squares of length $2i$ in a k-letter alphabet is thus $k^i \binom{2i}{i}$ as there are k^i many words of length i in Σ_k^+, which can be shuffled with themselves using $\binom{2i}{i}$ many conducting sequences $\beta \in \Sigma_2^+$ that contain i occurrences of 0 and 1. However, a word $s \in S_k$ might be obtained using different words $w \in \Sigma_k^+$ and different conducting sequences $\beta \in \Sigma_2^+$.

Example 5.12. The word $00110011 \in S_2$ can be obtained as $w_1 \sqcup\!\!\sqcup_{\beta_1} w_1$, where $w_1 = 0011$ and $\beta_1 = 00001111$, and as $w_2 \sqcup\!\!\sqcup_{\beta_2} w_2$, where $w_2 = 0101$ and $\beta_2 = 01010101$.

When shuffling a word w with itself, without losing generality we can always choose the next letter from the first copy of w, whenever we have used equally many letters from both copies of w in the shuffle so far. Therefore, we only need to count conducting sequences $\beta \in \Sigma_2^*$ that have the additional property that

$$\big|\beta[1]\beta[2]\cdots\beta[i]\big|_0 \geqslant \big|\beta[1]\beta[2]\cdots\beta[i]\big|_1 ,$$

for all $1 \leqslant i \leqslant |\beta|$, where $|w|_a$ denotes the number of occurrences of the letter

116

a in w. Binary words with equally many occurrences of 0 and 1 satisfying the inequality above are known as *Dyck words*, and there are $C_i = \frac{1}{i+1}\binom{2i}{i}$ many Dyck words of length $2i$, where C_i denotes the i-th Catalan number (see, for instance, Section 7.5 in [42]). This leads to the following:

Theorem 5.13. *Shuffle-squares are avoidable in* Σ_{10}.

Proof. Let $k \in \mathbb{N}$ and $c \in \left(\frac{1}{k}, 1\right)$, such that $\left|kc^2\right| < \frac{1}{4}$. (We will show later that such a c exists for $k = 10$)

Then we have:

$$\sum_{s \in S_k} c^{|s|} \leqslant \sum_{i \geqslant 1} C_i k^i c^{2i}$$

$$\leqslant \sum_{i \geqslant 1} \frac{1}{i+1}\binom{2i}{i}\left(kc^2\right)^i$$

$$= \frac{1 - \sqrt{1 - 4kc^2}}{2kc^2} - 1.$$

Now, if $k = 10$ and $c = \frac{127}{1000}$, then $\left|kc^2\right| = \frac{16129}{100000} < \frac{1}{4}$ and furthermore

$$\frac{1 - \sqrt{1 - 4kc^2}}{2kc^2} \leqslant kc,$$

as the left-hand side is around 1.2533 and the right-hand side is 1.27. Hence, by Theorem 5.11, shuffle-squares are avoidable on ten letters. $\qquad\square$

Recently Guégan and Ochem [43] proved that shuffle-squares are avoidable on seven letters. Their proof is based on the non-constructive power series approach by Bell and Goh [4], which proved to be a powerful tool in the area of avoidable patterns as exhibited by Rampersad [77], and Blanchet-Sadri and Woodhouse [11], and the proof benefits mainly from a better upper bound on the number of shuffle-squares that need to be avoided.

The idea we used to bound the number of conducting sequences, that need to be considered when creating shuffle-squares, can also be generalised to obtain a bound on the number of shuffle-powers of larger exponent. As an example, a *shuffle-cube* is an element of $u \sqcup\!\sqcup u \sqcup\!\sqcup u$ for some word u. There exists a natural bijection between Dyck words and a special form of a combinatorial object called

5. Shuffling square-free words

Young tableau [90]: a Young tableau of shape $(n_1, n_2, \ldots, n_k)$ is a left-aligned table with k rows and n_i elements in row i for all $1 \leqslant i \leqslant k$, with the property that the elements in the table are all pairwise different and the elements in each row are sorted in ascending order from left to right, while elements that form a column of the table are sorted in ascending order from top to bottom.

Example 5.14. A possible Young tableau of shape $(5, 3, 2)$ containing the numbers from one to ten is depicted in Figure 5.1.

1	3	4	7	8
2	5	9		
6	10			

Figure 5.1. A Young tableau of shape $(5, 3, 2)$.

The bijection is then established by mapping a Dyck word β of length $2i$ to a Young tableau of shape (i, i) in such a way that the positions of the letter 0 in β appear in increasing order in the first row, and the indices where 1 appears in β are put in increasing order in the second row.

Example 5.15. The Dyck word $\beta = 00100110100111$ of length 14 is mapped to the Young tableau of shape $(7, 7)$ depicted in Figure 5.2.

1	2	4	5	8	10	11
3	6	7	9	12	13	14

Figure 5.2. Young tableau of shape $(7, 7)$ corresponding to the word 00100110100111.

A conducting sequence β used to shuffle three copies of u to get a shuffle-cube is now a ternary word of length $3|u|$, with $|u|$ many occurrences of $0, 1$ and 2. As above, without loss of generality we can restrict ourselves to conducting sequences $\beta \in \Sigma_3^+$ satisfying

$$\left|\beta[1]\beta[2]\cdots\beta[i]\right|_0 \geqslant \left|\beta[1]\beta[2]\cdots\beta[i]\right|_1 \geqslant \left|\beta[1]\beta[2]\cdots\beta[i]\right|_2 \,,$$

for all $1 \leqslant i \leqslant |\beta|$. There exists a natural bijection between words of length $3i$ with this property and Young tableaux of shape (i, i, i), using the same ideas as above. Hence, we can upper bound the number of conducting sequences of length $3i$ that need to be considered by the number $Y_{(i,i,i)}$ of Young tableaux of shape (i, i, i). This number can be easily calculated using the so-called hook-length formula ([37], see also Section 5.1.4 in [59]):

$$Y_{(i,i,i)} = \frac{2 \cdot (3i)!}{(i+2)!(i+1)!i!}.$$

Therefore, if Q_k is the set of shuffle-cubes in Σ_k, then for $\left| kc^3 \right| < \frac{1}{27}$,

$$\sum_{s \in Q_k} c^{|s|} \leqslant \sum_{i \geqslant 1} Y_{(i,i,i)} k^i c^{3i}$$

$$\leqslant \sum_{i \geqslant 1} \frac{2 \cdot (3i)!}{(i+2)!(i+1)!i!} \left(kc^3 \right)^i$$

$$= \frac{{}_2F_1(-\frac{2}{3}, -\frac{1}{3}; 2; 27kc^3) - 1}{3kc^3} - 1,$$

where ${}_2F_1(a, b; c; z)$ is the hypergeometric function defined as

$$_2F_1(a, b; c; z) = \sum_{k \geqslant 0} \frac{a^{\bar{k}} b^{\bar{k}} z^k}{c^{\bar{k}} k!}.$$

Here, $a^{\bar{k}}$ denotes the rising factorial power $a^{\bar{k}} = a \cdot (a+1) \cdots (a+k-1)$. For more details about hypergeometric functions we refer to Section 5.5 in [42].

If $k = 6$ and $c = \frac{175}{1000}$, then $\left| kc^3 \right| < \frac{1}{27}$ is satisfied, and furthermore

$$\frac{{}_2F_1(-\frac{2}{3}, -\frac{1}{3}; 2; 27kc^3) - 1}{3kc^3} - 1 \approx 0.0396 < 0.05 = kc - 1,$$

which by Theorem 5.11 means that shuffle-cubes are avoidable in Σ_6.

5.7 Conclusions and open questions

A question that immediately suggests itself with respect to Theorem 5.7 is the following: For any square-free word $u \in \Sigma_3^\omega$, does there exist a β, such that $u \sqcup_\beta u$ is square-free? Here, the answer is negative:

Example 5.16. Let u be the lexicographically smallest square-free word. This is certainly a Lyndon word. According to [18], for every conducting sequence β, the word $u \sqcup_\beta u$ is lexicographically strictly smaller than u and thus can not be square-free.

However, before the word of Section 5.5 was found, the following weaker result was established, which is now mentioned here, as it evokes some question that is still interesting on its own:

Theorem 5.17. *There exist infinite square-free words $u, w \in \Sigma_3^\omega$ and a conducting sequence β, such that $u = u \sqcup_\beta w$.*

Proof. Let u be the infinite fixed point $h^\omega(0)$ of the following 18-uniform morphism h:

$$h(0) = 012021\mathbf{0}20102120210$$
$$h(1) = 120102\mathbf{1}01210201021$$
$$h(2) = 201210\mathbf{2}12021012102.$$

Both h and the morphism h' that is obtained by deleting the boldfaced letters from every image are square-free by Theorem 2.10. Furthermore, the sequence of bold-face letters in u equals u. Let now w be the word that consists of the non-boldfaced letters. As $w = h'(u)$, it is square-free, and furthermore $u = u \sqcup_\beta w$ for $\beta = (0^6 10^{11})^\omega$. □

Similarly to the question whether the existential statement of Theorem 5.7 can be turned into a universal one, one can ask if the word u in Theorem 5.17 could be any square-free word u:

Problem 5.18. For any square-free word $u \in \Sigma_3^\omega$, does there exist a square-free word $w \in \Sigma_3^\omega$, such that $u = u \sqcup_\beta w$ for some β?

So far, no answer to this question has been found. It is also desirable to find the minimal alphabet size for which shuffle-squares are avoidable.

Problem 5.19. What is the minimal m such that shuffle-squares are avoidable in Σ_m?

It is however not even easy to find lower bounds, as recent results by Buss and Soltys [15], as well as Rizzi and Vialette [84], show that it is generally NP-complete to decide if a given word is a shuffle-square. Hence, the usual backtracking approach seems to be unpractical already for $m = 4$. For $m = 3$ this backtracking search shows that every word in Σ_3^* of length at least 12 contains a shuffle-square.

Furthermore, the way how shuffle-squares of a given length are counted in Theorem 5.13 is rather naïve, and the ideas of Guégan and Ochem [43] are slightly more sophisticated and hence lead to a better bound on the alphabet-size needed to avoid shuffle-squares. One might be able to further improve their result, if a better way to upper bound the number of shuffle-squares is found, a problem which was already raised by Henshall, Rampersad, and Shallit [51].

Square-free shuffles of finite square-free words

> *"In God we trust; all others must bring data."*
>
> WILLIAM EDWARDS DEMING

This chapter lists the 335 square-free words mentioned in the proof of Theorem 5.5, each of which can be shuffled with itself to obtain a square-free word.

It can be checked that for $i \in \{3, 4, \ldots, 17\} \cup \{19, 20, 21, 26\}$, the word w_i of length i and the word $w_i \sqcup_{\beta_i} w_i$ are square-free:

$$w_3 = 012 \qquad\qquad \beta_3 = 0^2 101^2$$

$$w_4 = 0120 \qquad\qquad \beta_4 = 0^2 10^2 1^3$$

$$w_5 = 01201 \qquad\qquad \beta_5 = 0^3 1^2 0101^2$$

$$w_6 = 010212 \qquad\qquad \beta_6 = 0^4 10^2 1^5$$

$$w_7 = 0102120 \qquad\qquad \beta_7 = 0^6 1^4 01^3$$

$$w_8 = 01021201 \qquad\qquad \beta_8 = 0^6 1^4 01^2 01^2$$

$$w_9 = 010212012 \qquad\qquad \beta_9 = 0^6 1^4 01^2 0101^2$$

$$w_{10} = 0102120102 \qquad\qquad \beta_{10} = 0^6 1^4 01^2 0^3 1^4$$

$$w_{11} = 01210212021 \qquad\qquad \beta_{11} = 0^4 1^3 0^5 10^2 1^7$$

$$w_{12} = 010201202120 \qquad\qquad \beta_{12} = 0^{11} 1^{10} 01^2$$

$$w_{13} = 0102012021201 \qquad\qquad \beta_{13} = 0^{11} 1^{10} 0^2 1^3$$

$$w_{14} = 01210201202102 \qquad\qquad \beta_{14} = 0^2 10^3 10^2 1^5 0^4 1^3 0^2 1^2 01^2$$

A. Square-free shuffles of finite square-free words

$w_{15} = 012102012021201$

$\beta_{15} = 0^2 10^3 10^2 1^5 0^4 1^3 01^2 0^2 101^2$

$w_{16} = 0102012021012102$

$\beta_{16} = 0^{13} 1^4 01^6 0^2 1^6$

$w_{17} = 01020120210121020$

$\beta_{17} = 0^{13} 1^7 01^2 01^2 01^2 01^4$

$w_{19} = 0102012021012102012$

$\beta_{19} = 0^{13} 1^4 01^6 0^2 1^2 01^3 01^2 01^2$

$w_{20} = 01020120210121020102$

$\beta_{20} = 0^{13} 1^7 0^5 1^6 0^2 1^7$

$w_{21} = 010201202101210201021$

$\beta_{21} = 0^{13} 1^4 01^6 0^7 1^{11}$

$w_{26} = 0102012021012010210120210120$

$\beta_{26} = 0^{25} 1^{24} 01^2$

We apply compositions of the following square-free morphisms to these words (their square-freeness is checked using Theorem 2.10). Here, the notation $\sigma_i = \{u, v, w\}$ is used to denote that $\sigma_i(0) = u, \sigma_i(1) = v$, and $\sigma_i(2) = w$:

$\sigma_1 = \{1, 2, 0\}, \ \sigma_2 = \{2, 0, 1\}, \ \sigma_3 = \{1, 0, 2\}$

$\sigma_4 = \{2, 1, 0\}, \ \sigma_5 = \{0, 2, 1\}, \ \sigma_6 = \{0102012, 021012, 10212\}$

$\sigma_7 = \{0102012, 021012, 102010212\}$

$\sigma_8 = \{0102012, 0210201021012, 10212\}$

$\sigma_9 = \{0102, 01210120212, 012102010212\}$

$\sigma_{10} = \{0102012, 021012, 1020102101210212\}$

$\sigma_{11} = \{0, 102012021201021012, 10212021012\}$

$\sigma_{12} = \{0, 102012021012, 102120210201021012\}$

$\sigma_{13} = \{0102012, 0210201021012, 021201210212\}$

$\sigma_{14} = \{0102012, 0210201021012, 0210201210212\}$

$\sigma_{15} = \{0102, 012101201020120212, 012102010212\}$

$\sigma_{16} = \{0102012, 02101210201021012, 02102010212\}$

$\sigma_{17} = \{0, 102012021012102010212021012, 102012021201021202102010210212\}$

In the table, an entry $\sigma_{i_1 \cdot \ldots \cdot i_j}(w_k)$ is an abbreviation for $\sigma_{i_1} \circ \cdots \circ \sigma_{i_j}(w_k)$:

$w_{18} = \sigma_6(w_3)$ $w_{22} = \sigma_7(w_3)$ $w_{23} = \sigma_{6 \cdot 2}(w_4)$

$w_{24} = \sigma_{6 \cdot 1}(w_4)$ $w_{25} = \sigma_8(w_3)$ $w_{27} = \sigma_9(w_3)$

$w_{28} = \sigma_{7 \cdot 1}(w_4)$ $w_{29} = \sigma_{10}(w_3)$ $w_{30} = \sigma_{11}(w_3)$

$w_{31} = \sigma_{12}(w_3)$ $w_{32} = \sigma_{13}(w_3)$ $w_{34} = \sigma_{15}(w_3)$

$w_{35} = \sigma_{16}(w_3)$ $w_{37} = \sigma_{7 \cdot 1}(w_5)$ $w_{38} = \sigma_{15}(w_4)$

$w_{40} = \sigma_{14}(w_4)$ $w_{41} = \sigma_{11 \cdot 2}(w_4)$ $w_{42} = \sigma_{16}(w_4)$

$w_{43} = \sigma_{12 \cdot 1}(w_4)$ $w_{45} = \sigma_{10 \cdot 2}(w_4)$ $w_{46} = \sigma_{14 \cdot 1}(w_4)$

$w_{47} = \sigma_{6 \cdot 1}(w_8)$ $w_{49} = \sigma_{12 \cdot 2}(w_4)$ $w_{50} = \sigma_{9 \cdot 1}(w_5)$

$w_{53} = \sigma_{14}(w_5)$ $w_{56} = \sigma_{15}(w_5)$ $w_{58} = \sigma_{17}(w_4)$

$w_{59} = \sigma_{16}(w_5)$ $w_{61} = \sigma_{12 \cdot 1}(w_5)$ $w_{62} = \sigma_{12}(w_6)$

$w_{63} = \sigma_{16 \cdot 1}(w_5)$ $w_{64} = \sigma_{15 \cdot 1}(w_5)$ $w_{67} = \sigma_{6 \cdot 2}(w_{11})$

$w_{70} = \sigma_{16}(w_6)$ $w_{71} = \sigma_{13}(w_7)$ $w_{73} = \sigma_{14}(w_7)$

$w_{74} = \sigma_{10 \cdot 2}(w_7)$ $w_{79} = \sigma_{14 \cdot 1}(w_7)$ $w_{80} = \sigma_{12 \cdot 2}(w_7)$

$w_{82} = \sigma_8(w_{10})$ $w_{83} = \sigma_{13 \cdot 2}(w_8)$ $w_{86} = \sigma_{17 \cdot 2}(w_4)$

$w_{89} = \sigma_{11 \cdot 1}(w_8)$ $w_{94} = \sigma_{16}(w_8)$ $w_{97} = \sigma_{9 \cdot 1}(w_{11})$

$w_{98} = \sigma_{15 \cdot 1}(w_8)$ $w_{101} = \sigma_{11 \cdot 2}(w_{10})$ $w_{103} = \sigma_{13}(w_{10})$

$w_{106} = \sigma_{14}(w_{10})$ $w_{107} = \sigma_{9 \cdot 1}(w_{12})$ $w_{109} = \sigma_{13 \cdot 1}(w_{10})$

$w_{113} = \sigma_{17 \cdot 1}(w_5)$ $w_{118} = \sigma_{15 \cdot 1}(w_{11})$ $w_{122} = \sigma_{16 \cdot 1}(w_{10})$

$w_{127} = \sigma_{11 \cdot 1}(w_{12})$ $w_{131} = \sigma_{6 \cdot 2 \cdot 7}(w_3)$ $w_{134} = \sigma_{13 \cdot 3}(w_{12})$

$w_{137} = \sigma_{6 \cdot 6 \cdot 2}(w_4)$ $w_{139} = \sigma_{14}(w_{13})$ $w_{142} = \sigma_{17}(w_8)$

$w_{146} = \sigma_{16 \cdot 1}(w_{12})$ $w_{149} = \sigma_{6 \cdot 2 \cdot 8}(w_3)$ $w_{151} = \sigma_{6 \cdot 8}(w_3)$

$w_{157} = \sigma_{16 \cdot 1}(w_{13})$ $w_{158} = \sigma_{16}(w_{14})$ $w_{163} = \sigma_{7 \cdot 2 \cdot 7}(w_3)$

$w_{166} = \sigma_{15 \cdot 2}(w_{14})$ $w_{167} = \sigma_{13}(w_{16})$ $w_{173} = \sigma_{6 \cdot 1 \cdot 10}(w_3)$

$w_{178} = \sigma_{14 \cdot 1}(w_{16})$ $w_{179} = \sigma_{14}(w_{17})$ $w_{181} = \sigma_{10}(w_{19})$

$w_{191} = \sigma_{6 \cdot 2 \cdot 13}(w_3)$ $w_{193} = \sigma_{9 \cdot 7}(w_3)$ $w_{194} = \sigma_{6 \cdot 8}(w_4)$

$w_{197} = \sigma_{6 \cdot 3 \cdot 14}(w_3)$ $w_{199} = \sigma_{6 \cdot 14}(w_3)$ $w_{202} = \sigma_{17}(w_{12})$

$w_{206} = \sigma_{15 \cdot 1}(w_{17})$ $w_{211} = \sigma_{7 \cdot 10}(w_3)$ $w_{214} = \sigma_{7 \cdot 2 \cdot 10}(w_3)$

A. Square-free shuffles of finite square-free words

$$w_{218} = \sigma_{12\cdot7}(w_3) \qquad w_{223} = \sigma_{6\cdot7\cdot1}(w_5) \qquad w_{226} = \sigma_{7\cdot1\cdot12}(w_3)$$

$$w_{227} = \sigma_{7\cdot12}(w_3) \qquad w_{229} = \sigma_{7\cdot2\cdot12}(w_3) \qquad w_{233} = \sigma_{7\cdot1\cdot13}(w_3)$$

$$w_{239} = \sigma_{10\cdot8}(w_3) \qquad w_{241} = \sigma_{11\cdot8}(w_3) \qquad w_{251} = \sigma_{7\cdot2\cdot15}(w_3)$$

$$w_{254} = \sigma_{7\cdot1\cdot16}(w_3) \qquad w_{257} = \sigma_{8\cdot12}(w_3) \qquad w_{262} = \sigma_{8\cdot13}(w_3)$$

$$w_{263} = \sigma_{13\cdot8}(w_3) \qquad w_{269} = \sigma_{8\cdot14}(w_3) \qquad w_{271} = \sigma_{14\cdot8}(w_3)$$

$$w_{274} = \sigma_{9\cdot12}(w_3) \qquad w_{277} = \sigma_{8\cdot5\cdot14}(w_3) \qquad w_{278} = \sigma_{7\cdot15}(w_4)$$

$$w_{281} = \sigma_{8\cdot3\cdot14}(w_3) \qquad w_{283} = \sigma_{8\cdot1\cdot14}(w_3) \qquad w_{293} = \sigma_{9\cdot2\cdot13}(w_3)$$

$$w_{298} = \sigma_{9\cdot4\cdot14}(w_3) \qquad w_{302} = \sigma_{8\cdot10}(w_4) \qquad w_{307} = \sigma_{13\cdot2\cdot10}(w_3)$$

$$w_{311} = \sigma_{12\cdot12}(w_3) \qquad w_{313} = \sigma_{10\cdot13}(w_3) \qquad w_{314} = \sigma_{8\cdot15}(w_4)$$

$$w_{317} = \sigma_{14\cdot10}(w_3) \qquad w_{326} = \sigma_{10\cdot15}(w_3) \qquad w_{331} = \sigma_{11\cdot15}(w_3)$$

$$w_{334} = \sigma_{13\cdot8}(w_4) \qquad w_{337} = \sigma_{14\cdot12}(w_3) \qquad w_{346} = \sigma_{13\cdot14}(w_3)$$

$$w_{347} = \sigma_{11\cdot3\cdot14}(w_3) \qquad w_{349} = \sigma_{6\cdot1\cdot17}(w_4) \qquad w_{353} = \sigma_{12\cdot1\cdot15}(w_3)$$

$$w_{358} = \sigma_{12\cdot2\cdot14}(w_3) \qquad w_{359} = \sigma_{13\cdot15}(w_3) \qquad w_{362} = \sigma_{15\cdot1\cdot13}(w_3)$$

$$w_{367} = \sigma_{16\cdot1\cdot12}(w_3) \qquad w_{373} = \sigma_{11\cdot13}(w_4) \qquad w_{379} = \sigma_{16\cdot4\cdot14}(w_3)$$

$$w_{382} = \sigma_{15\cdot16}(w_3) \qquad w_{383} = \sigma_{8\cdot10\cdot2}(w_4) \qquad w_{386} = \sigma_{15\cdot2\cdot15}(w_3)$$

$$w_{389} = \sigma_{14\cdot1\cdot16}(w_3) \qquad w_{394} = \sigma_{11\cdot4\cdot14}(w_4) \qquad w_{397} = \sigma_{11\cdot1\cdot13}(w_4)$$

$$w_{398} = \sigma_{15\cdot2\cdot16}(w_3) \qquad w_{401} = \sigma_{17\cdot2}(w_{21}) \qquad w_{409} = \sigma_{9\cdot15\cdot2}(w_4)$$

$$w_{419} = \sigma_{7\cdot17}(w_3) \qquad w_{421} = \sigma_{7\cdot4\cdot17}(w_3) \qquad w_{422} = \sigma_{13\cdot3\cdot13}(w_4)$$

$$w_{431} = \sigma_{8\cdot14\cdot2}(w_5) \qquad w_{433} = \sigma_{11\cdot13\cdot1}(w_4) \qquad w_{439} = \sigma_{12\cdot1\cdot16}(w_4)$$

$$w_{443} = \sigma_{10\cdot14\cdot1}(w_4) \qquad w_{446} = \sigma_{8\cdot1\cdot13}(w_5) \qquad w_{449} = \sigma_{16\cdot4\cdot13}(w_4)$$

$$w_{454} = \sigma_{15\cdot16}(w_4) \qquad w_{457} = \sigma_{17\cdot8}(w_3) \qquad w_{458} = \sigma_{16\cdot5\cdot14}(w_4)$$

$$w_{461} = \sigma_{16\cdot1\cdot13}(w_4) \qquad w_{463} = \sigma_{9\cdot15\cdot1}(w_4) \qquad w_{466} = \sigma_{12\cdot15\cdot2}(w_4)$$

$$w_{467} = \sigma_{8\cdot4\cdot17}(w_3) \qquad w_{478} = \sigma_{8\cdot2\cdot17}(w_4) \qquad w_{479} = \sigma_{9\cdot2\cdot13}(w_5)$$

$$w_{482} = \sigma_{16\cdot3\cdot14}(w_4) \qquad w_{487} = \sigma_{13\cdot15\cdot2}(w_4) \qquad w_{491} = \sigma_{10\cdot16\cdot1}(w_4)$$

$$w_{499} = \sigma_{12\cdot7}(w_7) \qquad w_{502} = \sigma_{14\cdot14\cdot2}(w_4) \qquad w_{503} = \sigma_{10\cdot13\cdot2}(w_5)$$

$$w_{509} = \sigma_{9\cdot5\cdot17}(w_4) \qquad w_{514} = \sigma_{9\cdot4\cdot17}(w_3) \qquad w_{521} = \sigma_{9\cdot2\cdot17}(w_3)$$

$$w_{523} = \sigma_{9\cdot1\cdot17}(w_4) \qquad w_{526} = \sigma_{9\cdot4\cdot17}(w_4) \qquad w_{538} = \sigma_{9\cdot2\cdot16}(w_5)$$

$$w_{541} = \sigma_{17\cdot10}(w_3) \qquad w_{542} = \sigma_{10\cdot5\cdot17}(w_3) \qquad w_{547} = \sigma_{10\cdot1\cdot17}(w_4)$$

$w_{554} = \sigma_{11\cdot17}(w_4)$ $w_{557} = \sigma_{13\cdot14\cdot2}(w_5)$ $w_{562} = \sigma_{14\cdot16\cdot1}(w_4)$

$w_{563} = \sigma_{11\cdot4\cdot17}(w_3)$ $w_{566} = \sigma_{10\cdot5\cdot16}(w_5)$ $w_{569} = \sigma_{17\cdot1\cdot10}(w_3)$

$w_{571} = \sigma_{17\cdot12}(w_3)$ $w_{577} = \sigma_{11\cdot1\cdot17}(w_3)$ $w_{586} = \sigma_{9\cdot2\cdot13}(w_6)$

$w_{587} = \sigma_{11\cdot3\cdot17}(w_3)$ $w_{593} = \sigma_{10\cdot2\cdot16}(w_5)$ $w_{599} = \sigma_{17\cdot2\cdot12}(w_3)$

$w_{601} = \sigma_{17\cdot14}(w_3)$ $w_{607} = \sigma_{13\cdot4\cdot17}(w_3)$ $w_{613} = \sigma_{13\cdot2\cdot17}(w_3)$

$w_{614} = \sigma_{13\cdot3\cdot17}(w_3)$ $w_{617} = \sigma_{7\cdot17\cdot1}(w_4)$ $w_{619} = \sigma_{13\cdot4\cdot17}(w_4)$

$w_{622} = \sigma_{13\cdot1\cdot17}(w_4)$ $w_{626} = \sigma_{17\cdot2\cdot13}(w_3)$ $w_{631} = \sigma_{11\cdot15\cdot1}(w_5)$

$w_{634} = \sigma_{14\cdot10}(w_6)$ $w_{641} = \sigma_{14\cdot14\cdot1}(w_5)$ $w_{643} = \sigma_{8\cdot14\cdot2}(w_7)$

$w_{647} = \sigma_{13\cdot12\cdot1}(w_5)$ $w_{653} = \sigma_{17\cdot3\cdot14}(w_3)$ $w_{659} = \sigma_{16\cdot4\cdot17}(w_3)$

$w_{661} = \sigma_{16\cdot5\cdot17}(w_3)$ $w_{662} = \sigma_{16\cdot17}(w_4)$ $w_{673} = \sigma_{16\cdot14\cdot1}(w_5)$

$w_{674} = \sigma_{14\cdot12}(w_6)$ $w_{677} = \sigma_{7\cdot10\cdot1}(w_{10})$ $w_{683} = \sigma_{7\cdot1\cdot16}(w_8)$

$w_{691} = \sigma_{16\cdot4\cdot16}(w_5)$ $w_{694} = \sigma_{8\cdot17\cdot1}(w_4)$ $w_{698} = \sigma_{10\cdot2\cdot13}(w_7)$

$w_{701} = \sigma_{8\cdot17}(w_5)$ $w_{706} = \sigma_{8\cdot17\cdot2}(w_4)$ $w_{709} = \sigma_{8\cdot5\cdot17}(w_5)$

$w_{718} = \sigma_{15\cdot15\cdot1}(w_5)$ $w_{719} = \sigma_{8\cdot3\cdot17}(w_5)$ $w_{727} = \sigma_{6\cdot4\cdot13}(w_{11})$

$w_{733} = \sigma_{16\cdot2\cdot12}(w_7)$ $w_{734} = \sigma_{16\cdot1\cdot12}(w_6)$ $w_{739} = \sigma_{17\cdot1\cdot13}(w_4)$

$w_{743} = \sigma_{17\cdot4\cdot13}(w_4)$ $w_{746} = \sigma_{11\cdot10\cdot2}(w_7)$ $w_{751} = \sigma_{10\cdot13\cdot2}(w_7)$

$w_{757} = \sigma_{13\cdot15}(w_7)$ $w_{758} = \sigma_{16\cdot4\cdot14}(w_6)$ $w_{761} = \sigma_{13\cdot11\cdot2}(w_7)$

$w_{766} = \sigma_{17\cdot1\cdot14}(w_4)$ $w_{769} = \sigma_{17\cdot2\cdot13}(w_4)$ $w_{773} = \sigma_{14\cdot13}(w_7)$

$w_{778} = \sigma_{14\cdot1\cdot16}(w_6)$ $w_{787} = \sigma_{14\cdot14}(w_7)$ $w_{794} = \sigma_{17\cdot3\cdot14}(w_4)$

$w_{797} = \sigma_{17\cdot11\cdot2}(w_4)$ $w_{802} = \sigma_{12\cdot14\cdot2}(w_7)$ $w_{809} = \sigma_{12\cdot12\cdot2}(w_8)$

$w_{811} = \sigma_{13\cdot13\cdot2}(w_7)$ $w_{818} = \sigma_{15\cdot2\cdot15}(w_7)$ $w_{821} = \sigma_{9\cdot1\cdot11}(w_{10})$

$w_{823} = \sigma_{11\cdot17\cdot1}(w_4)$ $w_{827} = \sigma_{14\cdot16}(w_7)$ $w_{829} = \sigma_{17\cdot13\cdot1}(w_4)$

$w_{838} = \sigma_{10\cdot4\cdot17}(w_5)$ $w_{839} = \sigma_{7\cdot5\cdot17}(w_7)$ $w_{842} = \sigma_{7\cdot4\cdot17}(w_6)$

$w_{853} = \sigma_{17\cdot10\cdot2}(w_4)$ $w_{857} = \sigma_{12\cdot17\cdot1}(w_4)$ $w_{859} = \sigma_{14\cdot14\cdot2}(w_7)$

$w_{862} = \sigma_{15\cdot3\cdot14}(w_7)$ $w_{863} = \sigma_{10\cdot11\cdot1}(w_8)$ $w_{866} = \sigma_{9\cdot4\cdot16}(w_8)$

$w_{877} = \sigma_{12\cdot17\cdot2}(w_5)$ $w_{878} = \sigma_{11\cdot14\cdot1}(w_8)$ $w_{881} = \sigma_{7\cdot5\cdot13}(w_{11})$

$w_{883} = \sigma_{16\cdot13\cdot1}(w_7)$ $w_{886} = \sigma_{13\cdot5\cdot13}(w_8)$ $w_{887} = \sigma_{11\cdot5\cdot16}(w_8)$

$w_{898} = \sigma_{13\cdot5\cdot17}(w_5)$ $w_{907} = \sigma_{6\cdot6\cdot8}(w_3)$ $w_{911} = \sigma_{14\cdot13\cdot2}(w_8)$

A. Square-free shuffles of finite square-free words

$$w_{914} = \sigma_{17 \cdot 12 \cdot 2}(w_5) \qquad w_{1031} = \sigma_{10 \cdot 10}(w_{11}) \qquad w_{1033} = \sigma_{7 \cdot 12 \cdot 2}(w_{12})$$

$$w_{1039} = \sigma_{6 \cdot 5 \cdot 17}(w_{10}) \qquad w_{1042} = \sigma_{9 \cdot 2 \cdot 17}(w_6) \qquad w_{1046} = \sigma_{15 \cdot 2 \cdot 10}(w_{10})$$

$$w_{1049} = \sigma_{17 \cdot 3 \cdot 14}(w_5) \qquad w_{1051} = \sigma_{6 \cdot 6 \cdot 10}(w_3) \qquad w_{1061} = \sigma_{10 \cdot 4 \cdot 14}(w_{10})$$

$$w_{1063} = \sigma_{14 \cdot 9 \cdot 1}(w_{11}) \qquad w_{1069} = \sigma_{8 \cdot 1 \cdot 14}(w_{11}) \qquad w_{1082} = \sigma_{17 \cdot 10}(w_6)$$

$$w_{1087} = \sigma_{17 \cdot 14 \cdot 1}(w_5) \qquad w_{1091} = \sigma_{10 \cdot 5 \cdot 17}(w_7) \qquad w_{1093} = \sigma_{13 \cdot 4 \cdot 13}(w_{10})$$

$$w_{1094} = \sigma_{16 \cdot 10}(w_{10}) \qquad w_{1097} = \sigma_{10 \cdot 17 \cdot 1}(w_5) \qquad w_{1103} = \sigma_{10 \cdot 10}(w_{12})$$

$$w_{1109} = \sigma_{17 \cdot 3 \cdot 17}(w_3) \qquad w_{1114} = \sigma_{17 \cdot 4 \cdot 17}(w_4) \qquad w_{1117} = \sigma_{12 \cdot 11 \cdot 2}(w_{11})$$

$$w_{1373} = \sigma_{6 \cdot 7 \cdot 12}(w_3) \qquad w_{1381} = \sigma_{11 \cdot 11 \cdot 1}(w_{14}) \qquad w_{1382} = \sigma_{6 \cdot 6 \cdot 15}(w_4)$$

$$w_{1399} = \sigma_{10 \cdot 4 \cdot 17}(w_8) \qquad w_{1402} = \sigma_{16 \cdot 13}(w_{12}) \qquad w_{1409} = \sigma_{9 \cdot 7 \cdot 7}(w_3)$$

$$w_{1418} = \sigma_{13 \cdot 13 \cdot 2}(w_{12}) \qquad w_{1423} = \sigma_{16 \cdot 14}(w_{11}) \qquad w_{1427} = \sigma_{6 \cdot 7 \cdot 13}(w_3)$$

$$w_{1429} = \sigma_{17 \cdot 13 \cdot 1}(w_7) \qquad w_{1433} = \sigma_{16 \cdot 2 \cdot 12}(w_{11}) \qquad w_{1438} = \sigma_{8 \cdot 5 \cdot 17}(w_{10})$$

$$w_{1439} = \sigma_{11 \cdot 13}(w_{14}) \qquad w_{1447} = \sigma_{6 \cdot 11 \cdot 8}(w_3) \qquad w_{1451} = \sigma_{16 \cdot 1 \cdot 12}(w_{11})$$

$$w_{1453} = \sigma_{17 \cdot 2 \cdot 14}(w_7) \qquad w_{1454} = \sigma_{6 \cdot 6 \cdot 14}(w_4) \qquad w_{1459} = \sigma_{7 \cdot 6 \cdot 14}(w_3)$$

$$w_{1466} = \sigma_{15 \cdot 3 \cdot 14}(w_{11}) \qquad w_{1471} = \sigma_{7 \cdot 17 \cdot 2}(w_{10}) \qquad w_{1478} = \sigma_{7 \cdot 17 \cdot 1}(w_{11})$$

$$w_{1481} = \sigma_{6 \cdot 8 \cdot 10}(w_3) \qquad w_{1483} = \sigma_{17 \cdot 11}(w_8) \qquad w_{1486} = \sigma_{17 \cdot 8}(w_{10})$$

$$w_{1487} = \sigma_{12 \cdot 4 \cdot 17}(w_8) \qquad w_{1489} = \sigma_{13 \cdot 1 \cdot 14}(w_{13}) \qquad w_{1493} = \sigma_{16 \cdot 3 \cdot 14}(w_{11})$$

$$w_{1733} = \sigma_{12 \cdot 17 \cdot 1}(w_8) \qquad w_{1741} = \sigma_{11 \cdot 6 \cdot 10}(w_3) \qquad w_{1747} = \sigma_{6 \cdot 8 \cdot 16}(w_3)$$

$$w_{1753} = \sigma_{11 \cdot 5 \cdot 10}(w_{19}) \qquad w_{1754} = \sigma_{14 \cdot 1 \cdot 16}(w_{14}) \qquad w_{1759} = \sigma_{13 \cdot 16 \cdot 2}(w_{14})$$

$$w_{1762} = \sigma_{6 \cdot 2 \cdot 10}(w_3) \qquad w_{1766} = \sigma_{15 \cdot 7 \cdot 7}(w_3) \qquad w_{1774} = \sigma_{7 \cdot 6 \cdot 14}(w_4)$$

$$w_{1777} = \sigma_{9 \cdot 17 \cdot 2}(w_{10}) \qquad w_{1783} = \sigma_{10 \cdot 1 \cdot 16}(w_{17}) \qquad w_{1787} = \sigma_{11 \cdot 2 \cdot 13}(w_{17})$$

$$w_{1789} = \sigma_{10 \cdot 12}(w_{19}) \qquad w_{1801} = \sigma_{13 \cdot 14}(w_{16}) \qquad w_{1811} = \sigma_{10 \cdot 13 \cdot 1}(w_{17})$$

$$w_{1814} = \sigma_{6 \cdot 11 \cdot 8}(w_4) \qquad w_{1822} = \sigma_{7 \cdot 7 \cdot 15}(w_3) \qquad w_{1823} = \sigma_{7 \cdot 12 \cdot 8}(w_3)$$

$$w_{1831} = \sigma_{11 \cdot 2 \cdot 16}(w_{16})$$

Code listings

"I think the brain is like a pro-gramme in the mind."

STEPHEN WILLIAM HAWKING

This chapter contains source code listings for the computer programs that were used in some of the proofs of this thesis to perform checks on a finite, but sometimes large set of words. They are implemented in Ruby[1] and were tested with Ruby versions $\geqslant 1.9$.

B.1 Code for Chapter 3

common.rb, a library of commonly used functions

```ruby
1  #iterates the thue morse morphism i times and returns the resulting word
2  def thue_morse(i)
3      tm_word = '0'
4      i.times {
5          tm_word.gsub!(/[01]/) { |x| ['01','10'][x.to_i] }
6      }
7      return tm_word
8  end
9
10 #iterates the hall morphism i times and returns the resulting word
11 def hall(i)
12     h_word = '0'
13     i.times {
14         h_word.gsub!(/[012]/) { |x| ['012','02','1'][x.to_i] }
15     }
16     return h_word
```

---

[1]An interpreter can be downloaded at http://www.ruby-lang.org

B. Code listings

```
17  end
18
19  #replaces letters in w with the given images
20  #usage: phi(w, image of 0, image of 1, image of 2, ...)
21  #(variable number of arguments)
22  def phi(w, *images)
23      w.gsub(/./) { |x|
24          if(('0'..'9').find_index(x) < images.size)
25              images[('0'..'9').find_index(x)]
26          else
27              x
28          end
29      }
30  end
31
32  #checks whether a bijective morphism exists that maps f to t
33  def morphism_exists?(f, t)
34      #lengths have to be equal
35      return false if(f.length != t.length)
36      mapping = Hash.new
37      0.upto(f.length-1) { |pos|
38          #case1: the letter at f[pos] isn't mapped already
39          if(!(mapping.key?(f[pos])))
40              #return false if something else is mapped to the targetletter already
41              #(it's not injective then)
42              return false if(mapping.has_value?(t[pos]))
43              #otherwise map f[pos] -> t[pos]
44              mapping[f[pos]] = t[pos]
45          #case2: the letter is mapped already. check if it's mapped consistently
46          else
47              return false if(mapping[f[pos]] != t[pos])
48          end
49      }
50      #if no inconsistency is found
51      return true
52  end
53
54  #factorizes w into 3 parts of equal length for w of length 3k
55  def factorize(w)
56      third = w.length/3
57      return w[0,third], w[third,third], w[-third, third]
58  end
59
60  #short function that checks if x1=x2 and x1 can be mapped to f by a bijective morphism
61  def pattern?(x1, x2, f)
62      return (x1 == x2 && morphism_exists?(x1, f))
63  end
```

Lemma 3.2

```ruby
#!/usr/bin/env ruby
# We check that the word obtained by applying the morphism alpha:
#    0 -> 02110, 1 -> 02210
# to the Thue-Morse word does not contain any factor of the form
#    xxx or xf(x)x
# for permutation f with 3*|x| < 51.
# Since the length of this factor is at most 50, it is contained in the
# image of a factor of length 11 of the Thue-Morse word.
# We can easily check that all factors of length 11 of the Thue-Morse word
# already occur in the prefix of it that is obtained by iterating the TM-morphism
# on 0 six times. So it suffices to look for those patterns in this prefix.
# If there is no occurrence of such a pattern, the program will quit without
# producing any output.

require_relative 'common'

#check if w is of the form xf(x)x
#we assume that |w|=3k for some integer k
def checkxfx(w)
    x1, f, x2 = factorize(w)
    pattern?(x1, x2, f)
end

#check if w is of the form xxx
#we assume that |w|=3k for some integer k
def checkxxx(w)
    x1, x2, x3 = factorize(w)
    return w == x1 + x1 + x1
end

#checks if w contains a factor of length < 51 of the form xxx or xf(x)x at any position.
#note that we only have to check factors whose lengths are a multiple of 3.
def check(w)
    #d = length of u
    (1..16).each { |d|
        #starting position
        (0..w.length - 3*d).each { |i|
            u = w[i..i+d-1]
            fu = w[i+d..i+2*d-1]
            gu = w[i+2*d..i+3*d-1]
            if checkxxx(u+fu+gu) || checkxfx(u+fu+gu)
                puts "w contains factor of form xxx or xf(x)x: #{u}|#{fu}|#{gu}"
            end
        }
    }
end

#generate the prefix of the Thue-Morse word
t6 = thue_morse(6)
#apply the morphism alpha
t_alpha = phi(t6, "02110", "02210")
```

B. Code listings

```
52 #check for occurrences of xxx and xf(x)x
53 check(t_alpha)
```

Lemma 3.3 (1)

```ruby
 1 #!/usr/bin/env ruby
 2 # We check that the word obtained by applying the morphism beta:
 3 #   0 -> 012013213, 1 -> 012031023
 4 # to the Thue-Morse word does not contain any factor of the form
 5 #   uf(u)g(u)
 6 # for permutations f, g with  6 < |u| < 29.
 7 # Since the length of this factor is at most 84, it is contained in the
 8 # image of a factor of length 11 of the Thue-Morse word.
 9 # We can easily check that all factors of length 11 of the Thue-Morse word
10 # already occur in the prefix of it that is obtained by iterating the TM-morphism
11 # on 0 six times. So it suffices to look for those patterns in the image of this prefix.
12 # If there is no occurrence of such a pattern, the program will quit without
13 # producing any output.
14
15 require_relative 'common'
16
17 #checks if w contains a factor of form uf(u)g(u) with 6 < |u| < 29 at any position.
18 def check(w)
19     #d = length of u
20     (7..28).each { |d|
21         #starting position
22         (0..w.length - 3*d).each { |i|
23             u = w[i..i+d-1]
24             fu = w[i+d..i+2*d-1]
25             gu = w[i+2*d..i+3*d-1]
26             if morphism_exists?(u,fu) && morphism_exists?(u,gu)
27                 puts "w contains factor of form uf(u)g(u): #{u}|#{fu}|#{gu}"
28             end
29         }
30     }
31 end
32
33 #generate the prefix of the Thue-Morse word
34 t6 = thue_morse(6)
35 #apply the morphism beta
36 t_beta = phi(t6, "012013213", "012031023")
37 #check for occurrences of uf(u)g(u)
38 check(t_beta)
```

Lemma 3.3 (2)

```ruby
#!/usr/bin/env ruby
# We search for all factors of the word obtained by applying the morphism beta:
#    0 -> 012013213, 1 -> 012031023
# to the Thue-Morse word that are of the form
#    uf(u)g(u)
# for morphic permutations f and g with
#    |{ u[t], f(u)[t], g(u)[t] }| <= 2 for all t <= |u|
# when |u| < 7.
# Since the length of this factor is at most 18, it is contained in the
# image of a factor of length 4 of the Thue-Morse word.
# We can easily check that all factors of length 4 of the Thue-Morse word
# already occur in the prefix of it that is obtained by iterating the TM-morphism
# on 0 four times. So it suffices to look for those patterns in the image of this prefix.
# The program prints all factors of the desired form.

require_relative 'common'

#returns true if there is a position l such that u[l], fi[l] and fj[l]
#are pairwise different, false otherwise
def has_pos_with_3_different?(u, fi, fj)
    0.upto(u.length-1) { |l|
        if(u[l] != fi[l]) && (fi[l] != fj[l]) && (fj[l] != u[l])
            return true
        end
    }
    return false
end

#looks for factors of the form uf(u)g(u) with no position with 3 different letters in w
def check(w)
    occurrences = Array.new
    #d = length of u
    (1..6).each { |d|
        #starting position
        (0..w.length - 3*d).each { |i|
            u = w[i..i+d-1]
            fiu = w[i+d..i+2*d-1]
            fju = w[i+2*d..i+3*d-1]
            if morphism_exists?(u,fiu) && morphism_exists?(u,fju)
                if !has_pos_with_3_different?(u, fiu, fju)
                    occurrences << (u + fiu + fju)
                end
            end
        }
    }
    #remove duplicates and sort lexicographically (as listed in the proof)
    occurrences.uniq!
    occurrences.sort!
    occurrences.each { |v|
        u, fi, fj = factorize(v)
        puts "w contains factor uf(u)g(u) w/o pos with 3 diff letters: #{u}|#{fi}|#{fj}"
```

```
52     }
53 end
54
55 #generate the prefix of the Thue-Morse word
56 t4 = thue_morse(4)
57 #apply the morphism beta
58 t_beta = phi(t4, "012013213", "012031023")
59 #check for occurrences of the pattern
60 check(t_beta)
```

Lemma 3.4

```
 1 #!/usr/bin/env ruby
 2 # We check that there is no infinite word on an alphabet of 3 letters that avoids
 3 # the patterns xxx, xxf(x) and xf(x)x simultaneously.
 4 # Furthermore, we check that there is no infinite word on an alphabet of 3 letters
 5 # that avoids xxx, xf(x)f(x) and xf(x)x simultaneously.
 6 # We do this by trying to construct such words using a backtracking algorithm.
 7 # The program outputs the constructed prefixes and the occurrences where one of the
 8 # patterns appears.
 9
10 require_relative 'common'
11
12 #check if w is of the form xf(x)x, we assume that |w|=3k for some integer k
13 def checkxfx(w)
14     x1, f, x2 = factorize(w)
15     pattern?(x1, x2, f)
16 end
17
18 #check if w is of the form xxf(x), we assume that |w|=3k for some integer k
19 def checkxxf(w)
20     x1, x2, f = factorize(w)
21     pattern?(x1, x2, f)
22 end
23
24 #check if w is of the form xf(x)f(x), we assume that |w|=3k for some integer k
25 def checkxff(w)
26     x, f1, f2 = factorize(w)
27     pattern?(f1, f2, x)
28 end
29
30 #check if w is of the form xxx, we assume that |w|=3k for some integer k
31 def checkxxx(w)
32     x1, x2, x3 = factorize(w)
33     return w == x1 * 3
34 end
35
36 #checks if the word w contains a factor of the form xxx, xxf(x) or xf(x)x.
37 def checkxxx_xxf_xfx(w)
```

```
38    #factorlength
39    (1..(w.length/3).ceil).each { |d|
40        #starting position
41        (0..w.length - 3*d).each { |i|
42            u = w[i..i+d-1]
43            fu = w[i+d..i+2*d-1]
44            gu = w[i+2*d..i+3*d-1]
45            if checkxxx(u+fu+gu)
46                puts "#{w} contains factor of form xxx: #{u}|#{fu}|#{gu}"
47                return true
48            end
49            if checkxxf(u+fu+gu)
50                puts "#{w} contains factor of form xxf(x): #{u}|#{fu}|#{gu}"
51                return true
52            end
53            if checkxfx(u+fu+gu)
54                puts "#{w} contains factor of form xf(x)x: #{u}|#{fu}|#{gu}"
55                return true
56            end
57        }
58    }
59    return false
60 end
61
62 #checks if the word w contains a factor of the form xxx, xf(x)f(x) or xf(x)x.
63 def checkxxx_xff_xfx(w)
64    #factorlength
65    (1..(w.length/3).ceil).each { |d|
66        #starting position
67        (0..w.length - 3*d).each { |i|
68            u = w[i..i+d-1]
69            fu = w[i+d..i+2*d-1]
70            gu = w[i+2*d..i+3*d-1]
71            if checkxxx(u+fu+gu)
72                puts "#{w} contains factor of form xxx: #{u}|#{fu}|#{gu}"
73                return true
74            end
75            if checkxff(u+fu+gu)
76                puts "#{w} contains factor of form xf(x)f(x): #{u}|#{fu}|#{gu}"
77                return true
78            end
79            if checkxfx(u+fu+gu)
80                puts "#{w} contains factor of form xf(x)x: #{u}|#{fu}|#{gu}"
81                return true
82            end
83        }
84    }
85    return false
86 end
87
88 #try to produce an infinite word that avoids xxx, xxf(x) and xf(x)x by backtracking
89 puts "Trying to generate a word that avoids xxx, xxf(x) and xf(x)x:"
```

B. Code listings

```ruby
 90 def backtrack1(w)
 91    return if checkxxx_xxf_xfx(w)
 92    ["0","1","2"].each { |x| backtrack1(w+x) }
 93 end
 94 #without loss of generality the word starts with 0
 95 backtrack1("0")
 96
 97 #try to produce an infinite word that avoids xxx, xf(x)f(x) and xf(x)x by backtracking
 98 puts "Trying to generate a word that avoids xxx, xf(x)f(x) and xf(x)x:"
 99 def backtrack2(w)
100    return if checkxxx_xff_xfx(w)
101    ["0","1","2"].each { |x| backtrack2(w+x) }
102 end
103 #without loss of generality the word starts with 0
104 backtrack2("0")
```

Lemma 3.13

```ruby
 1 #!/usr/bin/env ruby
 2 # We check that the word obtained by applying the morphism alpha:
 3 #    0 -> 0011022, 1 -> 1100122
 4 # to the Thue-Morse word does not contain any factor of the form
 5 #    xxx or xf(x)x
 6 # for an antimorphic permutation f with |x| < 22.
 7 # Since the length of this factor is at most 63, it is contained in the
 8 # image of a factor of length 10 of the Thue-Morse word.
 9 # We can easily check that all factors of length 10 of the Thue-Morse word
10 # already occur in the prefix of it that is obtained by iterating the TM-morphism
11 # on 0 six times. So it suffices to look for those patterns in this prefix.
12 # If there is no occurrence of such a pattern, the program will quit without
13 # producing any output.
14
15 require_relative 'common'
16
17 #check if w is of the form xf(x)x, we assume that |w|=3k for some integer k
18 def checkxfx(w)
19    x1, f, x2 = factorize(w)
20    pattern?(x1, x2, f.reverse)
21 end
22
23 #check if w is of the form xx^Rx, we assume that |w|=3k for some integer k
24 def checkxxx(w)
25    x1, x2, x3 = factorize(w)
26    return w == x1 + x1.reverse + x1
27 end
28
29 #checks if the word w contains a factor of length < 66 of the form xx^Rx or xf(x)x.
30 #note that we only have to check factors whose lengths are a multiple of 3.
31 def check(w)
```

136

```
32    #d = length of u
33    (1..21).each { |d|
34        #starting position
35        (0..w.length - 3*d).each { |i|
36            u = w[i..i+d-1]
37            fu = w[i+d..i+2*d-1]
38            gu = w[i+2*d..i+3*d-1]
39            if checkxxx(u+fu+gu) || checkxfx(u+fu+gu)
40                puts "w contains factor of form xx^Rx or xf(x)x: #{u}|#{fu}|#{gu}"
41            end
42        }
43    }
44 end
45
46 #generate the prefix of the Thue-Morse word
47 t6 = thue_morse(6)
48 #apply the morphism alpha
49 t_alpha = phi(t6, "0011022", "1100122")
50 #check for occurrences of xxx and xf(x)x
51 check(t_alpha)
```

Lemma 3.17 (1)

```
1 #!/usr/bin/env ruby
2 # We check that the word obtained by applying the morphism zeta:
3 #    0 -> 012034, 1 -> 120324
4 # to the Thue-Morse word does not contain any factor of the form
5 #    uf(u)g(u)
6 # for permutations f (morphic) and g (antimorphic) |u| = 6.
7 # Since the length of this factor is 18 it is contained in the
8 # image of a factor of length 4 of the Thue-Morse word.
9 # We can easily check that all factors of length 4 of the Thue-Morse word
10 # already occur in the prefix of it that is obtained by iterating the TM-morphism
11 # on 0 four times. So it suffices to look for those patterns in the image of this prefix.
12 # If there is no occurrence of such a pattern, the program will quit without
13 # producing any output.
14
15 require_relative 'common'
16
17 #checks if the word w contains a factor of form uf(u)g(u) withg 6 < |u| < 9.
18 def check(w)
19     #d = length of u
20     d = 6
21     #starting position
22     (0..w.length - 3*d).each { |i|
23         u = w[i..i+d-1]
24         fu = w[i+d..i+2*d-1]
25         gu = w[i+2*d..i+3*d-1]
26         if morphism_exists?(u,fu) && morphism_exists?(u,gu.reverse)
```

B. Code listings

```
27              puts "w contains factor of form uf(u)g(u): #{u}|#{fu}|#{gu}"
28         end
29     }
30 end
31
32 #generate the prefix of the Thue-Morse word
33 t4 = thue_morse(4)
34 #apply the morphism zeta
35 t_zeta = phi(t4, "012034", "120324")
36 #check for occurrences of uf(u)g(u)
37 check(t_zeta)
```

Lemma 3.17 (2)

```
 1 #!/usr/bin/env ruby
 2 # We search for all factors of the word obtained by applying the morphism zeta:
 3 #    0 -> 012034, 1 -> 120324
 4 # to the Thue-Morse word that are of the form
 5 #    uf(u)g(u)
 6 # for permutations f (morphic) and g (antimorphic) with
 7 #    |{ u[t], f(u)[t], g(u)^R[t] }| <= 2 for all t <= |u|
 8 # when |u| < 7.
 9 # Since the length of this factor is at most 18, it is contained in the
10 # image of a factor of length 4 of the Thue-Morse word.
11 # We can easily check that all factors of length 4 of the Thue-Morse word
12 # already occur in the prefix of it that is obtained by iterating the TM-morphism
13 # on 0 four times. So it suffices to look for those patterns in the image of this prefix.
14 # The program prints all factors of the desired form.
15
16 require_relative 'common'
17
18 #returns true if there is a position l such that u[l], fi[l] and fj[l]
19 #are pairwise different, false otherwise
20 def has_pos_with_3_different?(u, fi, fj)
21     0.upto(u.length-1) { |l|
22         if(u[l] != fi[l]) && (fi[l] != fj[l]) && (fj[l] != u[l])
23             return true
24         end
25     }
26     return false
27 end
28
29 #looks for factors of the form uf(u)g(u) with no position with 3 different letters in w
30 def check(w)
31     occurrences = Array.new
32     #d = length of u
33     (1..6).each { |d|
34         #starting position
35         (0..w.length - 3*d).each { |i|
```

```ruby
                u = w[i..i+d-1]
                fiu = w[i+d..i+2*d-1]
                fju = w[i+2*d..i+3*d-1]
                if morphism_exists?(u,fiu) && morphism_exists?(u,fju.reverse)
                    if !has_pos_with_3_different?(u, fiu, fju.reverse)
                        occurrences << (u + fiu + fju)
                    end
                end
            }
        }
        #remove doubles and sort lexicographically
        occurrences.uniq!
        occurrences.sort!
        occurrences.each { |v|
            u, fi, fj = factorize(v)
            puts "w contains factor uf(u)g(u) w/o pos with 3 diff letters: #{u}|#{fi}|#{fj}"
        }
end

#generate the prefix of the Thue-Morse word
t4 = thue_morse(4)
#apply the morphism zeta
t_zeta = phi(t4, "012034", "120324")
#check for occurrences of the pattern
check(t_zeta)
```

Lemma 3.18 (1)

```ruby
#!/usr/bin/env ruby
# We check that the word obtained by applying the morphism beta:
#    0 -> 012013213, 1 -> 012031023
# to the Thue-Morse word does not contain any factor of the form
#    uf(u)g(u)
# for permutations f (antimorphic) and g (morphic) with  6 < |u| < 12.
# Since the length of this factor is at most 33, it is contained in the
# image of a factor of length 5 of the Thue-Morse word.
# We can easily check that all factors of length 5 of the Thue-Morse word
# already occur in the prefix of it that is obtained by iterating the TM-morphism
# on 0 five times. So it suffices to look for those patterns in the image of this prefix.
# If there is no occurrence of such a pattern, the program will quit without
# producing any output.

require_relative 'common'

#checks if the word w contains a factor of form uf(u)g(u) withg 6 < |u| < 9.
def check(w)
    #d = length of u
    (7..11).each { |d|
        #starting position
```

B. Code listings

```ruby
22          (0..w.length - 3*d).each { |i|
23              u = w[i..i+d-1]
24              fu = w[i+d..i+2*d-1]
25              gu = w[i+2*d..i+3*d-1]
26              if morphism_exists?(u,fu.reverse) && morphism_exists?(u,gu)
27                  puts "w contains factor of form uf(u)g(u): #{u}|#{fu}|#{gu}"
28              end
29          }
30      }
31 end
32
33 #generate the prefix of the Thue-Morse word
34 t5 = thue_morse(5)
35 #apply the morphism beta
36 t_beta = phi(t5, "012013213", "012031023")
37 #check for occurrences of uf(u)g(u)
38 check(t_beta)
```

Lemma 3.18 (2)

```ruby
1  #!/usr/bin/env ruby
2  # We check that the word obtained by applying the morphism eta:
3  #   0 -> 01234012431024301234012431023410243012431 0234,
4  #   1 -> 012340124310243012340123401243012341024310234
5  # to the Thue-Morse word does not contain any factor of the form
6  #   uf(u)g(u)
7  # for permutations f (antimorphic) and g (morphic) with 10 < |u| < 31.
8  # As mentioned in the proof, we have to check in the image of the word that is
9  # obtained by iterating the Thue-Morse morphism on 0 four times, since that word
10 # already contains all factors of length 3 that occur in the Thue-Morse word.
11 # If there is no occurrence of such a pattern, the program will quit without
12 # producing any output.
13
14 require_relative 'common'
15
16 #checks if the word w contains a factor of form uf(u)g(u) withg 6 < |u| < 9.
17 def check(w)
18     #d = length of u
19     (11..30).each { |d|
20         #starting position
21         (0..w.length - 3*d).each { |i|
22             u = w[i..i+d-1]
23             fu = w[i+d..i+2*d-1]
24             gu = w[i+2*d..i+3*d-1]
25             if morphism_exists?(u,fu.reverse) && morphism_exists?(u,gu)
26                 puts "w contains factor of form uf(u)g(u): #{u}|#{fu}|#{gu}"
27             end
28         }
29     }
```

```
30 end
31
32 #generate the prefix of the Thue-Morse word
33 t4 = thue_morse(4)
34 #apply the morphism eta
35 t_eta = phi(t4, "01234012431024301234012431023410243012431 0234", \
36                "01234012431024301234102340124301234102431 0234")
37 #check for occurrences of uf(u)g(u)
38 check(t_eta)
```

Lemma 3.18 (3)

```
 1 #!/usr/bin/env ruby
 2 # We search for all factors of the word obtained by applying the morphism eta:
 3 #    0 -> 01234012431024301234012431023410243012431 0234,
 4 #    1 -> 01234012431024301234102340124301234102431 0234
 5 # to the Thue-Morse word that are of the form
 6 #    uf(u)g(u)
 7 # for permutations f (morphic) and g (antimorphic) with
 8 #    |{ u[t], f(u)[t], g(u)^R[t] }| <= 2 for all t <= |u|
 9 # when |u| < 11.
10 # As mentioned in the paper, we have to search in the image of the word that is
11 # obtained by iterating the Thue-Morse morphism on 0 four times, since that word
12 # already contains all factors of length 3 that occur in the Thue-Morse word.
13 # The program prints all factors of the desired form.
14
15 require_relative 'common'
16
17 #returns true if there is a position l such that u[l], fi[l] and fj[l]
18 #are pairwise different, false otherwise
19 def has_pos_with_3_different?(u, fi, fj)
20     0.upto(u.length-1) { |l|
21         if(u[l] != fi[l]) && (fi[l] != fj[l]) && (fj[l] != u[l])
22             return true
23         end
24     }
25     return false
26 end
27
28 #looks for factors of the form uf(u)g(u) with no position with 3 different letters in w
29 def check(w)
30     occurrences = Array.new
31     #d = length of u
32     (1..10).each { |d|
33         #starting position
34         (0..w.length - 3*d).each { |i|
35             u = w[i..i+d-1]
36             fiu = w[i+d..i+2*d-1]
37             fju = w[i+2*d..i+3*d-1]
```

```
38              if morphism_exists?(u,fiu.reverse) && morphism_exists?(u,fju)
39                if !has_pos_with_3_different?(u, fiu.reverse, fju)
40                    occurrences << (u + fiu + fju)
41                end
42              end
43          }
44      }
45      #remove duplicates and sort lexicographically
46      occurrences.uniq!
47      occurrences.sort!
48      occurrences.each { |v|
49          u, fi, fj = factorize(v)
50          puts "w contains factor uf(u)g(u) w/o pos with 3 diff letters: #{u}|#{fi}|#{fj}"
51      }
52 end
53
54 #generate the prefix of the Thue-Morse word
55 t4 = thue_morse(4)
56 #apply the morphism eta
57 t_eta = phi(t4, "0123401243102430123401243102341024301243102 34", \
58                 "0123401243102430123401243012430123410243102 34")
59 #check for occurrences of the pattern
60 check(t_eta)
```

B.2 Code for Chapter 5

Lemma 5.2

```
1 #!/usr/bin/env ruby
2 # We check that all words in the image of every square-free word of length eight
3 # under the substitution g defined by
4 #    0 -> {01202120102120210, 012021020102120210},
5 #    1 -> {12010201210201021, 120102101210201021},
6 #    2 -> {20121012021012102, 201210212021012102}
7 # is square-free. The program produces no output, if all words in the image are
8 # square-free.
9
10 #checks if the word w is square-free
11 def is_squarefree?(w)
12     if (w =~ /(.+)\1/)
13         return false
14     else
15         return true
16     end
17 end
18
19 #create all square-free words of length eight over the alphabet {a,b,c,A,B,C}.
```

```ruby
20 #a will be mapped to the length 17 image of 0, A to the length 18 image of 0
21 #b will be mapped to the length 17 image of 1, B to the length 18 image of 1
22 #c will be mapped to the length 17 image of 2, C to the length 18 image of 2
23 $ts = Array.new
24 def bt(w)
25     return if !is_squarefree?(w.downcase)
26     if w.length == 8
27         $ts << w
28     else
29         ["a","b","c","A","B","C"].each { |x| bt(w+x) }
30     end
31 end
32 bt("")
33
34 #the substitution
35 def subst(w)
36     r = w.dup
37     r.gsub!(/[abcABC]/) { |x|
38         if(x == 'a')
39             "01202120102120210"
40         elsif(x == 'b')
41             "12010201210201021"
42         elsif(x == 'c')
43             "20121012021012102"
44         elsif(x == 'A')
45             "012021020102120210"
46         elsif(x == 'B')
47             "120102101210201021"
48         else
49             "201210212021012102"
50         end
51     }
52     return r
53 end
54
55 #try all words in the images for square-freeness
56 $ts.each{ |w|
57     puts "#{w} : #{is_squarefree?(subst(w))}" if ! is_squarefree?(subst(w))
58 }
```

Bibliography

[1]   J.-P. Allouche and J. Shallit. Automatic sequences: theory, applications, generalizations. Cambridge University Press, 2003.

[2]   K. I. Appel and F. M. Djorup. "On the equation $z_1{}^n z_2{}^n \cdots z_k{}^n = y^n$ in a free semigroup". In: *Trans. Amer. Math. Soc.* **134** (1968), 461–470.

[3]   D. R. Bean, A. Ehrenfeucht, and G. F. McNulty. "Avoidable patterns in strings of symbols". In: *Pacific J. Math.* **85** (2) (1979), 261–294.

[4]   J. P. Bell and T. L. Goh. "Exponential lower bounds for the number of words of uniform length avoiding a pattern". In: *Inform. and Comput.* **205** (9) (2007), 1295–1306.

[5]   J. Bernoulli. "Sur une nouvelle espece de calcul". In: *Recueil pour les astronomes* **1** (1771), 255–284.

[6]   J. Berstel. "Axel Thue's papers on repetitions in words: a translation". In: *Publications du Laboratoire de Combinatoire et d'Informatique Mathématique 20, Université du Québec à Montréal* (1995).

[7]   J. Berstel. "Axel Thue's work on repetitions in words". In: *Séries formelles et combinatoire algébrique*. Ed. by P. Leroux and C. Reutenauer. Vol. 11. Publications du Laboratoire de Combinatoire et d'Informatique Mathématique. Université du Québec à Montréal, 1992, 65–80.

[8]   J. Berstel. "Sur les mots sans carré définis par un morphisme". In: *Automata, Languages and Programming, 6th Colloquium, Graz, Austria, July 16-20, 1979, Proceedings*. Ed. by H. A. Maurer. Vol. 71. Lecture Notes in Computer Science. Springer, 1979, 16–25.

[9]   J. Berstel and D. Perrin. "The origins of combinatorics on words". In: *European J. Combin.* **28** (3) (2007), 996–1022.

[10] B. Bischoff, J. D. Currie, and D. Nowotka. "Unary patterns with involution". In: *Internat. J. Found. Comput. Sci.* **23** (8) (2012), 1641–1652.

[11] F. Blanchet-Sadri and B. Woodhouse. "Strict bounds for pattern avoidance". In: *Theoret. Comput. Sci.* **506** (2013), 17–28.

[12] A. Blondin Massé, S. Gaboury, and S. Hallé. "Pseudoperiodic words". In: *Developments in Language Theory - 16th International Conference, DLT 2012, Taipei, Taiwan, August 14-17, 2012. Proceedings.* Ed. by H.-C. Yen and O. H. Ibarra. Vol. 7410. Lecture Notes in Computer Science. Springer, 2012, 308–319.

[13] F.-J. Brandenburg. "Uniformly growing kth power-free homomorphisms". In: *Theoret. Comput. Sci.* **23** (1) (1983), 69–82.

[14] B. Brešar, J. Grytczuk, S. Klavžar, S. Niwczyk, and I. Peterin. "Nonrepetitive colorings of trees". In: *Discrete Math.* **307** (2) (2007), 163–172.

[15] S. Buss and M. Soltys. "Unshuffling a square is np-hard". In: *J. Comput. System Sci.* **80** (4) (2014), 766–776.

[16] A. Carpi. "On the size of a square-free morphism on a three-letter alphabet". In: *Inform. Process. Lett.* **16** (5) (1983), 231–235.

[17] J. Cassaigne, J. D. Currie, L. Schaeffer, and J. Shallit. "Avoiding three consecutive blocks of the same size and same sum". In: *J. ACM* **61** (2) (2014), 10:1–10:17.

[18] E. Charlier, T. Kamae, S. Puzynina, and L. Q. Zamboni. "Self-shuffling words". In: *Automata, Languages, and Programming - 40th International Colloquium, ICALP 2013, Riga, Latvia, July 8-12, 2013, Proceedings, Part II.* Ed. by F. V. Fomin, R. Freivalds, M. Z. Kwiatkowska, and D. Peleg. Vol. 7966. Lecture Notes in Computer Science. Springer, 2013, 113–124.

[19] E. Chiniforooshan, L. Kari, and Z. Xu. "Pseudopower avoidance". In: *Fund. Inform.* **114** (1) (2012), 55–72.

[20] D. D. Chu and H. S. Town. "Another proof on a theorem of Lyndon and Schützenberger in a free monoid". In: *Soochow J. Math.* **4** (1978), 143–146.

[21] M. Crochemore. "Sharp characterizations of squarefree morphisms". In: *Theoret. Comput. Sci.* **18** (2) (1982), 221–226.

[22] M. Crochemore, J. D. Currie, G. Kucherov, and D. Nowotka. "Combinatorics and algorithmics of strings (Dagstuhl seminar 14111)". In: *Dagstuhl Reports* **4** (3) (2014), 28–46.

[23]   M. Crochemore, C. Hancart, and T. Lecroq. Algorithms on strings. Cambridge University Press, 2007.

[24]   J. D. Currie. "Pattern avoidance: themes and variations". In: *Theoret. Comput. Sci.* **339** (1) (2005), 7–18.

[25]   J. D. Currie. "Infinite ternary square-free words concatenated from permutations of a single word". In: *Theoret. Comput. Sci.* **482** (2013), 1–8.

[26]   J. D. Currie. "Palindrome positions in ternary square-free words". In: *Theoret. Comput. Sci.* **396** (1–3) (2008), 254–257.

[27]   J. D. Currie. "Shuffle squares are avoidable". Unpublished manuscript. 2014.

[28]   J. D. Currie and N. Rampersad. "Cubefree words with many squares". In: *Discrete Math. Theor. Comput. Sci.* **12** (3) (2010), 29–34.

[29]   J. D. Currie and K. Saari. "Square-free words with square-free self-shuffles". In: *Electron. J. Combin.* **21** (1) (2014), P1.9.

[30]   E. Czeizler, E. Czeizler, L. Kari, and S. Seki. "An extension of the Lyndon Schützenberger result to pseudoperiodic words". In: *Developments in Language Theory, 13th International Conference, DLT 2009, Stuttgart, Germany, June 30 - July 3, 2009. Proceedings.* Ed. by V. Diekert and D. Nowotka. Vol. 5583. Lecture Notes in Computer Science. Springer, 2009, 183–194.

[31]   E. Czeizler, E. Czeizler, L. Kari, and S. Seki. "An extension of the Lyndon-Schützenberger result to pseudoperiodic words". In: *Inform. and Comput.* **209** (2011), 717–730.

[32]   E. Czeizler, L. Kari, and S. Seki. "On a special class of primitive words". In: *Theoret. Comput. Sci.* **411** (3) (2010), 617–630.

[33]   P. Dömösi and G. Horváth. "Alternative proof of the Lyndon-Schützenberger theorem". In: *Theoret. Comput. Sci.* **366** (3) (2006), 194–198.

[34]   P. Erdős. "Some unsolved problems." In: *Michigan Math. J.* **4** (3) (1957), 291–300.

[35]   A. Evdokimov. "Strongly asymmetric sequences generated by a finite number of symbols". In: *Dokl. Akad. Nauk.* **179** (1968), 1268–1271.

[36]   N. J. Fine and H. S. Wilf. "Uniqueness theorems for periodic functions". In: *Proc. Amer. Math. Soc.* **16** (1965), 109–114.

[37]   J. S. Frame, G. d. B. Robinson, and R. M. Thrall. "The hook graphs of the symmetric group". In: *Canad. J. Math.* **6** (1954), 316–324.

[38]   C. F. Gauß. Werke. Vol. XIII. Teubner, Leipzig, 1900.

[39]   P. Gawrychowski, F. Manea, R. Mercaş, D. Nowotka, and C. Tiseanu. "Finding pseudo-repetitions". In: *30th International Symposium on Theoretical Aspects of Computer Science, STACS 2013, February 27 - March 2, 2013, Kiel, Germany*. Ed. by N. Portier and T. Wilke. Vol. 20. LIPIcs. Schloss Dagstuhl - Leibniz-Zentrum für Informatik, 2013, 257–268.

[40]   P. Gawrychowski, F. Manea, and D. Nowotka. "Discovering hidden repetitions in words". In: *The Nature of Computation. Logic, Algorithms, Applications - 9th Conference on Computability in Europe, CiE 2013, Milan, Italy, July 1-5, 2013. Proceedings*. Ed. by P. Bonizzoni, V. Brattka, and B. Löwe. Vol. 7921. Lecture Notes in Computer Science. Springer, 2013, 210–219.

[41]   P. Gawrychowski, F. Manea, and D. Nowotka. "Testing generalised freeness of words". In: *31st International Symposium on Theoretical Aspects of Computer Science (STACS), STACS 2014, March 5-8, 2014, Lyon, France*. Ed. by E. W. Mayr and N. Portier. Vol. 25. LIPIcs. Schloss Dagstuhl - Leibniz-Zentrum für Informatik, 2014, 337–349.

[42]   R. L. Graham, D. E. Knuth, and O. Patashnik. Concrete Mathematics: A Foundation for Computer Science. 2nd. Addison-Wesley Longman Publishing Co., Inc., 1994.

[43]   G. Guégan and P. Ochem. "Nonconstructive methods for nonrepetitive problems". Preprint. 2014.

[44]   M. Hall Jr. "'Generators and relations in groups—The Burnside problem'". In: *Lectures on Modern Mathematics, Vol. II*. New York: Wiley, 1964, 42–92.

[45]   T. Harju. "A note on square-free shuffles of words". In: *Combinatorics on Words - 9th International Conference, WORDS 2013, Turku, Finland, September 16-20. Proceedings*. Ed. by J. Karhumäki, A. Lepistö, and L. Q. Zamboni. Vol. 8079. Lecture Notes in Computer Science. Springer, 2013, 154–160.

[46]   T. Harju and J. Karhumäki. "Many aspects of defect theorems". In: *Theoret. Comput. Sci.* **324** (1) (2004), 35–54.

[47]   T. Harju and M. Müller. "A note on short palindromes in square-free words". Submitted. 2013.

[48]   T. Harju and M. Müller. "Square-free shuffles of words". In: *CoRR abs/1309.2137* (2013).

[49]   T. Harju and D. Nowotka. "On the equation $x^k = z_1^{k_1} z_2^{k_2} \cdots z_n^{k_n}$ in a free semigroup". In: *Theoret. Comput. Sci.* **330** (1) (2005), 117–121.

[50]   T. Harju and D. Nowotka. "The Equation $x^i = y^j z^k$ in a Free Semigroup". In: *Semigroup Forum* **68** (3) (2004), 488–490.

[51]   D. Henshall, N. Rampersad, and J. Shallit. "Shuffling and unshuffling". In: *Bull. Eur. Assoc. Theor. Comput. Sci. EATCS* **107** (2012), 131–142.

[52]   M. Huova, J. Karhumäki, and A. Saarela. "Problems in between words and abelian words: k-abelian avoidability". In: *Theoret. Comput. Sci.* **454** (2012), 172–177.

[53]   J. Karhumäki and J. Shallit. "Polynomial versus exponential growth in repetition-free binary words". In: *J. Combin. Theory Ser. A* **105** (2) (2004), 335–347.

[54]   L. Kari and K. Mahalingam. "Involutively bordered words". In: *Internat. J. Found. Comput. Sci.* **18** (5) (2007), 1089–1106.

[55]   L. Kari and K. Mahalingam. "Watson-crick conjugate and commutative words". In: *DNA Computing, 13th International Meeting on DNA Computing, DNA13, Memphis, TN, USA, June 4-8, 2007, Revised Selected Papers.* Ed. by M. H. Garzon and H. Yan. Vol. 4848. Lecture Notes in Computer Science. Springer, 2007, 273–283.

[56]   L. Kari, B. Masson, and S. Seki. "Properties of pseudo-primitive words and their applications". In: *Internat. J. Found. Comput. Sci.* **22** (2) (2011), 447–471.

[57]   L. Kari and S. Seki. "An improved bound for an extension of Fine and Wilf's theorem and its optimality". In: *Fund. Inform.* **101** (3) (2010), 215–236.

Bibliography

[58] V. Keränen. "Abelian squares are avoidable on 4 letters". In: *Automata, Languages and Programming, 19th International Colloquium, ICALP92, Vienna, Austria, July 13-17, 1992, Proceedings*. Ed. by W. Kuich. Vol. 623. Lecture Notes in Computer Science. Springer, 1992, 41–52.

[59] D. E. Knuth. The art of computer programming, volume 3: sorting and searching. Addison-Wesley Professional, 1998.

[60] D. König. "Über eine Schlussweise aus dem Endlichen ins Unendliche". In: *Acta Sci. Math. (Szeged)* **3** (1927), 121–130.

[61] A. Lentin. "Sur l'équation $a^m = b^n c^p d^q$ dans un monoïde libre". In: *C. R. Math. Acad. Sci. Paris* **260** (1965), 3242–3244.

[62] J. Loftus, J. Shallit, and M.-w. Wang. "New problems of pattern avoidance". In: *Developments in Language Theory, Foundations, Applications, and Perspectives, Aachen, Germany, 6-9 July 1999*. Ed. by G. Rozenberg and W. Thomas. World Scientific, 1999, 185–199.

[63] M. Lothaire. Algebraic combinatorics on words. Cambridge University Press, 2002.

[64] M. Lothaire. Applied combinatorics on words. Cambridge University Press, 2005.

[65] M. Lothaire. Combinatorics on words. Cambridge University Press, 1997.

[66] R. C. Lyndon and M.-P. Schützenberger. "The equation $a^m = b^n c^p$ in a free group". In: *Michigan Math. J.* **9** (4) (1962), 289–298.

[67] G. S. Makanin. "The problem of solvability of equations in a free semi-group". In: *Sb. Math.* **32** (2) (1977), 129–198.

[68] F. Manea, R. Mercaş, and D. Nowotka. "Fine and Wilf's theorem and pseudo-repetitions". In: *Mathematical Foundations of Computer Science 2012 - 37th International Symposium, MFCS 2012, Bratislava, Slovakia, August 27-31, 2012. Proceedings*. Ed. by B. Rovan, V. Sassone, and P. Widmayer. Vol. 7464. Lecture Notes in Computer Science. Springer, 2012, 668–680.

[69]   F. Manea, M. Müller, and D. Nowotka. "On the pseudoperiodic extension of $u^\ell = v^m w^n$". In: *IARCS Annual Conference on Foundations of Software Technology and Theoretical Computer Science, FSTTCS 2013, December 12-14, 2013, Guwahati, India.* Ed. by A. Seth and N. K. Vishnoi. Vol. 24. LIPIcs. Schloss Dagstuhl - Leibniz-Zentrum für Informatik, 2013, 475–486.

[70]   F. Manea, M. Müller, and D. Nowotka. "The avoidability of cubes under permutations". In: *Developments in Language Theory - 16th International Conference, DLT 2012, Taipei, Taiwan, August 14-17, 2012. Proceedings.* Ed. by H.-C. Yen and O. H. Ibarra. Vol. 7410. Lecture Notes in Computer Science. Springer, 2012, 416–427.

[71]   F. Manea, M. Müller, D. Nowotka, and S. Seki. "Generalised Lyndon-Schützenberger equations". In: *Mathematical Foundations of Computer Science 2014 - 39th International Symposium, MFCS 2014, Budapest, Hungary, August 25-29, 2014. Proceedings, Part I.* Ed. by E. Csuhaj-Varjú, M. Dietzfelbinger, and Z. Ésik. Vol. 8634. Lecture Notes in Computer Science. Springer, 2014, 402–413.

[72]   J. Miller. "Two notes on subshifts". In: *Proc. Amer. Math. Soc.* **140** (5) (2012), 1617–1622.

[73]   M. Müller, S. Puzynina, and M. Rao. "Infinite square-free self-shuffling words". In: *CoRR abs/1401.6536* (2014).

[74]   P. A. B. Pleasants. "Non-repetitive sequences". In: *Math. Proc. Cambridge Philos. Soc.* Vol. 68. 02. Cambridge University Press. 1970, 267–274.

[75]   H. Prodinger and F. J. Urbanek. "Infinite 0-1-sequences without long adjacent identical blocks". In: *Discrete Math.* **28** (1979), 277–289.

[76]   N. Rampersad and J. Shallit. "Words avoiding reversed subwords". In: *J. Combin. Math. Combin. Comput.* **54** (2005), 157–164.

[77]   N. Rampersad. "Further applications of a power series method for pattern avoidance". In: *Electron. J. Combin.* **18** (1) (2011).

[78]   N. Rampersad. "Non-constructive methods for avoiding repetitions in words". In: *Combinatorics on Words - 9th International Conference, WORDS 2013, Turku, Finland, September 16-20. Proceedings.* Ed. by J. Karhumäki, A. Lepistö, and L. Q. Zamboni. Vol. 8079. Lecture Notes in Computer Science. Springer, 2013, 15–17.

[79]   N. Rampersad, J. Shallit, and M.-w. Wang. "Avoiding large squares in infinite binary words". In: *Theoret. Comput. Sci.* **339** (1) (2005), 19–34.

[80]   G. Richomme and F. Wlazinski. "Existence of finite test-sets for k-power-freeness of uniform morphisms". In: *Discrete Appl. Math.* **155** (15) (2007), 2001–2016.

[81]   G. Richomme and F. Wlazinski. "About cube-free morphisms". In: *STACS 2000, 17th Annual Symposium on Theoretical Aspects of Computer Science, Lille, France, February 2000, Proceedings.* Ed. by H. Reichel and S. Tison. Vol. 1770. Lecture Notes in Computer Science. Springer, 2000, 99–109.

[82]   G. Richomme and F. Wlazinski. "Some results on k-power-free morphisms". In: *Theoret. Comput. Sci.* **273** (1-2) (2002), 119–142.

[83]   M. Rigo and P. Salimov. "Another generalization of abelian equivalence: binomial complexity of infinite words". In: *Combinatorics on Words - 9th International Conference, WORDS 2013, Turku, Finland, September 16-20. Proceedings.* Ed. by J. Karhumäki, A. Lepistö, and L. Q. Zamboni. Vol. 8079. Lecture Notes in Computer Science. Springer, 2013, 217–228.

[84]   R. Rizzi and S. Vialette. "On recognizing words that are squares for the shuffle product". In: *Computer Science - Theory and Applications - 8th International Computer Science Symposium in Russia, CSR 2013, Ekaterinburg, Russia, June 25-29, 2013. Proceedings.* Ed. by A. A. Bulatov and A. M. Shur. Vol. 7913. Lecture Notes in Computer Science. Springer, 2013, 235–245.

[85]   D. Skordev and B. Sendov. "On equations in words". In: *Z. Math. Logik Grundlagen Math* **7** (1961), 289–297.

[86]   A. Thue. "Über die gegenseitige Lage gleicher Teile gewisser Zeichenreihen". In: *Norske Vid. Skrifter I. Mat.-Nat. Kl., Christiania* **1** (1912), 1–67.

[87]   A. Thue. "Über unendliche Zeichenreihen". In: *Norske Vid. Skrifter I. Mat.-Nat. Kl., Christiania* **7** (1906), 1–22.

[88]   F. Wlazinski. "A test-set for k-power-free binary morphisms". In: *RAIRO Theor. Inform. Appl.* **35** (5) (2001), 437–452.

[89] Z. Xu. "A minimal periods algorithm with applications". In: *Combinatorial Pattern Matching, 21st Annual Symposium, CPM 2010, New York, NY, USA, June 21-23, 2010. Proceedings.* Ed. by A. Amir and L. Parida. Vol. 6129. Lecture Notes in Computer Science. Springer, 2010, 51–62.

[90] A. Young. "On quantitative substitutional analysis". In: *J. Lond. Math. Soc.* **1** (1) (1928), 14–18.

[91] A. I. Zimin. "Blocking sets of terms". In: *Sb. Math.* **47** (2) (1984), 353–364.

www.ingramcontent.com/pod-product-compliance
Lightning Source LLC
LaVergne TN
LVHW022346060326
832902LV00022B/4279